Understanding Industry

Understanding Industry

Third Edition

Ian Marcousé

Foreword by Richard Branson

Hodder & Stoughton

A MEMBER OF THE HODDER HEADLINE GROUP

Acknowledgements

This book is updated regularly to keep abreast of recent thinking and events. This edition features six completely new case studies and a re-written final chapter.

Writing the book involved the help of many people at Understanding Industry, at Hodder and Stoughton and within the firms featured. I would especially like to thank: Charles Richardson and Layla Braithwaite at 3i; Bill Vestey at Sony; Alan George at Unilever; David Dimmock at Standard Life; Andrew Stevens and Les George at TI Group; William Record at Braebourne; Christine Street at Guinness; and Peter Cox of Dixons. Many thanks also to Jayne Stoyle at Understanding Industry and Justine Davis at Hodder and Stoughton.

Ian Marcousé

AEB assessment of Enhanced Course

In conjunction with the Understanding Industry Trust, the Associated Examining Board (AEB) has developed a test for sixth-form students following the Understanding Industry Enhanced Course, the syllabus of which is based on this book. The assessment consists of a one and a quarter hour test containing structured, short answer questions and is available in May annually. Schools and colleges wishing to enter candidates for the test should make their entries in the usual manner, with the AEB (tel: 01483 506506, Ext. 2342).

Activities in this publication may be photocopied for class use.

Orders: please contact Bookpoint Ltd, 39 Milton Park, Abingdon,
Oxon OX14 4TD. Telephone: (44) 01235 400414, Fax: (44) 01235
400454. Lines are open from 9.00 - 6.00, Monday to Saturday, with a
24 hour message answering service.
Email address: orders@bookpoint.co.uk

A catalogue record for this title is available from The British Library

ISBN 0 340 70155 2
ISBN Hodder & Stoughton 0 340 70154 4

First published 1989 as *Understanding Industry Now*

First published by Hodder & Stoughton Educational 1994
Second edition 1996
Third edition 1997
Impression number   10 9 8 7 6 5 4 3 2
Year   2000   1999   1998

Copyright © 1997 Understanding Industry Trust

All rights reserved. No part of this publication may be reproduced
or transmitted in any form or by any means, electronic or
mechanical, including photocopy, recording, or any information
storage and retrieval system, without permission in writing from
the publisher or under licence from the Copyright Licensing
Agency Limited. Further details of such licences (for reprographic
reproduction) may be obtained from the Copyright Licensing
Agency Limited, of 90 Tottenham Court Road, London W1P 9HE.

Typeset by Wearset, Boldon, Tyne & Wear.
Printed in Great Britain for Hodder & Stoughton Educational, a
division of Hodder Headline Plc, 338 Euston Road, London
NW1 3BH by Scotprint Ltd, Musselburgh, Scotland.

Contents

Introduction by Stuart Bishell	v
Foreword by Richard Branson	vi

Introduction
In association with GUINNESS PLC 1

Case study: Guinness Plc – The skills required for business success	7
Case study: ProShare – share ownership in the 1990s	11

Marketing and sales 12

Case study: The Solero success story	15
Case study: The launch of Chicken Tonight	21
Case study: Levi 501s – why was denim fading?	26
Case study: TI Group plc – marketing seals	28

Design and development
In association with SONY 32

Case study: Design-based innovation at Sony	33
Case study: Sony – the news studio in a briefcase	39
Case study: Cornetto – computer-aided ice cream	44

Production
In association with TI GROUP 48

Case study: Messier-Dowty – landing the world-leaders	50
Case study: Eurostar and the graduate engineer	56
Case study: Information technology at Marks & Spencer	62

Personnel
In association with STANDARD LIFE 65

Case study: Standard Life – recruiting tomorrow's managers	66
Case study: Kalmar – production on a human scale	71
Case study: Mitsubishi Electric Europe (B.V.) – managing change	75

Finance
In association with RAILTRACK 80

Case study: Price Waterhouse – financing the future	87
Case study: Railtrack – building long-term profitability	93

Management
In association with Dixons 95

Case study: Dixons – managing a service revolution	100
Case study: Leadership to win at Allied Domecq – the managing director's view	105
Case study: Virgin – effective management in action	108

Small business
In association with 3i 111

Case study: Richer pickings – a sound success	116
Case study: Braebourne Ltd – turning water into gold	120
Case study: Denby Pottery – a management buy-out success	125
Case study: The Body Shop – from little acorns . . .	128

Integration
In association with Unilever 130

Case study: Integration across the world – Magnum ice cream	132

Bibliography	136
Index	137

Logos of firms and organisations referred to in this book

The author and publisher would like to thank the following firms and organisations for their help in supplying information and/or illustrations for use in this publication:

- 3i Plc
- 3M United Kingdom Plc
- Airdata Limited
- Apple Computer UK Ltd
- Birds Eye Wall's
- The Body Shop International Plc
- Braebourne Ltd
- Chartered Institute of Marketing
- Clarks International
- The Denby Pottery Company Ltd
- Department of Trade and Industry
- Dixons Group Plc
- Ford Motor Company Limited
- GEC Alsthom
- Glaxo Pharmaceuticals UK Limited
- Grand Metropolitan Plc
- Guinness Plc
- Hewlett-Packard Limited
- Imperial Chemical Industries Plc
- J C Bamford Excavators Limited
- Kodak Limited
- Levi Strauss (UK) Limited
- Marks & Spencer Plc
- Messier-Dowty
- Mitsubishi Electric Europe (B.V.)
- Price Waterhouse
- ProShare
- Racal Electronics Group
- Railtrack
- Renishaw Plc
- Richer Sounds Plc
- Rolls Royce Plc
- Rover Group Ltd
- SmithKline Beecham
- Sony United Kingdom Limited
- Standard Life Assurance Company
- Tesco Stores Ltd
- Texas Instruments
- TI group
- Unilever Plc
- Vauxhall Motors Limited
- Virgin Management Limited
- Volvo Car UK Limited

Introduction

STUART BISHELL

I firmly believe that this book, *Understanding Industry*, is a valuable asset to all students, irrespective of their course studies or career choice. It informs students of how the world of industry and business operates by encouraging involvement in real and contemporary case studies and practical exercises. It may also encourage students to consider one of the many exciting and rewarding careers in industry and commerce.

When I was at school, my contemporaries and I were steered away from a career in industry and commerce. Only in the professions, it was implied, could we contribute to society and enjoy a rewarding vocation. I hope that this book will help to raise young people's awareness of the vital role played by industry and commerce in creating wealth and in maintaining a prosperous and civilised society.

We are grateful to all the companies and individuals who have contributed to this book. Their support enables industry and education to work together in delivering industry's message to the next generation of business managers and opinion formers.

Stuart Bishell
Chief Executive
Understanding Industry

ABOUT UNDERSTANDING INDUSTRY

Understanding Industry (UI) is an educational charity which works to increase knowledge, enhance skills and improve attitudes towards industry and commerce through the delivery of unique, high quality programmes designed to inform, involve and inspire 16–19 year old students. Over 1,500 companies from industry and commerce support the work of UI.

UI is unique because it provides a first-hand view, in the classroom, of the world of industry and commerce. Each session on a UI course is led by a working business manager and incorporates the most up-to-date business practice. The sessions are participative in style, involving exercises, case studies and business games. This book, *Understanding Industry*, is designed to cover the main areas of industry and commerce included in the UI course: marketing and sales, design and development, production, personnel, finance, management, small business and business integration. Courses are tailored to the particular needs and interests of the individual school or college, either as part of a general studies programme or as a support for examined subjects.

For more information about UI and its work please contact:

Understanding Industry
Enterprise House
59–65 Upper Ground
London SE1 9PQ
Tel: 0171 620 0735

Foreword

RICHARD BRANSON

This book is about industry: how it works and its relevance to our society. If you had asked most people 20 years ago what images they associated with industry they would probably have replied 'smoke', 'factories', 'pollution', 'chimneys'. Nothing could be further from the real picture of industry in our society today and thankfully attitudes to business in general are changing for the better.

Industry plays a crucial role in our economy and society. It provides us with wealth and affects the quality of life of all of us. Manufacturing industries drive the economy, and service industries flourish as a result. We all benefit when both prosper together; there are more jobs, more schools, more hospitals and more houses.

It is exciting and rewarding to work in industry. Innovation and the constant challenges that change bring are exciting. Industry is rewarding because you have the satisfaction of knowing that you are contributing to the wealth of the country. To be associated with industry no longer carries the stigma of profiteering, exploitation, and of being uncaring as it did when I was at school.

Our society needs all sorts and sizes of industry and commerce to be successful and make a profit. All of us at Virgin are proud to have made a contribution to the wealth of this country through our various business ventures. Since I was a teenager I have had the drive and ambition to succeed. As a young man I was running my own company and today manage a multimillion-pound business that is diverse and worldwide.

The talents of young people must not be stifled. Education is not just about getting the right grades in exams but it should encourage all students to develop to their optimum capacity, whatever that may be. Schools and colleges should prepare young people for life – that means making the understanding of industry and commerce more relevant and accessible.

I am proud to be associated with this book and hope that it will inspire you to succeed in one of the many interesting, challenging and varied careers that industry in Britain can offer. However, even if you decide not to enter this fascinating world of industry, perhaps *Understanding Industry* will leave a lasting impression about the importance of industry in all our lives.

Good luck to you, whatever your decision may be.

Richard Branson
Founder and Chairman of Virgin

Introduction

IN ASSOCIATION WITH

GUINNESS PLC

Wealth creation

Business is the process of making a profit by providing products or services which people want to buy. As a result of the drive to make a profit, firms create wealth which is then distributed within the economy. For example, Denby Pottery creates wealth by transforming raw Derbyshire clay into cups, saucers and other tableware bought throughout the world. In the process, 700 staff are employed directly, many others are employed indirectly (suppliers and distributors, for instance) and local and national government receive over £2 million a year in taxes.

The more initiative, invention and care taken by Denby staff, the more products they can sell and the more customers are prepared to pay for the Denby name. So, design and development, marketing, people and production are all key factors in wealth creation.

Statistics show that nearly 18 per cent of all the tax collected in Britain is from employers. That proportion is lower than in countries such as Japan and Germany, yet still represents a huge contribution towards government spending on such things as hospitals, roads, schools and old age pensions. So,

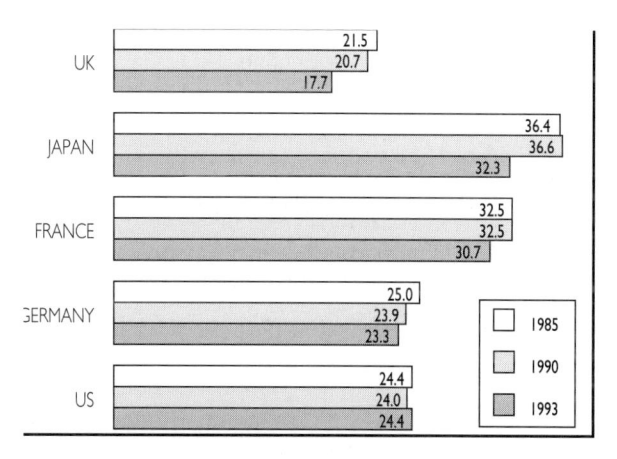

Country	1985	1990	1993
UK	21.5	20.7	17.7
JAPAN	36.4	36.6	32.3
FRANCE	32.5	32.5	30.7
GERMANY	25.0	23.9	23.3
US	24.4	24.0	24.4

Employers' tax and social security payments as a percentage of total taxation   Source: OECD

business does not only create wealth for shareholders, it also helps to provide the jobs and the public services we all rely on.

* * *

Over recent years, five factors stand out in their impact upon the economic environment for British businesses:

- Wide swings between boom and recession.
- Discovering and utilising North Sea oil.
- The arrival of Japanese companies and management ideas.
- A structural change towards service businesses.
- A shift towards flexible labour markets, partly through privatisation.

Economic background

At the time of writing (March 1997) Britain's economic prospects look sound. Industrial output is rising on the back of strong consumer demand. Investment levels are moving ahead and exports are holding up despite the strength of the pound. Later in this chapter there will be an analysis of why Britain is enjoying such favourable circumstances. First, a review of our recent economic and business past.

In 1899, Britain sold one in three of the world's exports of manufactured goods. She was the world's most important exporter by far. By the late 1970s Britain's share had fallen to 7.5 per cent, dwarfed by Germany, America and Japan. In fact, with only 1.5 per cent of the world's population, Britain's export performance was still quite impressive, but there was concern about her relative decline.

Partly as a response to this, the Conservative government of 1979 swept to power with a determination to revitalise the economy by:

- Lowering income taxes to restore people's incentive to work.
- Cutting inflation through tight monetary policy.
- Creating tough new laws to curb the power of trade unions.
- Establishing an 'enterprise culture' through **privatisation** and deregulation.

The overall approach was to reduce the role of government to give managers the right and the power to manage. Then people could be expected to set up their own businesses and to take pride in running them profitably.

The effect of these policies was dramatic. 1980 saw the sharpest recession for half a century as firms struggled to cope with high interest rates and exchange rates caused by the attempt to cut inflation. By the mid-1980s, however, a major recovery was underway. The rate of new business start-ups rose dramatically, as did the level of inward investment. American companies such as IBM and Motorola were joined by Japanese giants such as Mitsubishi, Nissan and Toyota. All were keen to set up factories in Britain – a member of the European Union with a government establishing favourable conditions for employers.

Despite a dramatic collapse in the stock market in October 1987, the economy kept moving ahead strongly. The government was convinced its policies had transformed the economic potential of the country, enabling it to grow faster than ever before. In the March 1988 Budget, the Chancellor of the Exchequer cut taxes for those in higher-earning brackets, to encourage enterprise still further.

Yet this proved a step too far. The tax cuts led to extra consumer spending, stoking up the already buoyant demand for imported goods and property. Rapid rises in house prices added to inflation, while the high level of imports pushed the balance between exports and imports severely into the red. In an attempt to control these excesses, interest rates were pushed up sharply, doubling between spring and autumn 1988.

Economies change course very slowly, so the effects only showed through in mid-1990. There was a fall in the demand for goods bought on credit, such as houses and cars. Firms cut back on investment and staffing, as they struggled to pay the high interest charges on their loans. The period between 1990 and 1993 proved the longest recession of the century, with economic output falling slowly but steadily, month after month.

Recovery came when Britain's withdrawal from the European Exchange Rate Mechanism (ERM) allowed the pound to fall by 15 per cent against all foreign currencies. This made British firms 15 per cent more competitive at a stroke. New export opportunities opened up, first in America and then in Europe.

Rising production for export started to lead Britain out of recession during 1993. Scarred by the recession, consumer and business confidence recovered very slowly, but by late 1994 an upward path was established. Unfortunately a series of interest rate rises made it unclear how long the upturn would last.

INTRODUCTION

The miracle of North Sea oil

Until the late 1970s, Britain had always been a huge net importer of oil. The mid-1970s discovery of oil in the North Sea changed that. By the end of the decade British oil production was rising fast, boosting exports and bringing huge tax revenues into the Treasury. This wealth helped the balance of payments (exports minus imports) in Britain, enabled the government to cut tax rates on items other than oil, and lifted British industrial production figures. Between 1977 and 1994 North Sea Oil was worth over £200 billion to the British economy.

In the early years, politicians worried about what would happen when the oil ran out. Now it is known that North Sea oil reserves should last for at least another 40 years so this eventual problem is no longer talked about.

The importance of oil in business and the economy should never be underestimated. As petrol, diesel and kerosene, it fuels cars, lorries and planes. Heavy oils are used in power stations to generate electricity. Furthermore oil is the major raw material for paint, plastics, vinyl, nylon and most of the synthetic fibres used in carpets, seat covers and clothes. Unsurprisingly, it is the world's most valuable export. Its unique importance means that an oil shortage could bring the economy to a halt or send inflation soaring. Alone among the major developed economies, Britain has the good fortune to be self-sufficient. Without North Sea oil, average living standards in Britain would be significantly lower.

Japanese firms in Britain – competitor or regenerator?

The first major Japanese company to establish a plant in the UK was YKK, the zip manufacturer, in 1971. This was followed in 1974 by the Sony television factory in South Wales. The trend continued in the 1970s, but accelerated in the 1980s as it seemed likely that moves to closer economic union within Europe might shut out Japanese exports. Japanese firms now employ over 30,000 British workers, mainly in areas of traditionally high unemployment, such as South Wales and the North East. Britain has been the most successful European country at bringing Japanese investment into new factories and financial services.

So why is Britain proving so attractive to Japanese companies?

- Due to the importance of the American market, English is the first foreign language taught in Japan.
- British wage rates for factory workers are the lowest among the developed European countries; in Holland and Germany, for example, wages are about 20 per cent higher.
- Non-wage costs are much lower for employers in Britain than elsewhere; in France, employers pay taxes that add more than a quarter to their wage bill.
- The attitude of successive British governments has been very welcoming to the Japanese; elsewhere there was mistrust of the motives and methods of Japanese firms.
- The industrial relations climate is seen as highly favourable; British unions have been willing to sign single-union, no-strike deals with Japanese firms.
- The success in Britain of the early pioneers such as Sony ensured that other Japanese firms felt happy to follow.

From the 1970s, there has been a fear that the Japanese would provide little of long-term benefit to the British economy. The concern was that Japanese factories in Britain would be 'screwdriver plants', merely assembling imported components. This would provide semi-skilled jobs, but not the professional tasks such as Research and Development (R & D), product design and production engineering.

Today firms such as Canon, Nissan and Sony have looked for more from their British employees. They have set up R & D operations here to boost the quality of their investment – away from assembly into high value-added activities. There has also been a beneficial spin-off from Japanese techniques for managing people and production. The success of Japanese managers at achieving high productivity with British workers has forced a rethink about management practices in this country.

In addition, most Japanese companies are committed to increasing the amount of components they buy from Britain. The Sony plant at Bridgend, for instance, now obtains over 90 per cent of its components locally. Typically, when Japanese firms first arrive they find it hard to obtain local supplies of the right quality and reliability. Yet within a year or two they build close relationships with small numbers of local producers whose competitiveness is boosted permanently from the work put into meeting the demands of the Japanese buyers.

Does manufacturing still matter?

Today, three quarters of those in work are engaged in the service sector. **Private sector** jobs in retailing, finance, and leisure and tourism are added to by **public sector** work in health and social care, education and the civil service. As the number of people employed in manufacturing fell during the 1980s, it became fashionable to believe that Britain's future rested with service industries. Table 1.1 shows how such a view could take hold. The only two categories showing job growth are services and the self-employed (most of whom provide services in any case). Nowadays, fewer than one fifth of jobs are in manufacturing.

So can the country afford to let manufacturing wither and die? Some people would say yes, believing that Britain can prosper solely by selling services to the world. They argue that services can create wealth as

TABLE 1.1 *Changes in the number of jobs by sector 1979–94*

	1979 (000s)	1994 (000s)	Change (000s)	Percentage change
Primary sector	705	326	−379	−54
Secondary sector:				
All production	8,642	5,314	−3,328	−38.5
Of which:				
Manufacturing	7,073	4,227	−2,846	−40
Services	13,240	15,210	+1,970	+15
ALL EMPLOYEES	22,587	20,850	−1,737	−8
Self-employed	1,842	3,230	+1,388	+75
TOTAL WORKFORCE IN EMPLOYMENT	24,429	24,080	−349	−1.5

Source: HMSO Annual Abstract of Statistics, *HMSO Employment Gazette*, January 1995

well as, if not better than, manufacturing. They point to Britain's huge overseas earnings from tourism, financial services, education, royalties and patents. Others disagree.

Sony's chairman, Akio Morita, has warned that 'in the long run an economy that has lost its manufacturing base has lost its vital centre. A service-based economy has no engine to drive it'. He goes on to add: 'When manufacturing prospers, all industries connected with it prosper – not only are more components, parts and salesmen needed, but more accountants, more dentists, more petrol stations, more supermarkets and more schools. Service industries cannot flourish in isolation – they depend on manufacturing to support them.'

Manufacturing industries, in turn, rely on a network of service industries within the key areas of banking and finance, law, distribution and marketing. Clearly, manufacturing and the service sector are dependent on each other. Consumer spending in developed economies tends to shift towards services such as transport and tourism, but manufacturing remains important.

Labour flexibility

Traditionally, British workplaces were organised in a rigid fashion. Employees were hired and trained to do one task and unless they were promoted might receive no further training. Tight **demarcation** lines showed where one job ended and the next one began. All that was expected of an employee was to work effectively at the task set out by the boss. Very few would feel involved enough to suggest ideas for improvements, nor did the employers expect this.

This rigid, narrow focus of work was also sought by trade unions. Employees working on single tasks maximised job numbers and therefore job security. Rigid job demarcation served the interests of employers, workers and trade unions equally.

Comparably rigid systems covered:

- Wage bargaining, with trade unions negotiating with employers on behalf of all employees (**collective bargaining**).
- Pay scales, with every employee on the same job grade receiving the same rate of pay.
- Terms and conditions of employment, with nearly all staff on full-time, permanent work status.

The 1980s and 1990s have seen dramatic changes towards greater flexibility. Japanese firms brought new employment practices to Britain, insisting that employees learn the skills to perform a wide variety of jobs. Multi-skilling replaced demarcation. The role of trade unions was also changed as many of the new firms demanded no-strike deals.

Also important has been high unemployment. Staff anxious to keep their jobs have proved willing to accept many changes in their conditions and terms at work. Firms have been able to reduce their numbers of full-time employees and top up their workforce with temporary or part-time staff as and when necessary for seasonal or other reasons.

Privatisation has also been a factor. First came the sale of the state-owned **nationalised** industries such as British Telecom, British Gas and British Steel. Shares in these giant businesses were sold to private investors through the stock exchange. Less public, but perhaps more important, was the move to contract out services to the private sector. Councils found private contractors to sweep the streets or run their accounts departments.

In both cases, the effects were similar. Strongly unionised public sector organisations switched to the private sector. Often, unions were no longer recognised by the private sector contractors, so employers found it easier to change working practices and terms of employment. The trend to flexibility was given a boost, sparking off similar actions by large private sector firms, contracting out services such as cleaning, security and deliveries.

From the point of view of employers, the job market of the 1990s has become very favourable. Large numbers of inflexible, full-time staff on set pay scales were transformed to become smaller, leaner and multi-skilled. In his book, *Inside*

Organisations, Charles Handy says that companies have increasingly taken on a shamrock shape. The shamrock's three leaves represent:

- The core workforce.
- The contractual fringe.
- The flexible labour force.

He believes that this will continue into the future, with job security only existing for the vital, highly educated, core workforce.

In which areas does Britain have a competitive advantage?

In *The Competitive Advantage of Nations*, Michael Porter compares the industrial nations of the world in order to identify their competitive strengths and weaknesses. In Britain's case, he identifies a range of areas where a strong national competitive position has been achieved.

The largest concentrations of British competitive advantage are in packaged goods (including food, alcoholic drinks and household products) and consumer goods retailing. Another important cluster is in financial or financially-related services such as insurance, trading and money management. Significant clusters are also present in pharmaceuticals, chemicals, computing equipment and software, entertainment and leisure products, defence and clothing.

It is encouraging for Britain's future prosperity that so many of these industries with a strong competitive position are in the fast growing 'sunrise' industries rather than the declining 'sunset' industries, such as metalworking and shipbuilding. Britain's successful sunrise industries include motor vehicles, electronics, aerospace, pharmaceuticals and consumer goods in general.

BRITISH BUSINESSES WITH INTERNATIONAL STRENGTH

Consumer products
- food and drink
- clothing
- household goods
- pharmaceuticals

Industrial products
- chemicals
- cars
- electronics
- aerospace

Services
- retailing
- insurance
- banking
- leisure

It is on these high-tech, high value-added industries, with their greater profit and export potential, that Britain's hopes for the future are pinned.

Many of the sunrise industries also have the important advantage of being knowledge- rather than labour-intensive. According to Professor Douglas McWilliams, the former chief economic adviser at the Confederation of British Industry (CBI), 'Low-skilled production is increasingly migrating to developing economies with rock-bottom labour costs, particularly those around the Pacific Rim. The only way we can remain competitive is by constantly up-skilling the manufacturing base. Companies must make themselves more innovative and high tech in order to compensate for the jobs that will inevitably disappear overseas.' In other words, those firms that do remain labour-intensive are likely to face an uncertain future.

What is the key to greater competitiveness?

Competing on a world-beating scale involves being successful in a number of key areas. The first step is to develop a strong consumer focus. This means listening to what customers want in order to respond to, or anticipate their needs. Then to develop and introduce innovative new products in order to stay ahead of the competition. This requires a large scale commitment of funds for research and development.

In addition, the selective use of automation can be beneficial, though large scale automation is not appropriate to all firms and all industries. There is a danger that if the production processes are not streamlined beforehand, automation will merely speed up the existing problems, not solve them. Nevertheless, automation can, if it is well planned, increase the rate of production and improve reliability.

However, the costs of developing innovative new products and of automating are so great that there may be a long period before the investment yields a profit. It is vital to the long-term competitiveness of industry that firms invest in the future, so City financiers must be prepared to lend 'patient money'. Unlike their Japanese and German counterparts, they have tended to be preoccupied with short-term profits at the expense of long-term investment.

Yet even if firms manage to improve their performance in all these areas, it will count for nothing if the quality of their products does not match that of their competitors. So what are the standards required for competing on a global scale?

British firms would certainly be vulnerable if they attempted to compete in world markets by virtue of low prices alone. In any case, studies have shown that buying decisions are rarely made solely on the basis of price. No less important are the quality of design and manufacture and the standards of customer service.

Competitiveness today depends on much more than low prices. It relies on a whole range of non-price factors, including good design, technological innovation, reliability, on-time delivery and after-sales service; in short, on quality. British firms such as Rover and Cadbury Schweppes have managed to transform their fortunes in recent years, through their success in getting all these aspects of quality right.

This does not mean, however, that they can now afford to sit back. The targets for world-class manufacturing are constantly expanding. As ever, it appears that the Japanese are setting the standards to beat. Simon Caulkin points out in an article in *Management Today* that, 'Already the Japanese are beginning to talk of "taken for granted" quality and product features, and are moving on to compete by "surprising" and "delighting" customers . . . quality and customer satisfaction are 1980's concepts. The aim now must be not just to meet customer needs but to exceed them.'

CASE STUDY

Guinness Plc – the skills required for business success

What factors have high achievers such as Richard Branson (Virgin), Anita Roddick (Body Shop) and Sir Ian MacLaurin (Tesco) in common? Is it their exam achievements? Their social contacts? Their inherited wealth? Or do they share some personal qualities that have been important in their successful business careers? Without question it is the latter; qualities that can benefit anyone starting out in business.

Guinness Plc has looked hard at defining the key personal qualities and how best to develop them. An analysis of the company's own managers has shown that success depends upon:

1 Commitment (to results, to quality, to excellence and to change).
2 Leadership (directing, motivating, inspiring and building cooperation).
3 Personal skills (confidence, maturity, communicating and influencing).

4 People development (counselling and developing others; reflecting on own strengths and weaknesses).
5 Problem solving (gets to the heart of issues; numerate; creative; good judgement; willing to take risks).
6 Strategic thinking (thinks about the whole business, about trends and about the future; copes with change).

Most of these qualities can be developed outside the classroom as well as within it. The captain of a school/college team will need to develop all the first four qualities to be really effective. Within the classroom, there should also be many opportunities to learn these personal qualities – whether through case studies, classroom presentations, project work or role plays.

Guinness identifies and develops these skills by setting demanding tasks for young high-flyers. In the past, university students were recruited for places on a two year management trainee course. Now the company favours a less formal 'business course'. The high achievers on this course may be hired for six months and given a project to complete. If this goes well and both sides like what they see, a management post will be offered. The benefits of this are its flexibility and the fact that it tests people's ability at work rather than at study.

In 1996 20-year-old Pasi Lankinen, from Finland, was selected for the programme. Guinness set him the task of devising a new 'knowledge programme' for the United Distillers sales force. The problem was that United Distillers sells so many different products (well over 1,000!) that new sales staff found it impossible to learn quickly about the traditions, the product qualities and the target customer for all the brands. This would make it impossible to sell effectively. So Pasi was set the important task of improving the existing training programme.

At the outset, Pasi assumed his task would be largely academic: interviewing, researching and writing. After reading everything he could about the whiskies, gins, brandies, liqueurs and many other alcoholic drinks made by United Distillers, Pasi had to start talking to the relevant sales and product managers. What were their needs?

To his surprise, Pasi found that he had to do much more than just phone up for appointments. Even though he was working on a task that would help the whole business and for a senior Head Office manager, almost everyone seemed too busy to see him. Only after careful discussions with, and coaching from, Guinness management development professionals was he able to see things from other managers' points of view. They had deadlines and targets to meet. Why should they spend time on something with no short-term payback run by a 20-year-old, fresh from college?

He learnt that he needed to *sell* his project to them before they would be helpful. This required a clear understanding of their goals and needs, careful planning and also a degree of assertiveness. He also learnt, the hard way, that he needed to be flexible about his style of approach. In Britain he could be quite informal, addressing managers by their first names. When he visited the Spanish subsidiary, however, using first names was regarded as disrespectful, even offensive.

Pasi also followed up his contacts by socialising after work and by keeping in touch by phone or in person. This was crucial because not only might he need to return for more information, but also these same people would be vital – later on – to the successful implementation of the new programme. As he came to know the staff better, he learnt who were the people who could 'get things done' (not necessarily because of their position) and which 'strings to pull'. In the terms of the six categories set out at the start, Pasi's experience pointed to the crucial role of categories one, three and four: commitment, personal skills and self-development.

To Christine Street, resourcing and development manager for Guinness, the exercise showed that 'people won't do things just because you're the boss'. Managing people effectively requires skills of persuasion and communication. You can achieve some things by telling staff what to do, but getting the best out of people requires everyone to believe in what is being done. Christine mentions a Guinness subsidiary overseas which underwent ferocious streamlining in order to meet an ambitious profit

INTRODUCTION

programme. He regarded the whole exercise as 'the most challenging thing I have ever done' and wants to return to the company once his degree is over. Guinness regards that as a compliment indeed.

ACTIVITY

How well do you perform against the Guinness criteria? What evidence is there that you have these qualities? What might you do to fill any gaps?

QUALITIES	EVIDENCE
1 Commitment (to results, to quality, to excellence).	Exam results......... Other.............
2 Leadership (directing, motivating, inspiring).	Captain/leader........ Other.............
3 Personal skills (confidence, maturity, communicating).	Telephone manner...... Influencing others......
4 Development (of others; and reflecting on own performance).	Trained others........ Self-knowledge........
5 Problem solving (analytic; numerate; risk-taker; creative)	Analytic/numerate...... Risk-taking..........
6 Strategic (thinks of whole business, trends and future).	Clear goals.......... Plan for achieving them..

The more evidence you have of fulfilling requirements such as these, the better. Can you think of ways to fill any of the gaps?

Pasi Lankinen

target. Although the target was met, much hard work was needed to sustain morale and to keep the commitment of the best people. The key managerial skills required were communication, motivation and the ability to build relationships.

And Pasi? Christine is clear that he will be an excellent catch for Guinness or any other company. He has returned to university to finish his degree, but left behind a well constructed slide presentation showing his recommendations for the new knowledge

The structure of industry

Britain has a mixed economy, which means that some firms operate in the private sector whilst others are

TABLE 1.2 *Types of business unit*

	Sole traders	*Partnership*	*Limited company*
Owners	One owner	Two to 20 owners – can be more in partnerships of solicitors and accountants etc.	Minimum of two shareholders
Management decisions	Owner	Partners	Board of directors elected by shareholders
Provision of funds	Owner's funds	Partners' funds contributed in amounts laid down in partnership agreement	Share capital up to maximum amount stated in memorandum – for public limited company the minimum to be **quoted** on the Stock Exchange is £50,000
Financial risk	Owner has unlimited liability	Partners have unlimited liability	Liability is limited to value of shareholding
Allocation of profits	Owner takes profits	Partners agree on how profit should be paid	Directors decide how much profit should be paid as dividends on shares and how much is ploughed back as investment
Duration	Ends on death of owner	Can be dissolved according to terms stated in partnership agreement, or ends on death of partner	Ends on liquidation, when assets are sold off and the company is legally wound up

under direct state control, these being the nationalised industries. Many of these have been privatised in recent years, such as BT and British Gas. There are three sectors within the economy:

- The primary sector – where resources are extracted from the ground, e.g. mining, quarrying, drilling for oil, farming and fishing.
- The secondary sector – where these primary products or raw materials are used to manufacture goods, e.g. electronics, steel, cars, clothes etc.
- The tertiary sector – where services are provided, e.g. banking, retailing, advertising, tourism and so on, and also public services such as health, education, defence etc.

Businesses in the private sector vary in size from small start-up firms to large multinational corporations. Yet, despite this diversity there are only three different legal forms of business: sole trader, partnership and limited company.

Most entrepreneurs operate as sole traders initially. This is the easiest way to start up, as no complicated legal formalities are involved. By definition, entrepreneurs are undertaking a risk in a new commercial venture. They have unlimited liability, which means that if the business fails, they may have to sell their home and personal possessions to pay outstanding bills. This is balanced by the fact that they keep any profits made and have complete freedom in decision making.

In time, sole traders may decide to form a partnership – a decision that is usually taken in order to raise more capital for expansion. In order to avoid disagreements, most partners draw up a formal partnership agreement. This includes details on, for instance, how much capital is contributed by each partner and the ratio in which profits and losses are to be shared.

As the business develops, further capital for expansion can be obtained by becoming a company and selling shares. Shares in private limited companies are not freely available to the general public and can only be transferred with the agreement of the directors. Shares in public limited companies, on the other hand, can be sold to the general public. Companies must have share capital of at least £50,000 before they can 'go public'. Only public companies are able to have their shares floated on the Stock Exchange.

In becoming a company the business acquires a legal identity which is separate from the shareholders. This means that it can be sued. Shareholders also have limited liability; if the business fails they are only responsible for an amount equivalent to their original investment. Therefore anyone owed money by a company that goes into liquidation may never receive a penny. For this reason, a private limited company must have **Ltd** after its name and a public company **Plc** after its name. This makes it clear to suppliers or anyone else dealing with them, that their liability is limited. Every company must also place a copy of its accounts at Companies House, so that anyone can check whether the firm is financially sound.

The essential differences between these three types of business units are shown in Table 1.2.

CASE STUDY

ProShare – share ownership in the 1990s

At the end of 1996 there were 9.5 million shareholders in Great Britain. Although down from its 1991 peak, the figure was more than treble the 1979 level. The increase was mainly the result of the major privatisation issues, such as the flotation of British Gas onto the London Stock Exchange. Ordinary householders were encouraged to buy shares for the first time, as the attractive share prices gave every chance of a profitable investment.

Investors buy shares for two reasons: the hope of capital gain (if the share price rises), and the expectation of regular and rising annual dividends paid by the companies out of their profits. But what benefit is share buying to industry?

Businesses only benefit from share buying when they issue fresh shares for sale. Broadly, this comes in two ways:

- When companies are floated on the stock market for the first time.
- When they make a rights issue, in other words raise extra share capital from existing shareholders.

In both cases the company receives an injection of capital which can be used to finance long-term investments such as new factories or new equipment. The share buyer puts money into the firm in return for the expectation of annual dividends and – hopefully – a rise in the value of the shares. In the five years to 1996, over £50 billion of share capital was raised by firms on the London stock market. This made a significant contribution to the investment spending upon which the future efficiency of British industry depends.

Sources of capital for UK firms

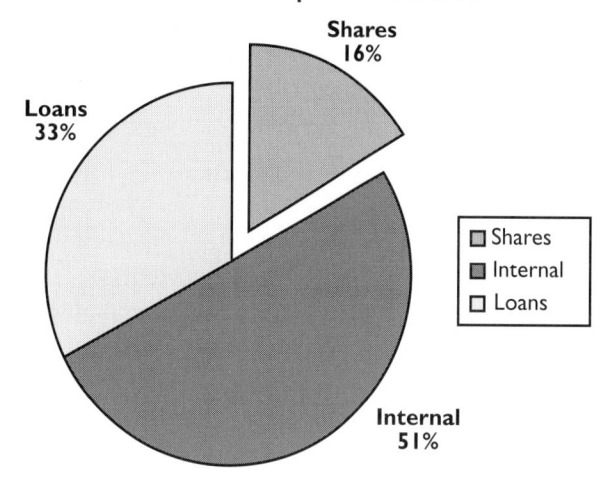

Shares 16%
Loans 33%
Internal 51%

Marketing and sales

Introduction: what is marketing?

Firms do not have a choice about whether or not to carry out any marketing. Every organisation markets itself, if only through the kinds of products and services it offers and the standard of its customer service. The only choice is between whether the marketing is done haphazardly or whether it is done systematically, through coordinating every aspect of the **marketing effort**. Marketing is often confused with selling or advertising. While both of these functions are involved, the total marketing effort also includes assessing customer needs and carrying out market research, together with the development of the product and its pricing, promotion and distribution.

The key task for any business is to get its marketing right, but this also means the company must be good at everything else from research and development to manufacturing and from quality control to financial control. Marketing does not function in isolation from other departments, but permeates the company. It is no more the exclusive responsibility of the marketing department than profitability is solely the responsibility of the finance department.

According to the Chartered Institute of Marketing, it is 'the management process responsible for identifying, anticipating and satisfying customer requirements profitably'. This means getting the right product or service in the right place at the right time, in the right quantities and at the right price, to ensure enough profit for the company.

WHY HAS MARKETING INCREASED?

In the early days of industrialisation, output could not keep pace with demand. Industries therefore operated in a **sellers' market**. This resulted in a **production orientation**, where firms concentrated on producing the goods they wanted to make. The disregard for consumer preferences at the time is summed up by the 'take it or leave it' attitude of Henry Ford. His comment, 'They can have any colour they like, as long as it's black', reveals an offhand approach which can largely be explained by the lack of competition – Ford had a 50 per cent share of the American car market in the 1920s.

However, particularly since the Second World War, firms have had to adopt a **marketing orientation**, in order to survive in today's fiercely competitive markets. Most industries now operate in a **buyers' market**, where consumers can choose what they want to buy from the immense variety of products and services on offer. Firms have to concentrate on producing the goods the market wants, rather than the ones they happen to make.

This changing orientation applies also to overseas markets. Firms can no longer presume, in these days of global competition, that the world will beat a path to their door. Competition has intensified as the open market in Europe presents a tremendous marketing opportunity, but also poses a huge potential threat for the unprepared firm.

What do people need and want?

Marketing starts with finding out what motivates customers to buy a particular product or service. As Peter Drucker, the American management expert, emphasises, 'The aim of marketing is to make selling superfluous. The aim is to know and understand the customer so well that the product or service sells itself.'

This means identifying the customer's **needs** and **wants**. Philip Kotler, in his book, *Principles of Marketing*, defines a need as 'a state of felt deprivation in a person' while wants are 'needs as shaped by our culture and personality'. In other words, all people need to eat, but one person may want beefburger and chips while another might want salmon and caviar. Wants only become **demand** when people have the resources to acquire what they want. For example, many people might want a Rolls Royce but only a few can afford to buy one, so the demand for Rolls Royces is small.

American psychologist AH Maslow has argued that people have different levels of needs. They seek to satisfy lower level needs, such as those for food, drink, shelter and safety, before trying to fulfil their higher order needs, for things such as social acceptance, status and self-fulfilment. However, people do respond differently in the way they satisfy a particular need according to their attitudes, social values and so on. The implication, therefore, is that consumers do not simply buy a product or service – they buy *solutions* to their perceived problems or needs. If the marketing effort is to be successful, it must emphasise the *benefits* consumers will gain by using the product or service.

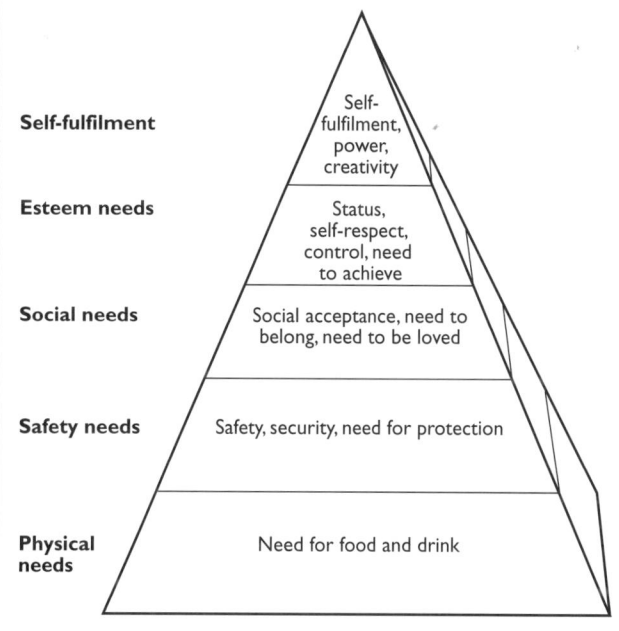

Self-fulfilment: Self-fulfilment, power, creativity
Esteem needs: Status, self-respect, control, need to achieve
Social needs: Social acceptance, need to belong, need to be loved
Safety needs: Safety, security, need for protection
Physical needs: Need for food and drink

Maslow's hierarchy of needs

In fact, what people want is usually far more than they need. In buying an expensive house, the successful person is making a statement about his or her status and position in society rather than just buying a shelter from the elements. Which marketing campaign for expensive houses is likely to be most effective – one which emphasises how structurally sound the houses are, or one which portrays a comfortable lifestyle with glamorous people in elegant room settings? In the same way most campaigns are cleverly aimed at subtly exploiting the often subconscious wants which influence people's buying decisions.

As most consumers' needs and wants are already being catered for, much effort also goes into creating new needs and wants by developing innovative products. Once introduced onto the market, these exploit wants which were **latent** and not expressed until the new product became available. How many people knew they wanted a personal stereo until Sony actually brought out their Walkman™?

Innovative products can therefore stimulate new consumer wants, but what about the reverse situation? Can new consumer wants stimulate innovative products being developed? In fact, this has already happened. For instance, in the plastics and synthetic fibre industries, the marketing people tell the researchers what properties they need and the researchers then design those materials. The implications of the fact that we can now 'innovate to order' are far reaching.

> **DISCUSSION POINTS**
>
> *1 Do advertisers encourage materialism by constantly exploiting people's needs and wants?*
>
> *2 What are some of the products and services which are advertised to exploit each level of Maslow's hierarchy of needs?*

Is market research essential?

Carrying out detailed market research, whether it concerns products and services aimed at domestic consumers or those aimed at industrial consumers, is the first step in any effective marketing campaign. Market research provides information which is sufficiently objective to form a basis for decision making. Firms generally start by looking at the information already available within their own company, from sales and account records and so on. These can show:

- Which products are most profitable.
- Whether sales fall into a pattern by type of product, by customer, by geographical area or by size of order.
- Whether the company is becoming too dependent on a few customers or products.
- Which customer accounts are most profitable.
- What proportion of sales quotations result in actual orders.

The next step for firms is to consult other sources of information which have already been published, such as government publications, media reports, newspapers and journals. These can show:

- Whether the total market for a particular product or service is growing, static or declining.
- What changes are taking place in the market.
- Who the main competitors are.

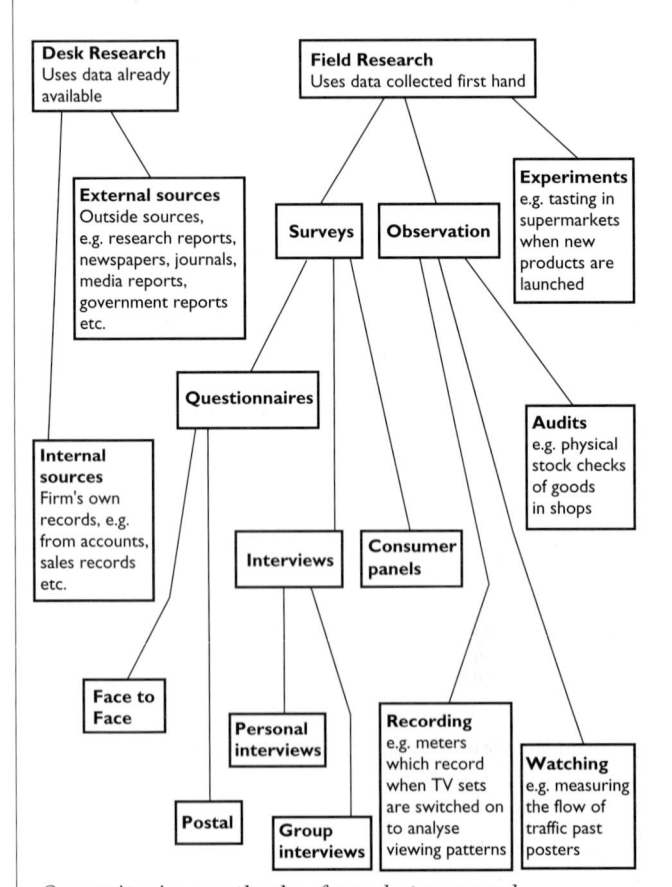

Quantitative methods of market research

If neither of these forms of **desk research** provides all the information required, the firm may then decide some **field research** is needed, which it can either do itself or commission a market research agency to carry out.

In any case, only a sample of people would be researched. It is not practical or even necessary to contact every person in the potential market! The group of people can be a random sample picked from the electoral registers, telephone directories and so on, or a stratified sample, where a representative cross-section of the population in terms of factors such as age, sex, income etc. is researched. Alternatively, interviewers may be given a quota. If they are conducting street interviews this means that they can choose whom to interview, providing they survey a certain number of people from, for example, each age group.

Once the size and type of sample has been chosen, firms can then carry out **quantitative research** to provide answers to such questions as *how many* people buy their product. They can also carry out **qualitative research** by means of group discussions and in-depth interviews, to establish such factors as *who* buys their products and *why*.

Market research cannot, of course, eliminate business risk, but it can greatly reduce the guesswork element.

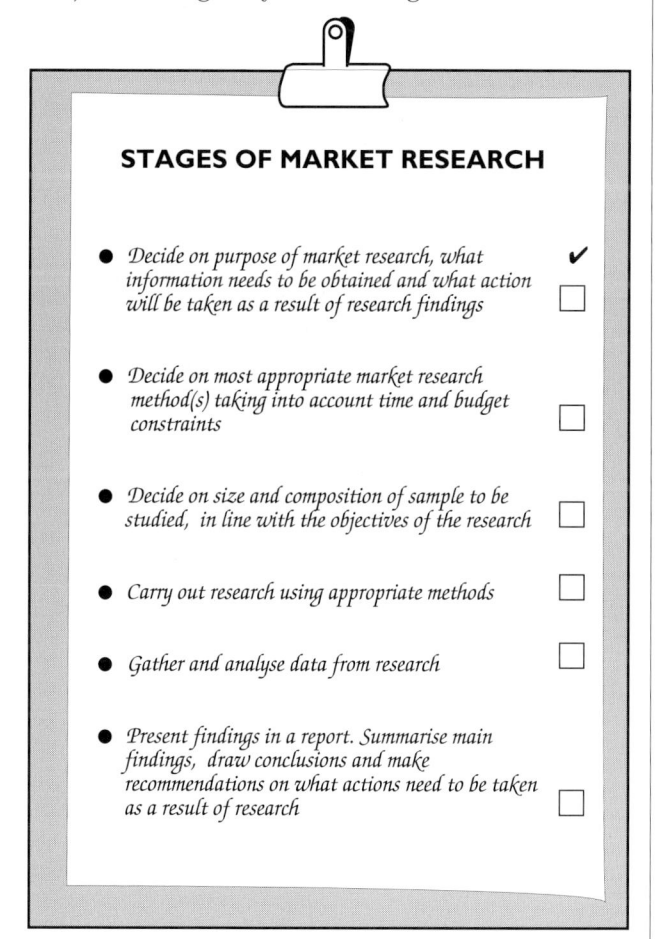

STAGES OF MARKET RESEARCH

- *Decide on purpose of market research, what information needs to be obtained and what action will be taken as a result of research findings* ✓

- *Decide on most appropriate market research method(s) taking into account time and budget constraints* ☐

- *Decide on size and composition of sample to be studied, in line with the objectives of the research* ☐

- *Carry out research using appropriate methods* ☐

- *Gather and analyse data from research* ☐

- *Present findings in a report. Summarise main findings, draw conclusions and make recommendations on what actions need to be taken as a result of research* ☐

Stages of market research

Potentially disastrous situations can thus be avoided, such as when a huge capital investment is made in a product for which there is no demand. This sounds unlikely, yet even highly innovative products have been known to fail because they are sold in a market which has not been correctly identified.

CASE STUDY

The Solero success story

Most new products hit the marketplace in a blaze of advertising and publicity. Wall's Solero was different. It arrived in retail freezer cabinets in June 1994 almost unannounced. Yet by August it was the UK's third fastest selling hand-held ice cream. Wall's were delighted by its success and decided that in 1995 it would be launched throughout Europe and supported by a £3 million marketing budget in the UK.

The Solero story started with a marketing decision to tackle the adult refreshment sector of the ice-cream market. The goal was to repeat the success of Magnum in the indulgence sector. Birds Eye Wall's dominated the market for impulse-purchase ice cream, so a product was needed that could stimulate total market growth by attracting new users. Research indicated that an opportunity existed for a premium quality product targeting 20–35-year-olds, which offered both refreshment and indulgence. As the brand mapping diagram on page 16 shows, Solero was to open up a new segment of the market.

An initial meeting was arranged in March 1993 to bring together product development, marketing and production staff. After their discussions, a product developer said, 'While you're all here, what do you think of this?' They were given a square, orange-coloured lolly on a stick. A couple of licks of the exotic fruit coating, and the discovery of dairy ice cream inside, convinced them that the right product had been found before they had even started looking. A target launch date was set for Spring 1995.

The development team explained that the smoothness of the fruit ice required a new, patentable production technique. Patents were immediately pursued and the implications for factory layout were examined.

The product's shape, taste and size were refined during the summer, using qualitative research. The whole product concept was then researched in Germany, Italy, Holland and Portugal in November 1993, to see how well it might perform as a Europe-wide brand. The results were so encouraging that the Birds Eye Wall's Board decided to rush the project forward for a 1994 test launch in Britain.

Meanwhile an appropriate brand name was sought that could be pronounced and registered throughout Europe. A specialist brand name agency found that only 42 from a 'shortlist' of 950 names could pass both tests. And the brand team liked none of them. Further work produced a final choice between two: Oasis and Solero. The Solero name was not available in Belgium, but its association with the sun and its exceptional pronounceability made it the winner. (In Belgium, you will have to ask for Soledo.)

At the same time, the packaging design had been decided upon and the price set at 80p – between Opal Fruits at 65p and Magnum at 90p. The product was ready for launch.

As June 1994 approached it was still not certain whether the factory would be able to produce this new style of ice cream in sufficient numbers. So it was decided that no advertising would be run until it was clear that production could keep up with demand. This was fortunate, because although factory output proved buoyant, an exceptionally hot July sent demand rocketing for all refreshment products.

The market share graph shows Solero's rise to a 20 per cent sector share in its first, rushed season. Pleasingly for Birds Eye Wall's, it hit the share held by Mars Opal Fruits brand and – surprisingly – Mars

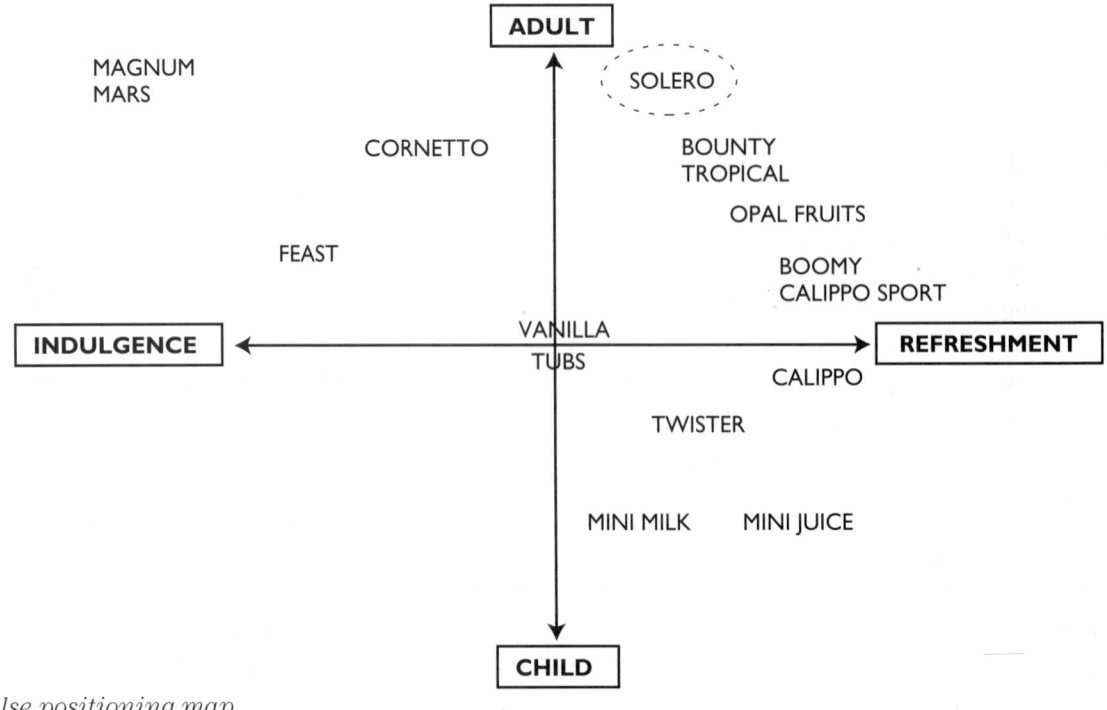

Impulse positioning map

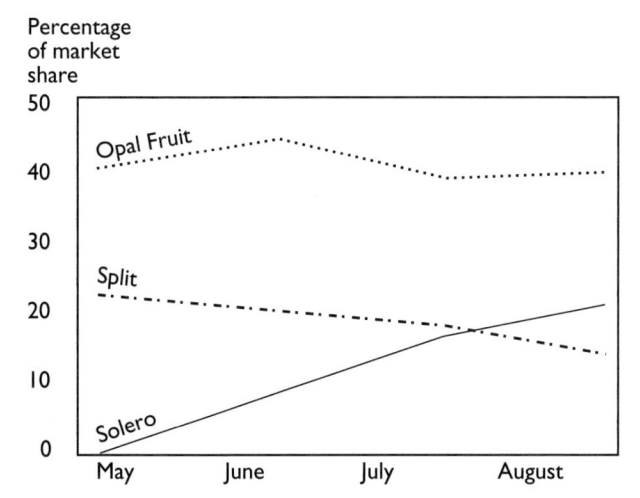

Market share within adult refreshment sector – 1994

ice cream. Most important of all, however, Solero achieved its target of expanding the market for ice cream. One quarter of Solero buyers were not previously ice cream impulse buyers at all. For Melanie Heap, Solero's brand manager, the product launch is now history. Her task now is to keep the upward momentum going.

How is the market divided up?

The pattern of replies drawn from market research provides clues as to the kinds of people who are likely to buy that product or service. Several distinct groups of customers are revealed who make up sections or **segments** within the total market. Once the characteristics and buying behaviour of these groups is known, marketing can then be directed at the particular segments or **target groups** which have been identified as containing the most potential customers.

The firm can then establish its market position by concentrating the marketing effort on the particular segment which is likely to yield the highest sales for its products or services. The advantage of identifying target groups is that the sales effort can be directed by means of a 'rifle shot' approach at the people who are most likely to buy. This is far more effective than aiming the sales effort at the market in general, as in the scattered 'shotgun' approach.

Market segments are divided up on the basis of demographic factors, such as age, sex and geographical area, and also on consumers' income, occupation and ethnic group. Segments can also be divided up in terms of many other factors, such as whether people are heavy or light users of the product or service.

One of the most common ways of defining market segments is by **socio-economic group (SEG)**. Table 2.1 on page 18 illustrates this. People within the same SEG tend to show certain similarities in their expectations, values and behaviour compared with members of other groups. However, this is a very general classification and some overlapping does occur. For example, some people from the lower SEGs may earn more than those from higher SEGs.

The markets for most **fast-moving consumer goods** tend to be highly segmented, for example, soaps, shampoos, cigarettes, biscuits etc. Some companies try to offer a range of products which exploits all segments. However, they need to be aware of the danger of **fragmentation**. This occurs if they try to cater for too many segments, and each segment becomes so small that very little profit is generated.

Small firms generally find it easier to break into a specific segment of a wider market. This enables them to survive by concentrating on supplying a specialised product or service, rather than trying to compete with bigger firms who have cornered the mass market. This strategy of identifying a specialist segment at which marketing can be targeted is called **niche marketing**.

Markets should, however, always be segmented on the basis of what customers want or need, not on the basis of the products they buy. This is an important distinction. Firms who think they are just in the business of making slide rules and concentrate all their efforts on improving their slide rules are in danger of going out of business when a firm comes

TABLE 2.1 *JICNARS social grade definitions*

Social grade	Social status	Occupation
A	Upper middle class	Higher managerial, administrative, or professional
B	Middle class	Intermediate managerial, administrative or professional
C1	Lower middle class	Supervisory or clerical, and junior managerial, administrative or professional
C2	Skilled working class	Skilled manual workers
D	Working class	Semi-skilled and unskilled manual workers
E	Those at lowest level of subsistence	State pensioners or widows (no other earner), casual or lowest-grade workers

Source: *JICNARS National Readership Survey*

along which makes calculators. They have ignored the fact that what customers actually want is a product that carries out calculations quickly. They do not want a slide rule as such, so if a better product becomes available which does calculations quickly, consumers will buy that instead.

ACTIVITY

Identifying target groups

1 Decide what target group each of the following products or services is aimed at and the needs which are being catered for in each case.

- Spray furniture polish
- Building society accounts
- Ford Fiestas
- Ready meals
- Rolls Royces
- TV rental shops
- *Oh Boy!* magazine
- Polyfilla
- Life insurance
- Season tickets
- The *Financial Times*

2 What are some of the market arguments for the following products or services?

- Shampoos (e.g., normal, dry, greasy, permed, dandruff, frequent wash, baby shampoo etc.)
- Breakfast cereals
- Package holidays
- CDs
- Cheap Day returns
- Cars
- Watches

Who are a firm's main customers?

In many cases, it is common to find that 20 per cent of customers account for 80 per cent of sales. This is known as the 80/20 Rule or **Pareto Effect**.

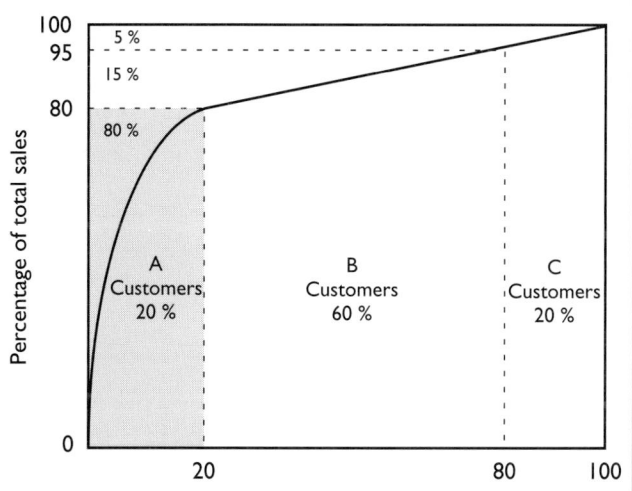

The Pareto Effect

The diagram shows the typical ratio of sales to customer groups found in the Pareto Effect. The A group constitutes 20 per cent of customers and accounts for 80 per cent of total sales. The B group constitutes 60 per cent of customers and accounts for 15 per cent of sales, whilst the C group makes up 20 per cent of customers, but only accounts for 5 per cent of sales. Clearly, firms that are successful in identifying the A group can make their advertising considerably more effective by targeting these important customers. However, they should not forget that some B or C group customers can become A group customers with good service and attention.

The marketing mix

After considering the market research findings and identifying the market segment it intends to target, the firm then needs to offer a total package to meet customers' needs and wants. Four key areas are blended to produce the required response in the target audience: product, price, place and promotion. These elements make up the **marketing mix**, or 'offering' to the customer.

The right product

A new product is distinct from a **line extension**, such as a 'new' lemon version of a shampoo. Ideas for new products can come from anywhere – the company's own research and development programme, competitors' products and so on. A constant supply of new ideas or **concepts** is needed, as only a small percentage survives screening and test marketing to be launched nationally.

Sometimes it takes marketing flair to think of a good use for an invention. The highly successful yellow Post-it™ notes were born when 3M invented an adhesive that had low stickiness but retained its properties after repeated use. It wasn't what they were looking for so it was put on the shelf, until years later when another researcher suggested using it for a notepad with pages that stuck but could be peeled off easily. Post-it™ notes went on to become one of their best sellers – quite a feat in view of the fact that 3M make about 60,000 different products!

Of course, only a handful of new products ever become winners. One reason many products fail is that they are not distinctive enough. If a new product is to succeed, it should have certain features which make it stand out from the competition, so that it forms a **unique selling proposition (USP)**. In reality, these distinguishing features are often very minor. For instance, all shampoos contain the same basic ingredients. It is only the additives which vary slightly. The differences are more in the way each shampoo is packaged, priced and advertised. Creating a unique identity in this way turns a product into a **brand**, which means it can then be sold for more. A comparison between prices of branded goods and supermarket own-label goods illustrates the point.

Companies can increase their total **market share** by introducing many **brand variants** aimed at different segments of the market. For example, Van den Berghs have done this with their margarine brands, such as Stork, Blue Band, Echo, Flora, Krona etc. However, firms must be careful not to introduce brands with a low profit margin that **cannibalise** market share away from their other products which may be brand leaders with higher profit margins.

THE PRODUCT LIFE CYCLE

Any product will pass through various stages in its life cycle, just as humans and animals do, although the time span between when it is first introduced and when it is finally withdrawn from the market varies greatly.

As products reach maturity in a market which has been fully exploited and has therefore become **saturated**, they start to decline. In some cases, the firm may decide to delay the end by using various **extension strategies**. The product can be given a new lease of life by being repackaged or reformulated. A good example of a long-running brand is Lux soap which is over 80 years old. Its

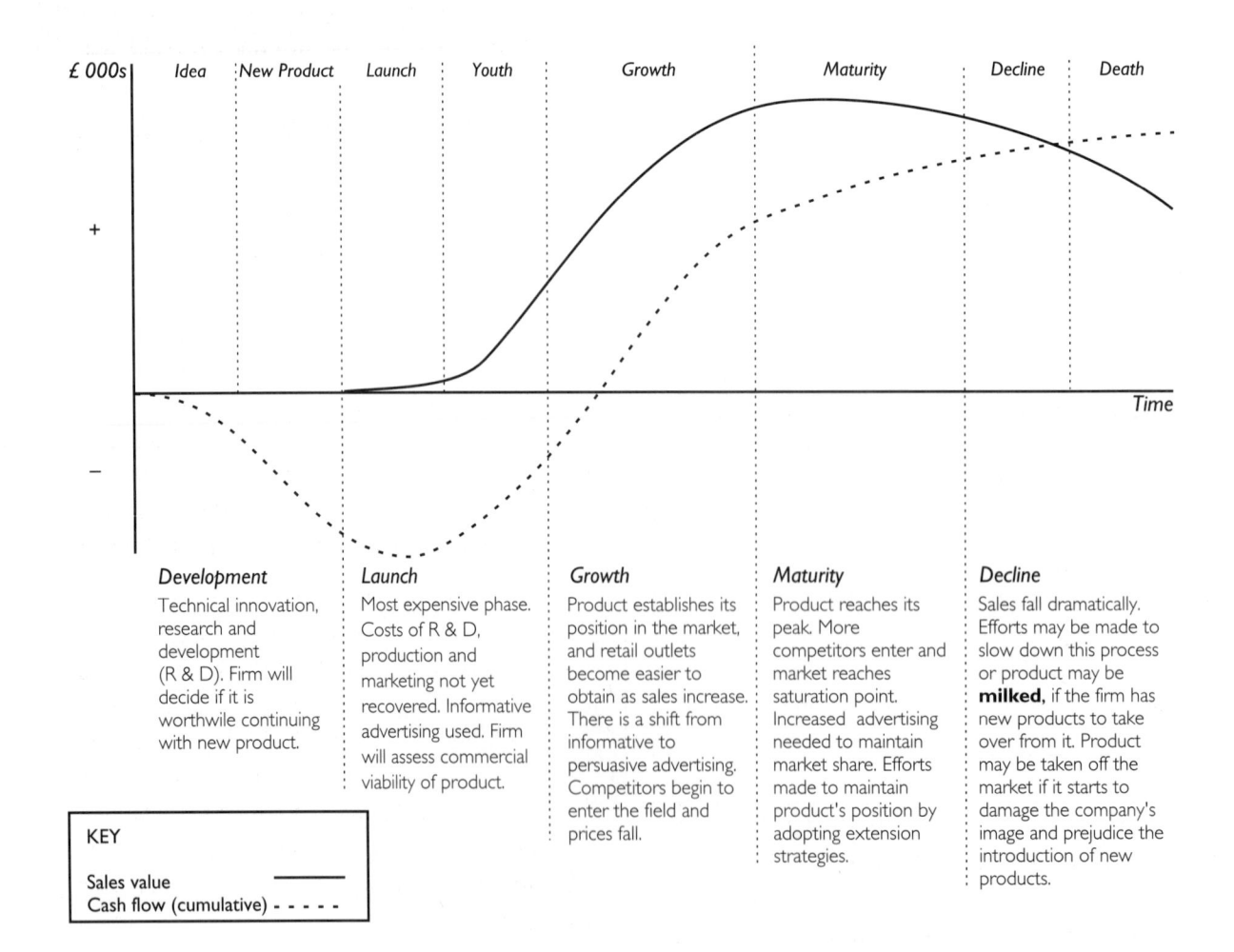

Development
Technical innovation, research and development (R & D). Firm will decide if it is worthwhile continuing with new product.

Launch
Most expensive phase. Costs of R & D, production and marketing not yet recovered. Informative advertising used. Firm will assess commercial viability of product.

Growth
Product establishes its position in the market, and retail outlets become easier to obtain as sales increase. There is a shift from informative to persuasive advertising. Competitors begin to enter the field and prices fall.

Maturity
Product reaches its peak. More competitors enter and market reaches saturation point. Increased advertising needed to maintain market share. Efforts made to maintain product's position by adopting extension strategies.

Decline
Sales fall dramatically. Efforts may be made to slow down this process or product may be **milked**, if the firm has new products to take over from it. Product may be taken off the market if it starts to damage the company's image and prejudice the introduction of new products.

KEY
Sales value ———
Cash flow (cumulative) - - - - -

The product life cycle

shape, perfume, colour and packaging have changed continuously during that time. Other strategies include finding new uses or markets for the product or bringing out new accessories for it.

Some brands seem to live forever – your parents and maybe even your grandparents will probably remember such classics as Bisto, Oxo, Dettol, Ovaltine, or Colman's mustard.

Most products do, of course, eventually die. Often this is just because of changing consumer tastes, but increasingly it is because of the rapid pace of technological change. Life cycles are getting shorter and shorter, especially in areas such as the electronics industry. New products become obsolete; often within months rather than years, as each technically more advanced version is brought out.

THE BOSTON MATRIX

A single-product business is very vulnerable in the market place, particularly if it only has a few major customers. Most businesses are therefore **multi-product** firms with a **portfolio** or variety of products, which they try to ensure are all at different stages in their life cycles in order to avoid great fluctuations in profit levels. A well-balanced portfolio also means that the revenue generated by older products can help to nurture new products through their introduction.

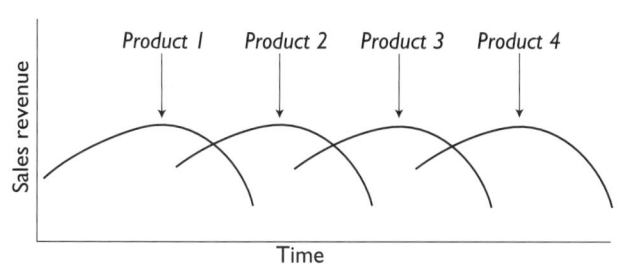

The importance of successive product launches

The Boston Consulting Group in Massachusetts, USA, have devised a matrix for classifying products in order to analyse whether a firm's product portfolio is well balanced.

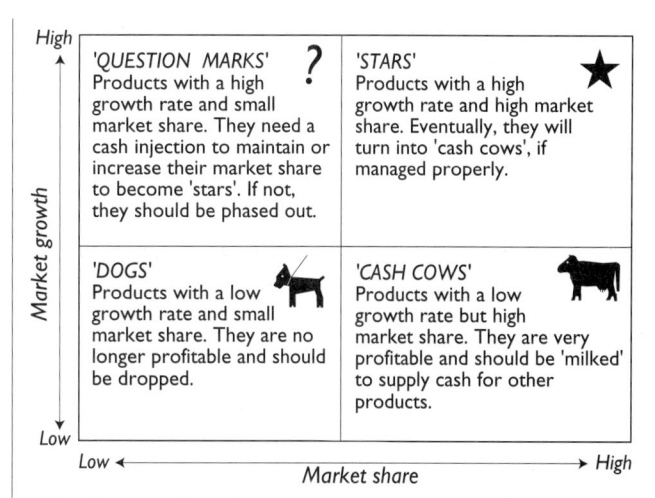

'QUESTION MARKS' Products with a high growth rate and small market share. They need a cash injection to maintain or increase their market share to become 'stars'. If not, they should be phased out.

'STARS' Products with a high growth rate and high market share. Eventually, they will turn into 'cash cows', if managed properly.

'DOGS' Products with a low growth rate and small market share. They are no longer profitable and should be dropped.

'CASH COWS' Products with a low growth rate but high market share. They are very profitable and should be 'milked' to supply cash for other products.

The Boston Matrix

CASE STUDY

The launch of Chicken Tonight

In September 1993 a new product 'came out flapping'. A £10 million blitz announced the arrival of Chicken Tonight, a range of recipe sauces for chicken pieces. The high-profile launch campaign shot Chicken Tonight to brand leadership in the market for cooking sauces, boosted the whole market size, and won industry awards for 'launch of the year'.

The story began in 1992, with the successful introduction of Chicken Tonight in America by a sister company of Brooke Bond Foods. Brooke Bond, already a force in the fast-growing cooking sauce market with its pasta sauce, decided to test Chicken Tonight in Britain. The first priority was to ensure that the recipes met British tastes and regulations. After market research, all varieties were adjusted to suit British tastes, such as adding real cream to the 'Creamy' varieties.

With the new products performing well in research, Brooke Bond decided to launch the product as quickly as possible. The salesforce was set a target of getting the product into at least 65 per cent of grocery shops. In fact they managed to persuade 85 per cent of retailers to stock the brand before the first commercial appeared.

The brand manager also set a sales target – to achieve a 12 per cent market share. This was beaten comfortably, with Chicken Tonight enjoying a 21.6 per cent market share by the first quarter of 1994. Furthermore, the launch boosted sales within the whole market from £90 million to £120 million, increasing the value of each market share percentage.

The sales success was based upon a two-pronged approach: first, achieve high product trial; then maximise repeat purchase. The brand management team, Claire Potter and William Brown, knew it would be hard to gain product trial. There were already 130 sauces crowded onto the market, yet fewer than half the households in the country ever bought one. Furthermore there were strongly established brands such as Homepride and Uncle Ben's. It was decided that the launch advertising campaign would have to be bigger and have more impact than any rival, involving a major TV campaign. In addition it would need heavy support from trial gaining sales promotions.

The television campaign proved a tremendous success, with its memorable song and slogan 'I feel like Chicken Tonight'. Research showed it to be six times more memorable than other cook-in sauce advertisements. The launch sales promotion was also important. It offered cash back on the first purchase, an offer taken up by 18 per cent of customers.

To maintain customer interest, Brooke Bond developed the wing-flapping theme of the advertising into a nationwide 'flapper roadshow'. Shoppers were recorded doing chicken impersonations for TV commercials. As many as 25,000 people attended each roadshow. Repeat purchase was also achieved through the quality of the product itself, the range of six recipes, and by the launch of three new versions at the start of 1995.

Chicken Tonight succeeded partly because of the heavy marketing spending and excellent distribution levels, but also because Brooke Bond's marketing team worked to bring together the right products and promote them in a unique and interesting way.

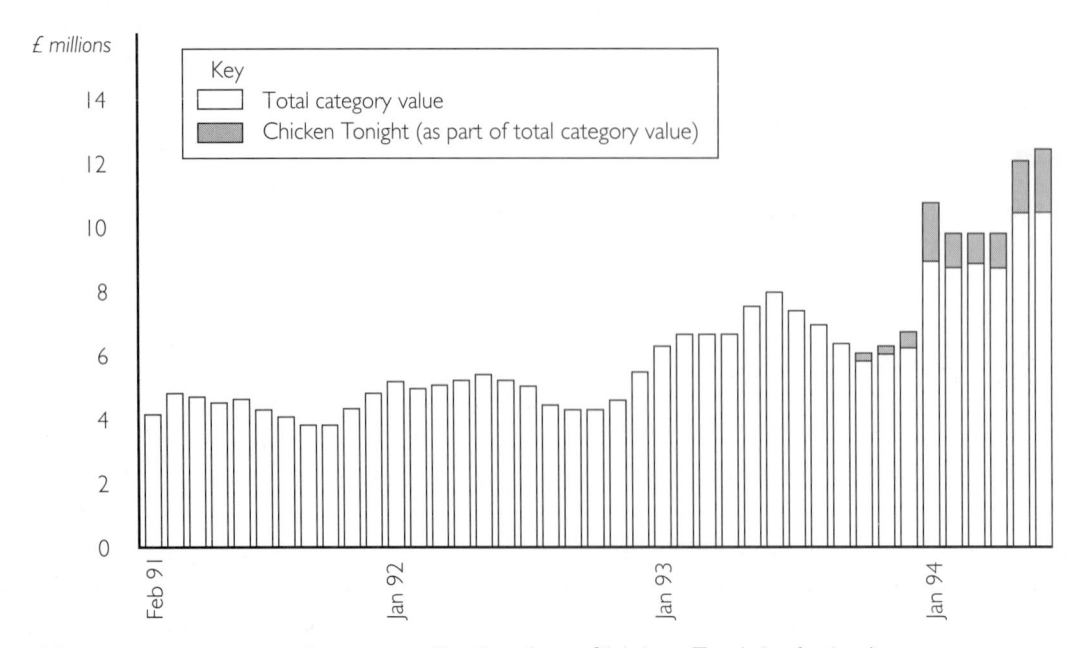

Wet cooking sauce category value – contribution from Chicken Tonight (value)

MARKETING AND SALES

> ## ❝ DISCUSSION POINTS ❞
>
> *1* What marketing mix did Brooke Bond use in their launch of Chicken Tonight?
>
> *2* Conduct a SWOT analysis on Chicken Tonight to identify its Strengths, Weaknesses, Opportunities and Threats.

In-store promotion for Chicken Tonight

The right price

The price of a product or service is another element of the marketing mix, which interacts with the other factors to determine whether or not consumers will buy. The model of demand and supply in the diagram shows how the market works.

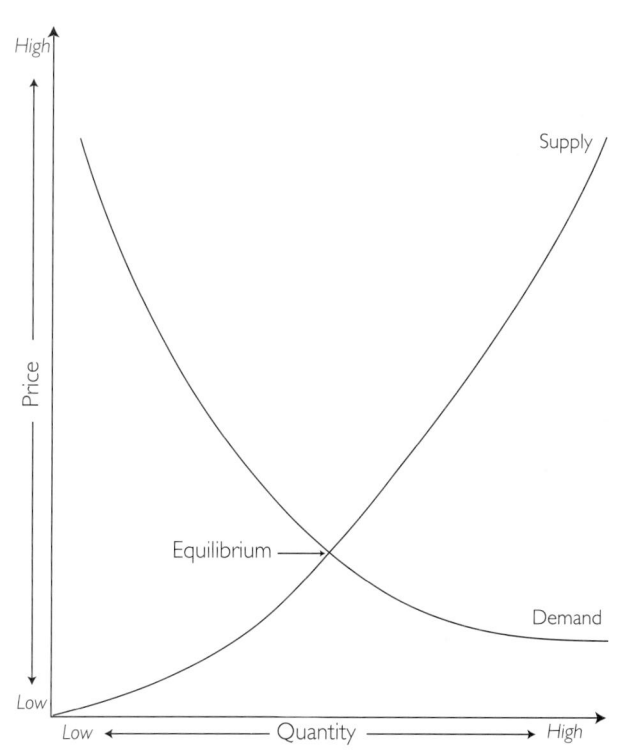

Demand curve – shows more goods are bought when prices are low.
Supply curve – shows suppliers offer more goods when prices are high.
Equilibrium – the market price is set where supply equals demand.
Glut – when an excess of supply pushes prices down.
Shortage – when supply is too low to meet the demand, forcing prices up.

Supply and demand curves

This overall view of the market provides a simple view of how demand and supply interact. However, a firm's decision as to which pricing strategy to adopt is complicated by many other factors. The pricing strategy will vary according to the stage reached in the product's life cycle and its **position** in the market relative to its competitors. If the product can be **differentiated** from rival products, perhaps by its good design, or by the quality of the after-sales service offered, then it can be sold for more.

So what pricing strategies might be used?

- **Market penetration** A price is set which is below that of competitors, in order to capture a share of the market. A short-term loss is sometimes accepted, in the hope that the price can be raised after **brand loyalty** has been gained and customers start to reorder the brand by name. The actual products may be priced cheaply in order to encourage customers to buy, but the accessories to go with it may be priced expensively, as with the film for instant cameras. However, if prices are pitched too low, customers may become suspicious about quality. Another danger of price cutting is that competitors may retaliate by lowering their prices as well. Firms tend to avoid getting into such a price-cutting war, because the end result is that they all achieve the same market share as they had before, but at a lower price level. A low price strategy may also prove dangerous for products which are expected to have a short life span.

- **Skimming**   A high price is set to recover the development costs of new products quickly. Consumers are prepared to pay high prices for products which are innovative and for which there are no substitutes. CD players, for example, were priced at £1,000 when first launched, yet within two years were available for £200. Similarly, video recorders, calculators, computer games and telephone answering machines all commanded high prices when they were first introduced onto the market. The danger of pricing products too highly is that sales may be lost.
- **Price discrimination**   A price is set which varies for different segments of the market – for example, pensioners can get cheap tickets.
- **Competitive pricing**   A price is set which is at the same going rate as competitors' prices. This is common when goods or services provided are very similar and not capable of being differentiated very much, as with home mortgages or petrol.

Having worked out their pricing strategy, firms then need to calculate what price to charge for their goods. A common pricing method is **cost plus**, which is when the total costs incurred are added together and a suitable percentage **mark-up** added on for profit. In the final analysis, though, the 'right' price should not just be based on the firm's costs. It must relate to the price that sufficient numbers of customers are prepared to pay – that is, the price that the market will bear – which in turn is dependent on how customers perceive the value of the product.

The right place

Having decided on the right product and price, the company has to get the product to the industrial user or final consumer by way of an efficient and cost-effective distribution system.

The traditional **channel of distribution** is from manufacturer to wholesaler to retailer to consumer. Wholesalers, because they are in the middle, have the advantage of **breaking bulk**. This means that retailers can buy in smaller quantities from them, rather than from manufacturers who tend to prefer to make one large delivery.

In recent years this chain has been shortened as many manufacturers have started to sell directly to large retailers who buy in bulk, such as the supermarket chains with their own depots, or to retailers who can carry huge stocks themselves, such as the hypermarkets like Asda. A shorter distribution channel is also used when the product is fragile and handling must be minimised, as with frozen foods, or where the product is bulky, as with furniture. Some manufacturers sell directly to the consumer using mail order.

The method of transport is also important. Cost-effective physical distribution can result in significant savings for the company. The choice of transport method is determined by weight, bulk, value and perishability of the goods and by the needs of the company. Road tends to be the most popular as it is the most flexible method, offering a door-to-door service without the restrictions of rail transport. Rail is cheaper for bulky goods and can compete with road over long journeys where the door-to-door factor becomes less critical. Air is used for light, expensive and perishable goods. Sea is used for bulky commodities like oil transported over long distances. In recent years the widespread use of containers has streamlined distribution considerably.

The choice of **distribution outlet** is partly influenced by the image and nature of the product. Expensive perfume would obviously not be sold through supermarkets. Products that have a low unit cost, are purchased frequently and are easily substituted, such as crisps and baked beans, must be widely available or sales are lost.

Retail outlets include supermarkets, hypermarkets, department stores, multiple stores, cooperatives and discount stores. Goods can also be sold by mail order and door-to-door selling. A recent development has been the growth of **franchising**, where the **franchisees** own their own business but the **franchiser** provides the name, products and expertise to run it, with the benefits of economies of scale like bulk buying and national advertising.

The Body Shop group provides a good example of the benefits of franchising where the franchiser is able to expand by functioning, in effect, as a wholesaler. Anita Roddick, 1984's Businesswoman of the Year, has made her Body Shop group something of a retailing legend, with sales accelerating to £195 million in 1994 and numerous applicants waiting for a franchise. With only £4,000 start-up capital, she has managed to expand the business through the franchise route, yet still kept tight control on all the outlets.

The right promotion

Having got the right product and determined the right price the firm must design an effective promotion strategy. There are three aspects of promotion: advertising, sales promotions and public relations.

ADVERTISING

This is the most common type of promotion and one of the earliest forms. As mass production increased in the latter stages of the Industrial Revolution and economies of scale were made, high volume sales were needed, which meant firms had to advertise in order to attract large numbers of customers. As living standards improved still further, encouraging the production of more goods, it was no longer a sellers' market and firms had to compete with each other to persuade customers to buy their product.

Not all advertising is aimed at consumers as the **end users**. Increasingly, advertisers are having to sell to the retailer, which necessitates a different kind of advertising, where the degree of trade acceptability already achieved by the product is emphasised in order to persuade the retailer to stock it.

In the field of industrial marketing, the text of advertisements or **advertising copy** tends to be less emotive and more informative. This is because industrial buying decisions often tend to be made by groups of people rather than individuals, unlike those made by domestic consumers. The decisions also tend to be made in a more formal and methodical way. There is a greater emphasis on advertising in the trade press, trade fairs and exhibitions and on the use of technical brochures.

Commercial television is the most expensive medium to use but is also the most popular because of its effectiveness. Although TV advertising in Britain is only 40 years old, it has produced slogans and catch phrases that have become part of our language, familiar jingles and lasting images. The demands of telling an interesting story in a short space of time are such that it is no accident that one of our most successful directors, Alan Parker of *Bugsy Malone*, *Midnight Express* and *Shoot the Moon* fame, began in films as a director of TV commercials.

Other media that are less expensive include commercial radio, posters, cinema, magazines, journals and newspapers.

ACTIVITY

Identifying types of advertising

Give examples of products and services which are advertised by using the following methods:

- **Persuasive** – glamorous images and persuasive language used to encourage consumers to buy.

- **Informative** – used to make consumers aware of the existence and identity of the product. May provide technical information.
- **Corporate** – where a company promotes its name and image rather than an individual product. Benefits overall sales of all products.
- **Generic** – where a group of manufacturers promotes a whole industry or type of product.
- **Competitive** – where companies subtly imply that rival firms' products are inferior to their own.

SALES PROMOTIONS

These are used to generate short-term increases in sales by encouraging consumers to try the product once, in the hope of generating repeat sales. They include:

- Coupons, vouchers, and percentage reduction (such as 25p off, £1 cash refund, etc.).
- Free samples. These are often used for new products.
- Self-liquidating offers. Goods are offered at cost price for a certain number of tokens or packet tops.
- Free offers, such as free gifts at petrol stations.
- Bargain packs such as '20 per cent extra free', 'Buy two, get one free' etc.
- Charity promotions. On receipt of a certain number of proofs of purchase, a donation is made to charity.
- Prize promotions and newspaper bingo.

Point-of-sale promotions encourage customers into the shop. A well-known type of price promotion is the use of **loss leaders**, where customers are attracted into the shop by a few products priced cheaply in the hope that they will then buy other products priced normally.

PUBLIC RELATIONS

This is the process of obtaining favourable publicity via the editorial columns of press media or in television or radio braodcasts. The PR expert has the contacts within the media to ensure that the client's story or side to a dispute is reported sympathetically. Public relations can be a positive process of organising interviews on Breakfast TV shows or setting up launch parties for new products. However there have also been cases where PR personnel have been engaged in spreading negative, even malicious stories about rival firms. PR can also backfire if it is *too* successful. For example, some pop bands are so 'hyped' that their music cannot live up to the advance publicity.

CASE STUDY

Levi 501s – why was denim fading?

The scene is an American laundromat in the 1950s. A young man wearing jeans walks in, calmly takes off his jeans and puts them in the machine. He then sits down amongst the other customers in his boxer shorts and carries on reading while he waits for his jeans to be washed.

This advert, 'Launderette', which was part of the campaign that advertising agency Bartle Bogle Hegarty (BBH) produced for the relaunched Levi 501s, has become a cult classic – one of the most successful adverts of all time. It made the actor, Nick Kamen, an overnight star. In the UK alone, sales rocketed by 800 per cent within the first year. The factory in Scotland where the jeans were stitched together could not meet demand, even by working 18-hour shifts and taking on extra staff. Levi's sold three months' stock of 501s in just three weeks. Shops were besieged by people asking to try on the jeans that 'the bloke in the launderette wears'.

Yet before the decision was taken to relaunch the original 501 classic design, Levi Strauss, who are the world's biggest manufacturer of jeans, were suffering from a serious downturn in the jeans market. The main problem was that by the early 1980s, the 16- to

MARKETING AND SALES

24-year-olds who buy half of all jeans sold had begun to see denim jeans as a tired legacy of their parents' younger years. Sales in the European jeans market slumped from 250 million pairs in 1981 to 150 million pairs in 1985. Levi's reaction to the declining market was to **diversify** their product base. The trouble was that having moved away from jeans into products ranging from socks to flannel shirts, it got to the point where the Levi's brand name was in danger of being diluted.

Something had to be done. Levi's made the bold decision to go back to basics, reverse the diversification and concentrate on selling jeans. The job of designing the European promotion to accompany the relaunch of the 501 design was given to BBH. The objectives of the campaign were to increase the profitability of the company and to lower the age profile of the brand's consumers, which had been creeping up and away from the **core** of the jeans market as the brand's image had worsened. According to Tim Lindsay, the director in charge of the Levi Strauss account at BBH, 'The **creative brief** was to persuade the 15- to 20-year-old males, who represent the core of the jeans market, that 501s were the right look and the only label.' The campaign had to be designed to appeal to this **target market**. The message also had to be clear without the use of speech, as the adverts were to be shown across Europe.

Market research carried out by BBH revealed a growing desire amongst the young for clothes and objects with a genuine heritage. They also uncovered a fascination for a mythical America of the past – 'the America that had produced Dean and Presley, the '57 Chevrolet and Sam Cooke'.

Further research confirmed that the campaign based around the fifties nostalgia theme was liked. Accordingly 'Launderette' and 'Bath' (with actor James Mardle getting into a bath to shrink his 501s) went on air in December 1985. They were quickly followed by 'Parting' and 'Entrance'. The later commercials, 'Cochrane', 'Refrigerator' and 'Pick up', also invoke the nostalgia theme.

The series of commercials for 501s has won many industry awards, both in the UK and internationally.

They have been discussed on 23 different TV programmes, thus providing additional free advertising. Most importantly, the campaign achieved its original objectives of returning the company to profitability and of adjusting the brand's **consumer profile** back to the core of the market.

In addition, Levi's **market share** rocketed from 13 per cent to 18 per cent. Competitors did not complain. They also benefited from the rejuvenated jeans market, which expanded from being worth £550 million in 1985 to £800 million in 1987. Sales of other products also increased. The 'golden oldies' which formed the soundtracks of the adverts all got into the UK top ten when re-released. According to trade sources, 'Launderette' also created a major fashion trend, with over two million pairs of boxer shorts being sold in 1986!

A scene from Levi's advertisement, 'Creek'

Since then, Levi's have cemented their position as market leaders, gaining a 26 per cent share of a market worth £1.11 billion by 1994. The campaign has also gone from strength to strength, with the series of advertisements 'Night and Day', 'Procession', 'Tackle' and 'Campfire' capturing the mood and style of modern day America.

'Creek', focusing on a staid Middle American Sunday picnic opens with a Ma, Pa and their two daughters in a horse-drawn buggy. Enjoying a few moments of freedom, as they run through the woods the girls are stopped in their tracks by the sight of a bare-torsoed man bathing in the creek and a pair of trousers drying on a rock in the sun. From their hiding place the girls watch as our hero wades to the shore and it is revealed that he is wearing a pair of original shrink-to-fit Levi's 501s.

Industrial marketing

Industrial marketing means offering the right product at the right price at the right place to sell profitably to *business* customers. In other words, selling goods and services that are not aimed directly at consumers.

Industrial marketing is used for:

- Selling finished goods such as aeroplanes, lorries or office furniture.
- Selling raw materials or components such as steel or plastic computer casings.
- Selling services to businesses, such as waste disposal or legal and auditing services.

In any of the above, industrial marketing is likely to imply a finely targeted approach – honing in on the few people in companies who will be involved in making the buying decision. So whereas consumer marketing tends to aim at mass markets, industrial marketing is more focused. A single industrial customer may be responsible for buying millions of pounds worth of a single product.

So how does industrial marketing differ from consumer marketing? Clearly the marketing mix will be affected. When dealing with fewer, more expert buyers, products must be tailored precisely to customer requirements and provide exceptional levels of quality, service back-up and reliability. With industrial marketing, the product becomes the primary element of the mix; although price and place remain very important, promotion often takes a secondary role.

Increasingly, though, progressive British companies are rethinking their approach to the promotion of industrial goods. They have come to appreciate that to keep existing customers and develop new ones requires more innovation and product development. New products can only generate new business if customers are made aware of the developments and their benefits. That can eventually be achieved through salesforce links with existing clients, but product promotion through direct mail, trade exhibitions and trade magazines can also be highly effective.

Many of Britain's biggest and most successful manufacturing companies sell exclusively to industrial buyers. Therefore the general public are unaware of names such as the TI Group, GKN or GEC Alsthom. Yet they are among Britain's biggest export earners and heaviest investors in research and development. Industrial marketing is their way of sustaining this success.

CASE STUDY

TI Group plc – marketing seals

When the State of California passed a law demanding zero industrial pollution emissions, businesses throughout the world were horrified. Here was a State which, on its own, represented the world's sixth largest economy, acting in a way that could threaten the very existence of many factories and thousands of jobs.

Fortunately, some firms took a more positive view, deciding to take up the challenge of cleaning up their manufacturing. One was Britain's TI Group plc, through its subsidiary John Crane. John Crane manufactures sealing systems for pumps. Although this may sound a minor product line, in 1995 John Crane's sales were more than £500 million – more than twice the worldwide turnover of The Body Shop.

Virtually every production process requires liquids to be pumped from one place to another. Often it is just water acting as a coolant, but sometimes the liquid being pumped around might be a dangerous acid or other hazardous, even toxic liquids. The propellor of the pump sits inside the pump's casing and pushes the liquid forward. The external environment, motor and bearings must be protected from the liquid, which is where the sealing system comes in. If the liquid is as harmless as water, a cheap seal will do the job adequately. If it is a hazardous or toxic liquid, however, a very strong and highly reliable sealing system will be needed.

John Crane has provided a wide range of sealing products for over 75 years, but all involved the emission of minute quantities of liquid. This was thought inevitable because the pump *inside* the pipe was being driven by a rod turned by the motor *outside* the pipe. To protect the motor entirely from the liquid would require a plug so rigid that the rod would be unable to turn.

John Crane's invention is of a 100 per cent effective seal that allows zero pollution emissions. The firm's technological breakthrough is complex, but, in short, involves the use of a safe gas such as nitrogen being pumped under pressure through special spiral grooves cut into the seal. This acts as a safe barrier, allowing only nitrogen to escape in small quantities. As nitrogen is a component of air, it is not a pollutant.

Having tested and patented this process, John Crane was able to launch this important new product onto the world market in 1993. The seal had been developed in anticipation of customers' zero emission requirements in the wake of strict government pollution laws. Other features of the new seal included longer life, reduced maintenance costs, lower energy costs and ease of installation – resulting in a lower total cost for customers, despite the higher price of the seal itself.

John Crane's 100 per cent effective seal

The approach to the launch was bound up in a new marketing strategy. After careful analysis of its product and market strengths and weaknesses, John Crane decided to focus its efforts upon specific markets such as chemicals, petrochemicals and oil refining. Here, hazardous and expensive fluids require high technology seals with high value added. These target markets would be served by specialist sales engineers who would be briefed to provide exceptional service.

The new pump seals were therefore developed first for customers within the core market. Selling a leading-edge, high technology product also required the use of a high technology selling technique. An impressive multimedia computer presentation was produced to explain with graphics and sound, the benefits of the new seal. This, together with John Crane's detailed knowledge of customer needs, made it quite easy to sell the new product – even though the cost is far more than that of an ordinary seal.

To gain new customers, the company featured its new seal (the Type 2800) at the June 1995 Eurochem trade exhibition at Birmingham's huge National Exhibition Centre. With special spiral groove carpet and etched glass partitions, the large stand created a great deal of interest, generating over 150 new business leads. Great care was taken over press releases to trade magazines, ensuring a good level of favourable (and free) publicity.

A further consequence of John Crane's new marketing strategy was to make more effort to win market share in the fast-growing economies of the Far East. The company set up new service centres in the region and hired and trained new sales engineers. The unique Type 2800 offered a marvellous opportunity to make new customer contacts which might lead on to a whole range of sales opportunities.

John Crane has set an ambitious, multimillion-pound sales target for the Type 2800. It expects sales to grow 20 times between 1995 and the year 2000! Industrial marketing may not have the glamour of the consumer side, but it has just the same opportunities.

" DISCUSSION POINTS "

1 Every business has many stakeholders (groups with an interest in the firm's success or failure). Which of the following stakeholders are affected by John Crane's marketing success?
- Shareholders
- Employees
- The Government
- Local residents
- Society generally

2 Many people think that the interests of stakeholders inevitably conflict. Discuss this view in the light of the John Crane case study.

ACTIVITY

Pace Designs: designing a promotional campaign for a new product

BRIEF

You work for the advertising agency of Marston, Davis and Longton, who have just been approached by Pace Designs to produce a new promotion campaign for the national launch of their exciting new range of unisex jeans aimed at the 16- to 24-year-old target group.

1. Decide on a new name for the jeans and an appropriate slogan to be used in all the promotions. These must be in keeping with the image of the product and its market positioning.

2. Two commercials will be produced by your agency, to be shown on TV and in the cinema, which will cost £300,000 each to make. Suggest an outline idea or theme on which the adverts could be based.

3. Decide how you will allocate your promotion budget of £1.5 million between TV and press in order to reach the target group most effectively. Use Tables 2.2 and 2.3, which show advertising rates and circulation figures. Decide if any other sales promotions are to be used.

4. Design a full-page advertising spread for a newspaper or magazine, based on the theme you have chosen and incorporating all the necessary details.

MARKETING AND SALES

Advertising rates for selected TV regions

ITV Region	Maximum cost of a 30 second spot at weekday peak times (£)	Audience (number of ITV households '000)
Carlton/LWT (London)	74,000	4,565
Central TV (Midlands)	35,000	3,668
Granada TV (North West)	21,000	2,590
Yorkshire TV (Yorkshire)	15,000	2,301
Meridian (South and South East)	28,000	2,134
HTV (Wales and West)	15,000	1,842
Anglia TV (East)	20,000	1,665
Scottish TV (Central Scotland)	11,000	1,400
Tyne Tees TV (North East)	5,000	1,184
West Country TV (South West)	6,000	660
Ulster TV (Ulster)	3,000	491
Grampian TV (North Scotland)	2,000	479
Border TV (Border)	1,200	271

Source: British Rate and Data (BRAD), June 1994, BARB Establishment Survey Report Q4 1993

Advertising rates for selected TV regions

Advertising rates for selected newspapers and magazines

Newspaper or magazine	Cost of full page spread at standard rate (£)	Circulation (Average number of sales per month)
Daily Express	31,500	1,491,077
Daily Mail	32,760	1,758,994
Daily Mirror	32,800	2,695,266
Sun	34,500	3,521,855
Daily Telegraph	43,500	1,033,573
News of the World	40,000	4,664,092
Radio Times	17,950	1,485,759
TV Times	14,400	1,021,966
Cosmopolitan	10,920	456,703
Mizz	7,750	183,960
Just Seventeen	7,930	226,562
Options	9,800	163,455

Source: British Rate and Data (BRAD), June 1994

Advertising rates for selected newspapers and magazines

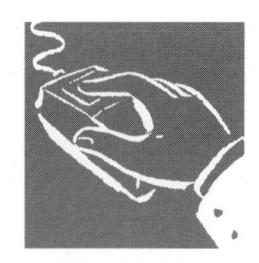

Design and development

IN ASSOCIATION WITH

SONY

Introduction: what does design involve?

In the face of mounting evidence that buying decisions are rarely made on price alone, it is becoming increasingly obvious that good design is a powerful and competitive weapon for business. Good design can also add value to a product, enabling it to be sold for more. Enlightened firms are already realising that good design can be one of the most powerful forces in creating distinctiveness, not just in terms of the features or look of the product, but also in terms of its quality and performance.

Good industrial design can influence not just what a product looks like, but how easily and cheaply it is made, how efficiently and reliably it functions and how well it can be displayed at the point of sale. Product design is therefore not only about **form** and **aesthetics** – that is, shape and appearance – but also about **function** – that is, performance. However, industrial designers can only contribute fully if they are given a pivotal role in the development team rather than just being brought in as stylists at the end. They should be fully involved in every stage of the development process right through to advising on tooling and production systems.

Ideally, designers should work towards meeting a **design brief** or specification that describes the criteria or standards which the product design should achieve; though inevitably, any product design always represents a compromise solution between all the factors which have had to be reconciled. It is also influenced by a variety of constraints which place limitations on the designer.

Paul Kotler, in a recent article, 'Design: A powerful strategic tool', argues that in order to succeed a company must 'seek to creatively blend the major elements of the **design mix**, namely performance, quality, durability, appearance and cost'.

Concorde – this design has taken into account function as well as form and aesthetics (© Adrian Meredith)

ACTIVITY

Analysing the factors involved in designing a new product

Look at the questions below, which might be asked by a design team working on a new product. State which element of the design mix is being considered in each one.

- How will inspection and testing for faults be carried out?
- Is the styling in keeping with the image of the product?
- Does the product have the latest technical functions the market wants?
- Can the design be simplified to make production easier?
- Are the properties of the materials and components suitable for the product's expected life?
- Can fewer moving parts be used?
- Is the product comfortable/practical to use?
- Can this design be made with the existing production facilities?
- Will the investment in the product be recovered over its life cycle?
- How good are the materials and components from suppliers?
- What are the distinguishing features of the product's exterior?
- How regularly will the product need maintenance/servicing?
- What operating/storage conditions will the product have to stand up to?
- Are the materials and components in line with the retail price?
- What safety standards and regulations will the product have to comply with?
- Can maintenance be carried out easily?

CASE STUDY

Design-based innovation at Sony

These days it is hard to visualise a world without videos and personal stereos. Yet there were doubts about the potential of each of these products. In the case of the personal stereo, it took the commitment of the Sony chairman, Akio Morita, to ensure that the Walkman™ was developed.

Innovations such as the Walkman™ start with product design. 'The job of the designer is to visualise people's future needs', says Katsumi Yamatogi, design manager at Sony's Design Centre Europe. Design means 'imagining how a product will look and perform', linking human beings and engineering. It requires a combination of forward-looking creativity and practical engineering know-how.

Sony established its Design Centre Europe in Britain in early 1993, as part of a strategy of providing for local tastes and needs. More than three quarters of Sony's sales are outside Japan yet, until recently, almost all its designers have been Japanese working in Tokyo. Mr Yamatogi believes that design is 'culture-based technology', so long-term success in Europe requires European design input.

So how does a design idea come about? Mr Yamatogi believes there are three main sources:

1 Imagining a use: the product and the people using it (such as a TV watch).
2 Technological breakthrough: when Sony's R & D department announced the development of a miniature, flat TV screen, Sony's designers identified hand-held TVs and videophones as likely design opportunities.
3 Identifying the person: developing a design idea based upon a particular type of person, for example Sony's product range for children, called 'My First Sony'.

After an idea has been sounded out on the rest of the design team, the product concept is sketched. A computer-aided design (CAD) system can then be used to mock up the dimensions and workings of the product. Sony designers in Britain have a direct digital line to the Tokyo head office. At the end of office hours, a new idea can be transferred instantly to Japan – just in time for the start of the working day. Designers in Tokyo can develop it further, give feedback and, eventually, approval to the European idea. All this can be ready for the British designer on arrival the next morning. So Sony designs can be developed 24 hours a day.

A good example of Sony design in Europe is the new 'Casual Traveller' radio cassette alarm clock (see right). The idea stemmed from design concepts produced in 1992 based on European lifestyles. Sony designers thought of audio products to suit bikers, hikers, campers and even footballers! This provided discussion material for a brainstorming session between Sony's designers, marketing staff, engineers and product planners. At this stage, Sony encourage younger, more junior employees to become involved, to maximise the creative input.

From the meeting emerged the idea of a portable radio cassette designed for the 'Eurokid' – the frequent travelling, inter-railing student. It would need to be a personal stereo, a clock and an alarm, but also have a built-in high quality speaker to share music with friends. The other key requirements were for it to be tough, durable and light.

Another key factor at this stage is to agree a target price: an estimate of what the likely customer can afford to pay. This provides a ceiling to the production cost which may restrict the designers to less expensive materials or features. For the Casual Traveller, a target price of around £60 was agreed between the marketing and design staff.

After several months of CAD drawings and discussion, Sony's Business Group in Tokyo not only agreed that the product should proceed to launch in Europe, but also decided that it would have sales potential in Japan.

Once the project had been approved, design, engineering and manufacturing staff had to work

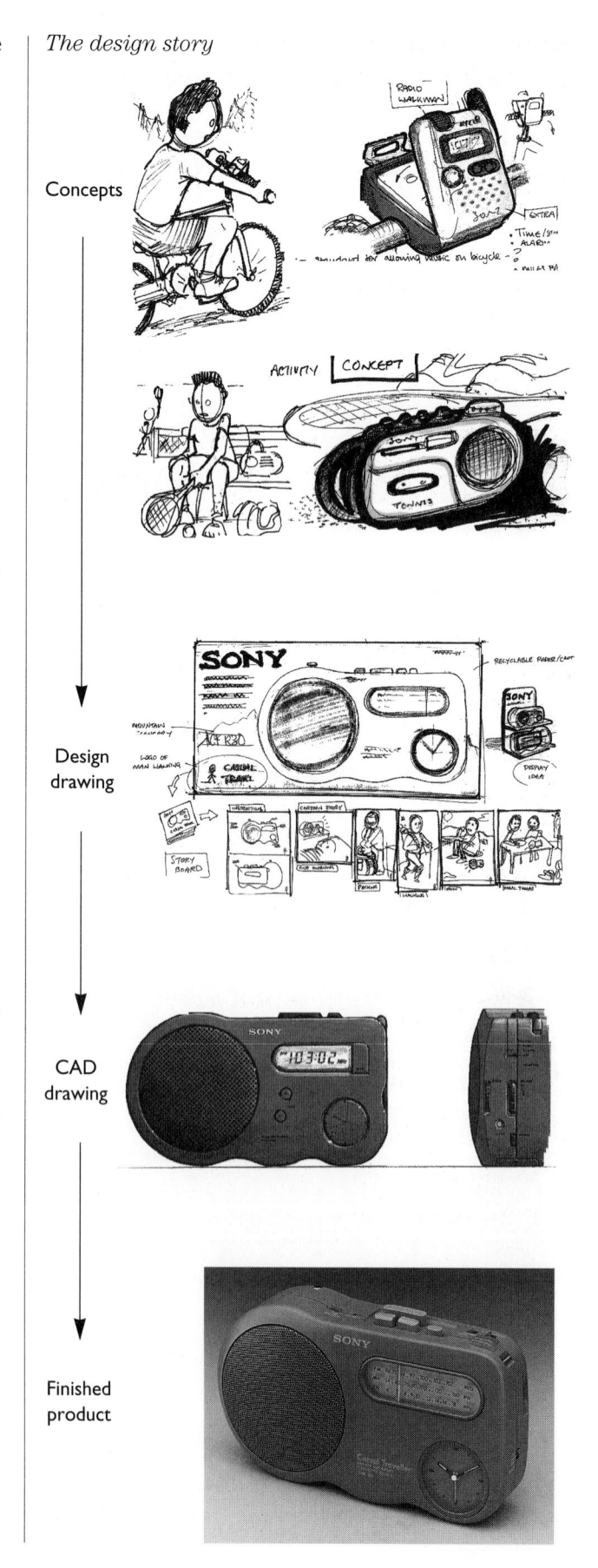

The design story

Concepts

Design drawing

CAD drawing

Finished product

closely to turn drawings into high volume production. This took less than a year, which is regarded as impressively fast. Mr Yamatogi feels that teamwork at this stage (often called simultaneous engineering) is crucial. The Casual Traveller came out in Japan before its Autumn 1994 European launch and is proving a considerable sales success in both markets.

This was exactly what Sony's strategists hoped for when setting up the Design Centre Europe – local ideas not only boosting Sony's market share in the European Union, but also bringing new designs to Japan.

ACTIVITY

Analysing the stages involved in introducing a new product

Decide on the most logical order for the sequence of events involved in introducing a new product from the list below. What factors could influence the best order?

- Full-scale production
- Working samples made up and tested
- Models or prototypes made up
- Design chosen from concepts presented
- Design brief for product prepared
- Patent applied for
- Consumer trials on target group carried out
- Original idea or concept
- Gap in market identified
- Own designers or outside consultants from design agency approached
- Raw materials organised
- Tooling made up for manufacture
- Market research on consumer needs carried out

Products must satisfy consumer needs

The first requirement of a successful new product is that it must be geared to satisfying consumer needs. However, this is more easily said than done. In affluent western societies today, a vast range of products and services exists to serve consumer needs. Many innovative firms are therefore going one stage further by attempting to stimulate subconscious needs. This new focus is evident in the approach adopted by one company, (quoted by the DTI in their survey of innovative companies), who argue that, 'You must get into the mind of the customer even when the customer does not know their own mind!' The challenge now facing marketers is that these **latent needs** are awakened only when the new product is first introduced onto the market. After all, how many people thought they needed a personal stereo, compact disc player or microwave oven until these products actually became available?

In his book, *The Design Dimension*, Christopher Lorenz describes the approach adopted by Sony. When Sony unveiled their new portable black-and-white TV set with an eight-inch screen in the USA during the 1960s, it was an immediate success. Yet only weeks earlier, General Electric had completed a major piece of market research on the potential of small, portable TVs and their findings included conclusions like 'people do not place a high value on portability of the TV set'. Rather than asking consumers to predict their feelings towards an unfamiliar product, Sony had instead observed the growing number of sets sold and the increasing number of TV channels and realised that these two factors would create a demand for a second set in many homes. Lorenz went on to add that, 'In effect, the company had looked beyond consumers expressed needs to their underlying behaviour patterns and had led the market by stimulating a new want. It has since done precisely the same with the video cassette recorder, Walkman™ personal stereo and the Watchman™ flat-tube TV.'

Clearly, companies with a successful record of product innovation are those who consistently manage to introduce products which satisfy the existing or latent needs of a target market. This sounds a very straightforward recipe for success. The fact is there are many pitfalls for the unwary. For one thing, the findings of market research surveys often provide a poor indication of the true sales potential of highly innovative products. It is notoriously difficult to gauge consumer reaction to radically different products which are unlike anything else on the market, since consumers invariably dislike products they cannot visualise.

The example of the Post-it™ notepads developed by 3M is typical, where the marketing people were ready to scrap the project at an early stage because the product had performed so badly in the initial research studies. In this instance, the use of trial samples proved to be the key factor in gaining consumer acceptance and the familiar yellow notepads have since become one of 3M's most successful products.

Some would argue that if companies always heeded market research findings they would never launch radically different products at all. Certainly the lesson appears to be that damning research findings in the case of innovative products should be treated with a degree of caution in order to avoid the danger of rejecting potential winners. Decisions made on the strength of market research recommendations should, in any case, always be taken in the light of managers' experience and judgement. In the most innovative companies, their 'feel' for the market is legendary. For instance, the Sony Walkman™ was launched despite research that warned it would be a complete flop. In the event, Sony went on to reap the marketing coup of the decade.

However, these examples do not indicate that market research evidence should be ignored as a matter of course. In the majority of cases properly conducted research is a reliable predictor of market potential. In fact, the penalty for introducing products which have been developed without reference to consumer needs can be high. The Sinclair C5 is a classic example of a product which, although it was extremely innovative, failed within a very short time of being launched. This was largely because the market need for an electronic vehicle with a limited carrying capacity and performance was never properly established.

A full-scale market research survey was out of the question because of the emphasis on secrecy. Instead, a small sample of 63 families was shown the vehicle and allowed to drive it around a large room. The C5 was launched on the basis of this limited research and of course the personal conviction of Sir Clive Sinclair.

In October 1985 the *Financial Times* reported that the receiver put the debts of Sinclair's C5 concern at £7.75 million. Nevertheless, it is interesting to speculate whether the C5 might have succeeded if it had been promoted as a golf trolley or invalid wheelchair. In other words, could it have survived if it had been designed to meet a specific consumer need?

The Sinclair C5

ACTIVITY

Needs catered for by different innovations

What are the needs and requirements catered for by the following innovations?

- Car phones
- Low-calorie drinks
- Cash machines
- Non-stick pans
- Infra-red alarm detectors
- Video-cassette recorders
- Solid emulsion paints
- Personal computers
- Personal stereos
- Disposable kitchen towels
- Frozen ready meals
- High speed trains
- Satellite dishes
- Photocopiers

The role of technology

The pace of technological change is such that new products are quickly superseded as competitors scramble to bring out even more advanced versions. In the nature of things it is inevitable that successful products are going to attract imitators. However, it is the scale of competition today that is unprecedented. As Richard Brookes points out in his book, *The New Marketing*, 'Five years after the launch of its personal computer, IBM was fighting a new battle – not with the Japanese as everyone originally expected, but with low-wage companies in Taiwan and South Korea. By 1986 IBM's PC had become a commodity product and was being copied by more than two hundred firms.'

Firms need, therefore, to introduce a constant stream of new products. Few can aim to be as prolific as Hewlett Packard, who manage to generate ideas for eight new products a week! Yet all the signs suggest that UK firms, particularly in terms of creative ability, have the potential to exceed this performance. A survey by the Japanese Ministry of International Trade and Industry, quoted in *Winning Ways* by James Pilditch, claims that of the significant innovations since the Second World War, 6 per cent were Japanese, 14 per cent were French, 22 per cent came from the USA and a staggering 55 per cent were from the UK.

State-of-the-art technology has certainly been the key factor determining the success of Renishaw Plc, a British manufacturer whose touch-trigger probe is capable of measuring machined steel to accuracies of millionths of a metre. The probe, which has a 70 per cent share of the world market for such tools, is used on products ranging from car engines to the US space shuttle, where the accurate fit of the heat-shielding tiles is vital to the survival of the shuttle as it passes through the earth's atmosphere.

The role of technology is essential in stimulating a high level of innovation, particularly amongst the motor vehicle, electronic, aerospace, pharmaceutical and consumer goods industries. New technological advances can determine:

- **The kinds of products and services that are offered**, e.g. fax machines, satellite TV, digital audio tapes, cash dispensing machines, antibiotics, etc.
- **The kinds of raw materials that are available**, e.g. man-made fibres, biodegradable plastics, ceramic parts for car engines, aseptic packaging for products like fruit juices which previously required refrigeration, etc.
- **The ways in which products are designed and manufactured**, e.g. techniques like CAD have dramatically reduced the time taken to design and engineer new products and the use of robots has revolutionised production lines in industries like car manufacturing.

Given the crucial role played by technology in innovation it is obviously vital that companies keep an open mind towards emerging technologies. In 1938, an amateur physicist living in New York called Chester Carlson developed a process which he called 'electro-photography'. Carlson approached more than 20 companies to try and get them to develop his product, including RCA, IBM and General Electric, but was turned down by every one. Eventually, a small company called Haloid agreed to develop his process commercially. Haloid, which later became Xerox, is now one of the largest corporations in the USA – a success due in no small measure to the fact that the company was the first to spot the huge potential of photocopiers.

Clearly, then, firms need to be flexible enough to respond to each wave of technological progress as it occurs. Ultimately, those who are unwilling or unable to adapt to the rapidly accelerating pace of change are likely to face an increasingly uncertain future – witness the fate of many of the Swiss watchmakers who were slow in adopting quartz digital technology. However, market conditions are complex and there are many reasons why even products that are technologically superior do not automatically succeed. In the case of the Apple Macintosh computer, what should have been a huge sales advantage (that is, that anyone, not just computer experts, could learn how to operate the computer in as little as 20 minutes) counted for very little in a market where the need for IBM compatibility was the major consideration.

is all too easy to get left behind when yesterday's radical new extras, such as VCRs with Nicam digital stereo, become today's taken-for-granted features. The motor car industry illustrates the scale of this competition. Japan's eight car manufacturers change their models on average every 4.6 years. This compares with an average figure of 8.1 years for the three major US car makers and 12.2 years for European manufacturers.

UK firms clearly face a formidable challenge. By definition, those who do not view innovation as a priority have effectively opted for stagnation and eventual decline. The role of management is critical in nurturing a culture that actively fosters change and innovation. 'Our job', according to one chairman of a highly innovative company, 'is to make our products obsolete before our competitors do.' Innovation is often confused with invention and assumed to be the sole province of the research and development (R & D) department. The popular image of boffins in white coats conjuring up new inventions is clearly outdated. The reality is that innovation does not have to be technology-led. People from a wide variety of departments within an organisation are capable of thinking up ideas for new products or modifications to existing products.

The importance of innovation

In the fiercely competitive trading conditions of the 1990s, innovation has emerged as the main battleground, with success being determined by the ability of companies to bring a constant stream of ever-more sophisticated products to the market ahead of their competitors. The rules of the game have moved on. Innovation was once regarded as essential for growth; today it has become essential for survival.

Rising standards of living and the pace of technological change mean that companies need to constantly update their products and services in order to cater for the latest customer expectations. It

Something old, something new

The innovation process is not just about radical new inventions, although these do sometimes occur. The existence of well-known examples of innovations based on *revolutionary* technological changes, such as the invention of robots, fibre optics, lasers and silicon chips, has unfortunately tended to perpetuate the myth that most innovations stem from this kind of creative breakthrough. In fact, the reality behind most product introductions is far less dramatic.

Innovations tend to develop more as a result of an *evolutionary* process: once a product has been introduced onto the market, the information provided as feedback from users is incorporated into later modifications and improvements, through continuous redesigns. The product thus evolves gradually in stages, via a series of small incremental steps, rather than as a giant technical quantum leap forward. The so-called 'blockbuster discoveries' are, by definition, few and far between. After all, radically different products such as the TV, computer or aeroplane cannot be invented very often!

Most 'new' designs have in fact evolved from this process of continuous redesign or **iteration**, which refines the product into a version that is cheaper, offers more sophisticated features and is better designed in some way. Innovation therefore involves modifying old products as well as developing new ones.

Japanese firms, such as Sony, have consistently adopted a policy of re-innovation. In a recent speech, Sony's chairman, Akio Morita, summed up the company's attitude: 'The technology of one product spawns the more advanced technology for another. We would not have been able to develop the Trinitron TV, or compact disc and digital recording, if we had not known how to design and manufacture the generation of products preceding them.' He went on to add that creativity in **product planning** was also important: 'There was no new technology involved in the Sony Walkman. What we did was see the technology we already had in a totally new configuration.'

In this context, it is obviously essential for firms to develop products which are capable of being redesigned. Gardiner and Rothwell, in their report on innovation for the Design Council, distinguish between **lean** and **robust** designs. Robust designs can be stretched to produce a variety of versions for different requirements which form a **product design family**. The Boeing 707 and Ford Cortina are both examples of designs which gradually evolved into a family of models, each new stage incorporating the latest technological developments. Robust designs like this have a greater degree of flexibility than lean designs which are not capable of being adapted when customers need change.

Should firms just stick, then, to redesigning and developing their tried and tested products? Clearly, this offers less financial risk in the short term, but without a flow of new products a company is likely to stagnate and decline. Companies need, obviously, to get the balance right between revamping old products and introducing new ones. Manufacturers of coated products, 3M, who have a formidable reputation for innovation, demonstrate what can be achieved. With about 60,000 individual products ranging from Scotch™ tape to Post-it™ notes, they consistently achieve their target of deriving 27 per cent of their sales revenue each year from products or services that are less than five years old.

CASE STUDY

Sony – the news studio in a briefcase

When watching a TV news reporter, how do you think the pictures got to you? Remember that they may only be an hour old.

If the video is freshly shot and the news story very important, the clips are sent by satellite and edited in the newsroom. When the news reporters have time, they edit the video (complete with voice-over) on location using two video recorders, picture monitors and loudspeakers. The result is then sent through as a complete news clip, electronically by satellite, or by telecom line or courier. The whole system has to cope with the speed and flexibility required by TV news programmes. It works well, but now new multimedia technologies are about to revolutionise the way news is produced.

In 1994, the chairman of Sony's Broadcast Products Company came to Europe to visit some of the major TV news studios. When chatting about the future, a senior TV executive said that what was wanted was a news editing studio in a briefcase. The chairman returned to Japan, told his staff, and a new product was born.

In July 1994, key sales, marketing, design and engineering executives from Britain, Japan and America met at Sony's annual 'product line-up' meeting. They decided to develop a completely new electronic news gathering and editing system, of which the portable editor would be a crucial part. Sony's R & D centre at Basingstoke would be responsible for developing the portable editor. A timetable was set that meant producing a working prototype for discussion with potential clients at the TV industry's main trade fair in April 1995.

The Basingstoke team agreed on a design specification to provide a highly portable, user-friendly editing studio that could marry video, sound and text to very high technical standards. It would provide 40 minutes running time on batteries, to enable editing to take place anywhere. It would be far less bulky than existing equipment, be quicker and more flexible in use, and provide a higher standard of editing. This would make the product essential equipment for all foreign and many local news reporters.

The reporter (plus camera operator) would:

1. Video the story and send the raw footage electronically to the news studio.
2. Transfer the video clips to the Sony portable editor and carry out the editing anywhere – in a hotel room, airport etc.
3. Record the voice-over, write any introductory script and send it, together with editing recommendations, through to the news studio via a modem link.

On receipt of the material the news producer could either implement the reporter's instructions directly, or make his/her own editing decisions.

Sony is the world's leading supplier of electronic news gathering equipment, with a substantial market share. So the company's experience in this market – together with its customer contacts – ensured a full understanding of the product requirements. Development engineers were able to discuss the detailed specification directly with TV news staff. For example the original design included a headphone socket in the editing computer, to enable editors to marry the sound with the pictures. Journalists and professional editors stated their preference for a small loudspeaker to allow more than one person to listen, so that was included.

The result – Sony's portable editor

Throughout the product's development, Sony benefitted from its multinational organisation. Sony's Broadcast Products Company has R & D and design development facilities in England, America and Japan. This helped the designers' understanding of how each country's TV news programmes are put together. The BBC, for instance, starts with the reporter's script, then finds pictures to illustrate the points being made. In America, the starting point is often the video and sound, around which a script is written.

With this full understanding of different customer needs, Sony was able to develop a product equally applicable in any country.

Technically, the new product incorporates three main developments:

- Digitisation – the ability to record video and sound digitally, so that it can be transferred easily to a computer; this helps the editor work faster and with more flexibility and precision.

DESIGN AND DEVELOPMENT

- Compression, enabling huge quantities of information to be stored on a 3.5 inch disk (whereas ordinary floppy disks store less than two megabytes of information, the Sony portable editor uses 650 megabyte disks – developed by Sony engineers in Japan).
- A laptop computer with the power to cope with a large number of colours (invaluable when editing several pieces of colour film on the computer screen at the same time).

In addition the engineers had to write a great deal of software, including the design of a Windows-based user-friendly operating programme. This was very important, as the product had to provide all the facilities expected by professional editors plus the ease of operation required by journalists.

For Vince Harradine, principal engineer and project leader, the coordination of a project being developed in Britain and Japan required many business trips and constant communication via E-mail. For both Vince and his divisional director, David Creed, the whole project has been a terrific challenge. Both are convinced that they and their design teams have developed a world-beating multimedia product.

At the April 1995 trade fair, the portable editor was presented privately to major TV news broadcasters. The response was very positive. After further discussions, Sony's Basingstoke design centre agreed a final product proposal with colleagues in Japan. The product launch date was set for April 1996.

Of course, this is not a product that will sell millions of units. It is designed for a market niche – the world's TV newsrooms and their journalists. Yet with the market for mass products such as TVs and videos becoming ever-more competitive, Sony wants to keep ahead by adding more 'intelligence' to its products. In this case, a huge amount of value is added to the electronic components by tailoring them to the precise needs of one small segment of the electronics market. The TV stations can afford to pay the high price needed to repay Sony for the design and development work involved.

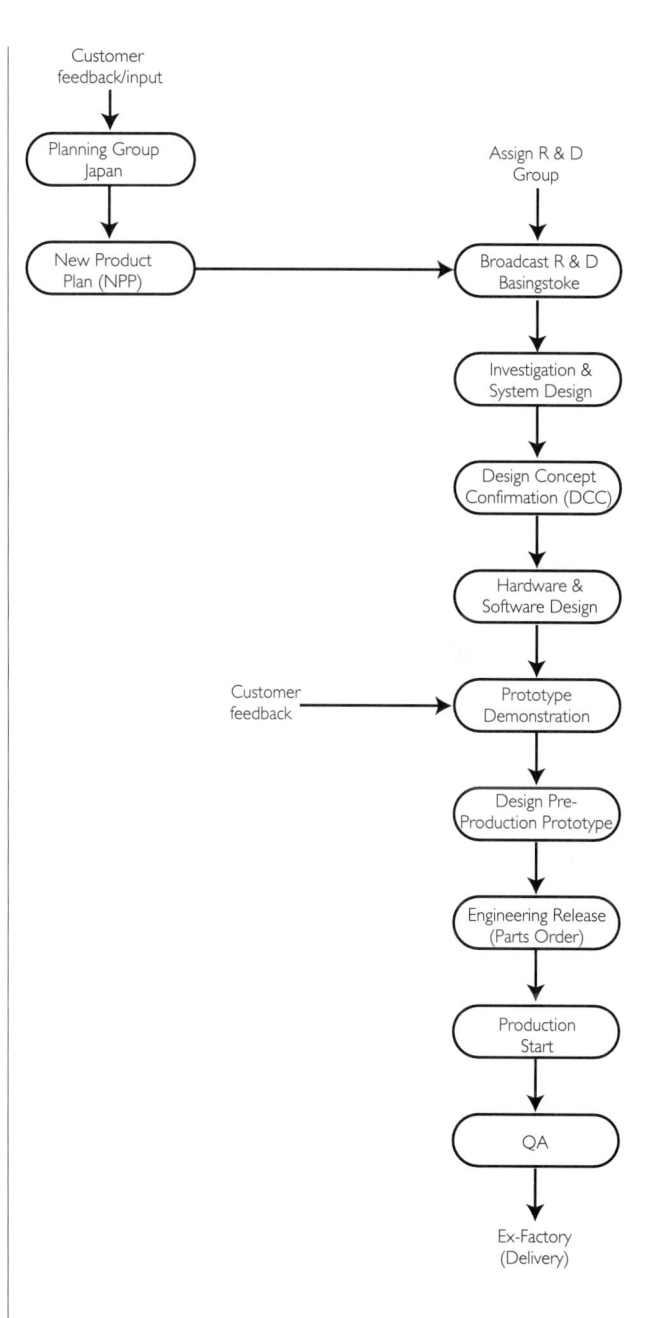

DNE-50 design flow chart

The need for teamwork

The lone inventor concept and the 'Eureka!' syndrome of product innovation are no longer applicable today, particularly as industrial engineering becomes more complex. Great design engineers like Robert Stephenson, the locomotive builder, and Isambard Kingdom Brunel, the civil engineer, possessed formidable abilities. However, with the information explosion that has occurred since their time, it is debatable whether one person is capable any longer of mastering all the specialist knowledge found in a variety of disciplines.

Teamwork is the approach adopted in today's enlightened companies who are committed to design, as being the best way to refine, develop and implement a complicated project. How should such multidisciplinary teams be organised? As David Bernstein, who runs a successful design agency, pointed out in a talk given at the London Business School, 'When a project is begun in one department and handed over to another, then inevitably some of the impetus is lost and much of the continuity and sense of ownership. The answer is frequently to create a matrix structure, a horizontal band across the vertical divisions, a project group, for example, cutting across the department divisions and consisting of members from each department.' The aim now is to change the traditional **linear** or sequential approach, where the research, design, production and marketing departments are brought in one after the other as the project progresses, to a **matrix** or teamwork approach whereby people drawn from different departments work together simultaneously on developing a project. The comparison is between running a relay race or playing in a football team.

Teamwork is vital in helping firms to maintain their competitive position. When Fuji first launched its throw-away camera, Kodak responded to the lucrative market sector which had been opened up by introducing its own disposable camera. A teamwork approach enabled Kodak to design and develop their new 'Fling' camera in record time. The company's computer-aided design system was *networked* so that all the people involved, including an outside firm of toolmakers, could work together simultaneously on the project.

Large companies organised on a **pyramidal** structure can often stifle innovation in their efforts to minimise risk. However, as James Pilditch points out in his book, *Winning Ways*, innovative companies go to great lengths to cut through this hierarchy. At Texas Instruments they run an IDEA programme (Identify, Define, Expose, Act). Any young engineer can get $20,000 to test a new idea simply by convincing any one member of a large group of authorised technical staff that it is worth following. 'Speak'n'Spell', the voice synthesising device, was developed in this way. He goes on to add that 'The essential point is to create teams that cut across all the usual departmental walls, then to free them from the normal procedures of the company's main business.' These teams in companies such as 3M and Hewlett Packard are like small entrepreneurial start-ups which are put together to come up with new products in any way they want. They let many ideas develop, then test them quickly on the market. Basically, they are a way of getting small company vitality into an established corporation.

The dangers of poor coordination

The use of teams of people brought together from different departments to develop a new product has proved highly effective at APV Baker (formerly Baker Perkins), a heavy engineering company manufacturing machinery for baking and biscuit making. A development team might consist of members from different areas of engineering and from the sales, finance, marketing, manufacturing and industrial design departments. Such cooperation improves communication, avoiding the dangers of various departments pulling in different directions. These dangers are amusingly illustrated by Michael Smith, who runs APV Baker, in a series of diagrams on 'How not to design a swing', or 'The perils of poor coordination', quoted in Christopher Lorenz's book *The Design Dimension*.

DESIGN AND DEVELOPMENT

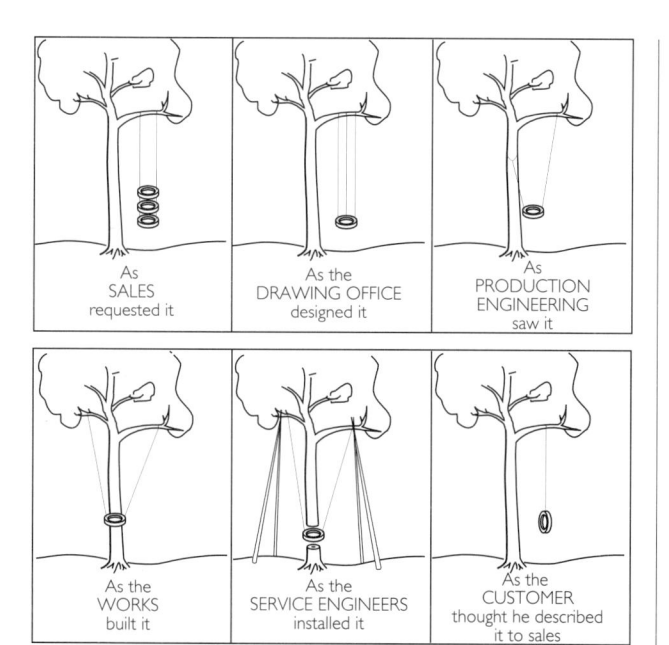

How not to design a swing

The need to shorten lead times

Olivetti used to take two years to introduce a new typewriter; now they can start to produce new designs in about two months. When IBM first introduced personal computers, they cut their normal development time from 24 months to 14 months forcing other competitors to try and follow suit. Cutting development times does not mean introducing poor products. In *A Passion for Excellence*, American authors Tom Peters and Nancy Austin describe how Xerox created a new product in 28 days that has since earned them £3 billion.

Once the decision has been taken to launch a new product, it is vitally important that the development time or **lead time** between initial design and full production is reduced as much as possible. If companies take too long to introduce a product, competitors will enter the market with similar products and erode potential profits. A study has shown that in consumer electronics, distributing a product six months late can cut life-cycle profits by about a third. More and more businesses today are therefore trying to cut lead times, a common aim being to halve them.

Those leading companies who have succeeded in meeting this challenge have done so by cutting product introduction times to the bone, making use of **computer-aided design (CAD)** techniques. These have revolutionised the time needed to design and develop a product.

Advanced CAD facilities used in the design of products at Renishaw Plc

There are many advantages of CAD:

- Designers can create a greater variety of products. All dimensions within the design can be varied radically or by the merest fraction, as the designer wishes. The designer can sketch a basic shape for a product, produce a wire-frame model and a three-dimensional shaded model and show how all the parts used for the product are assembled together.
- The time previously spent on making models and prototypes to test the feasibility of the design can be saved, because the performance characteristics of the computer design, such as resistance to stress, can be analysed to a high degree of probability.
- The design can be modified at this early stage in the light of any problems which emerge, thus preventing the need for expensive reworking later. There is therefore a greater likelihood of the product specification being *right first time* when manufacture begins.

UNDERSTANDING INDUSTRY

CASE STUDY

Cornetto – computer-aided ice cream

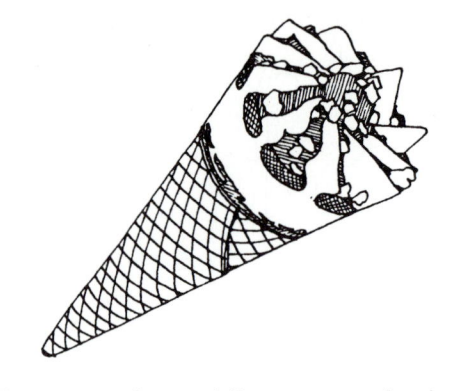

The Cornetto – the world's most popular ice cream

Cornetto is one of the great success stories of the ice-cream world. It is the world's most popular ice cream. In 1992, 85 million units were sold in Britain alone. The Cornetto is produced in Gloucester in Europe's biggest ice-cream factory. The factory makes more than 100 million litres of ice cream a year – enough to fill Wembley stadium to the brim! Birds Eye Wall's uses computer-aided design (CAD) and computer-aided manufacture (CAM) to provide the efficiency and flexibility to cope with changes in demand for ice cream. Consumption can vary by 14 times, depending on the weather.

Birds Eye Wall's uses its CAD workstations to plan every aspect of the production layout. This makes it easier to identify the knock-on effects of any suggested changes to one part of the manufacturing process. CAD systems offer a potential drawing accuracy level of 0.000001 mm. Precision is vital to a high-speed production process because slight

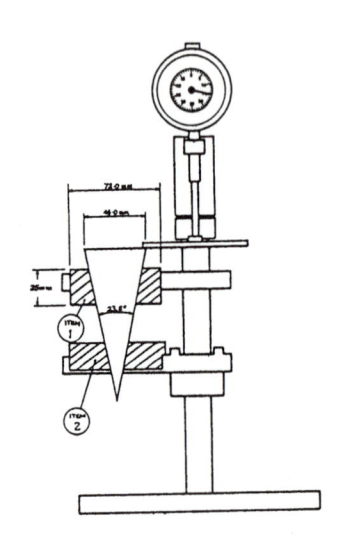

The cone checker

1. DISPENSE CONES
2. SEAT CONES
3. DOUBLE CHOCOLATE SPRAY
4. ICE CREAM FILL
5. TOP DECORATION FILL
6. NUT DEPOSIT
7. LID INSERTION
8. CRIMP CONES OVER LID
9. REMOVE

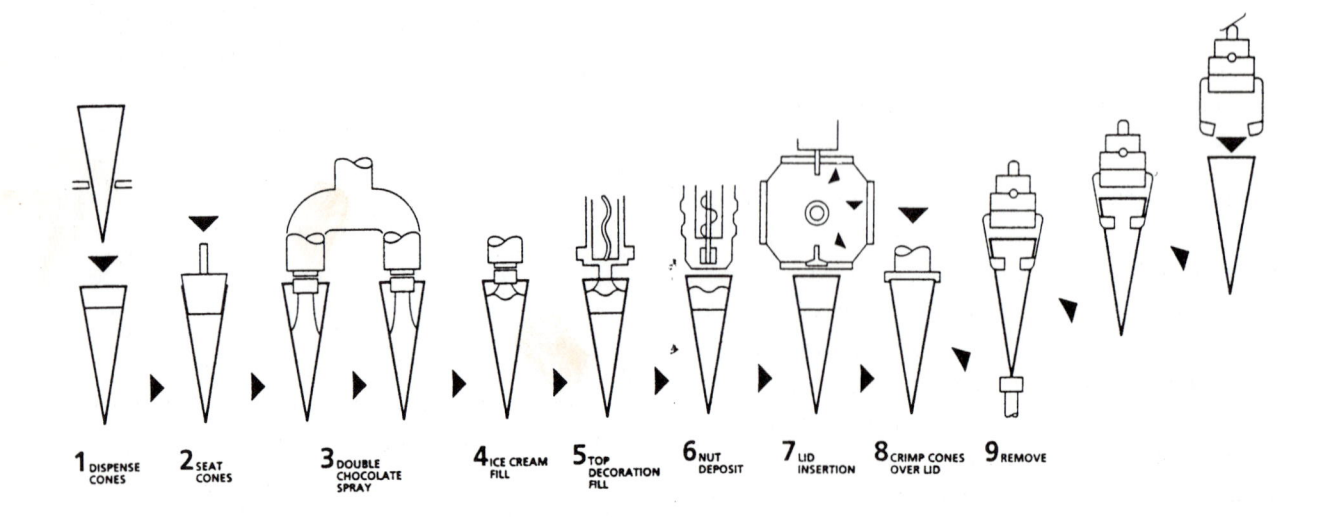

Cornetto production

inaccuracies can lead to poorly presented, or even damaged, products.

The Cornetto cone is a rolled sheet of wafer. A secret recipe batter is baked between two carefully designed hotplates in a rotary oven. It has to be a constant thickness and the right size and shape to produce a sheet of wafer which will roll into a cone to an accuracy of plus or minus 2mm. On the page opposite is a CAD drawing of a device for checking the tolerance of the cones used in the production of Cornetto.
The ability to produce up to half a million Cornettos a day requires some remarkable technology. The production line is constantly being developed to make it more efficient. The CAD illustration opposite shows how automated the production process has become.

The need for long-term investment

The costs of developing innovative new products in high technology industries and of installing automation and robotics are so great that there is generally a long **payback period** before the investment can be expected to yield any returns. It follows from this that if UK firms wish to match the performance of aggressive overseas competitors, they may need to forgo short-term profits in order to make the long-term investments which are essential for survival.

A report on innovation for the Design Council, by Paul Gardiner and Roy Rothwell, pointed to 'the problem of British firms adopting an increasing "cash flow" view of development activity, focusing on short-term projects that yield quick results instead of taking the longer-term view and investing in innovation'. They went on to add that British firms are often at a disadvantage compared to German and Japanese firms, because of the lack of City investors who are willing to take a long-term view and lend 'patient money'. In other words, City investors generally expect a quick return and are less prepared to make investments which take years to yield any profits – the so-called 'jam today' mentality.

Private companies generally find it easier to adopt a committed policy of reinvestment than public companies, which have to explain to shareholders that their dividends are going to be lower for a few years because of money invested in developing new products. Tax policies in the UK are not very helpful either. Whereas companies can 'write off' spending on research, investment in product design and development is not allowable against tax.

The Staffordshire-based firm of JC Bamford Excavators, which manufactures earth-moving equipment, reinvests more than £20 million a year. Clearly, JCB's priorities of building up a sound operational base, rather than being concerned with short-term profits, are a lesson to other firms.

Testing stability on different gradients at JCB

Many more UK firms will need to take a long-term view in order to keep up with the competition. This is especially important if firms are to invest in new technology such as computer-aided design and manufacturing or robotics, where the pay-back period is likely to be five years or longer. In view of this, firms who are concerned only with better and better figures over the next quarter or six months are likely to find themselves being gradually squeezed out by those who *have* invested in the future.

Taking the long-term view does of course mean

accepting that though a new innovation can bring in vast profits it can also fail. As Gardiner and Rothwell emphasise, 'Innovation is inherently a high-risk undertaking and one of the things we can be sure about is that there will be failures. Management must accept this and not use one failure as an excuse for withdrawing from the innovation race altogether.' It goes without saying that innovation is more likely to thrive in companies where people involved in projects that fail are not thought any less of.

The importance of research and development

The pace of innovation in today's marketplace is such that it has become vital for firms to invest heavily in **research and development (R & D)** in order to maintain their competitive edge. Firms which do not accord R & D a central role in their operations have effectively made a decision not to be in business in 10 or 15 years' time. It is within the high technology 'sunrise' industries such as computers, automobiles, electronics, pharmaceuticals and aerospace that the costs of such investment are particularly large. By the same token, however, the potential rewards, if a new product does prove to be a winner, are also much greater.

Within the automobile industry, the R & D costs for a new car can amount to around £300 million. The bill for taking a new model from design to production can be as much as £700 million. With outlays like these, car manufacturers obviously have to produce in huge volumes in order to make a profit. According to one estimate, a minimum of five million vehicles needs to be produced simply to recover the investment in R & D. Philips, the Dutch electronics group, argue that many electronics products today must capture an 8 per cent share of the world market simply to break even on R & D costs. Not surprisingly, even the largest companies find it difficult to produce in such volumes, which is why they tend to use components such as a particular engine across a number of models.

The time and level of investment required to introduce a new drug onto the market is also phenomenal. One study has estimated that on average it takes about 13 years and £85 million to take a drug from basic research to product launch. Some of this investment goes on the early 'weeding out' process. The pharmaceutical division of ICI considers approximately 10,000 new chemical compounds each year. Of these, probably no more than four will be taken into development. Only about one in ten eventually make it through the development process to reach the market. Even then, there is no guarantee of success. Inevitably, there are only a handful of drugs which are capable of generating enough profit to offset not only their own development costs but also those of the failures, as well as the 'non-starters' which never get past the development stage.

However, the rewards can be great for those companies which are successful in producing world-beating products. The anti-ulcer drug, Zantac, produced by Glaxo, the UK's leading pharmaceutical company, is a prime example. It has become the world's top selling prescription medicine, generating over £2 billion in revenues in 1993 and accounting for almost 50 per cent of the company's sales.

Within the aerospace industry, developing a new aero engine from drawing board to eventual delivery can cost as much as £2 billion. For this reason, aero engine manufacturers such as Rolls Royce are now seeking to improve and modify existing engines rather than incur the expense of designing completely new ones from scratch. For instance, their latest engine is said to have been developed at the relatively modest cost of £100 million. The development costs were reduced by taking the core of an existing engine, fitting it out with parts adapted from other units and then incorporating all the latest modifications. In addition, whereas in the past the company built as many as 39 test engines when developing a new aero engine, today eight or ten is enough as much of the early testing is done by computer simulation.

The importance according to R & D within Rolls Royce, where spending rose to a high of £253 million in 1993, has obviously been a crucial factor in explaining the company's expanding share of world markets. In the space of 10 years, Rolls Royce has increased its share from 5 per cent to the point where it now accounts for 20 per cent of civil engines made worldwide.

These examples taken from very different industries demonstrate clearly that despite the phenomenal costs, an increasing number of companies at the leading edge of technology view their commitment to research and development as an essential investment in the future.

ACTIVITY

Johnson Ceramics: designing a new product

GENERAL BACKGROUND

You work as a product designer for a design agency called First Editions and have just been consulted by a new client, Johnson Ceramics, who are based in Stoke-on-Trent, Staffordshire, and manufacture crockery. Martin Johnson, the firm's founder, has come to see you because he wants to extend the firm's product base by introducing a new range of coffee mugs. The company already has products catering for most needs, which retail through department stores, supermarkets and gift shops. However, Martin thinks there is a gap in the market for a really well-designed mug aimed at the 16–20 age group. The new coffee mug must be a good shape and size, practical to use and cheap to manufacture. It must also have a graphic design likely to appeal to this target group.

THE BRIEF

Bearing in mind the client's requirements you will need to prepare a presentation to the company, which will include a design drawing for your coffee mug, together with a written list of all the factors you took into account in planning the design which you are going to recommend to them.

The list below suggests some possible areas you will need to think about before you start designing.

1. List five questions which you would expect a short market research questionnaire to include.

2. What is the product specification for your mug?

   a) Shape: Wide or narrow? Rounded or angular? Heat loss minimised? Easy to hold? Stability? Stand to protect surfaces? Stackable when stored?

   b) Size: Capacity held? Weight when carried full? Size of handle?

   c) Materials: Made from stoneware, bone china, special glass or plastic? Resistant to what temperatures? Resistant to staining? Porosity? Expected life? Easily breakable? Microwave/dishwasher safe? Suitable for everyday or occasional use? Cost?

   d) Graphic design: On one side or both? Colours or black and white? A few colours or a riot of them? Pastels or bold primaries? Distinctiveness? Theme — landscapes, birds, flowers, cartoons, people, geometrics? Can design be extended for a whole range? Overall style geared to target group?

3. Which factors do you think are going to be most important for your brief?

4. What production methods would you advise your client to use? Mass production or craft methods? Glazed or unglazed? Interior and exterior finish? Handle fixed on or moulded in one piece?

5. Why would you make up prototypes of your design?

6. How should samples be tested?

7. How much do you think your design of coffee mug should retail for?

Production

IN ASSOCIATION WITH

TI GROUP

Introduction: the role of production

By definition, manufacturing firms exist to manufacture or make a product. It is the value added by firms during the production process which enables them to sell their finished product at a much higher price than the pure cost of the raw materials used in their manufacture. For example, car tyres sell for far more than the rubber that they are made from, furniture for far more than the cost of the timber alone.

In order to increase the amount of value added, firms need to make the best possible decisions in four key areas of production: **scale**, **method**, **quality** and **location**.

In addition, they are continually striving to improve efficiency and productivity, in order to survive in a climate of increasing overseas competition.

Are firms getting bigger?

There is a growing trend, both within individual industries and in terms of total manufacturing output within the UK, for production to be concentrated more and more into the hands of a few large firms. The 100 largest manufacturing companies employ roughly one third of the labour force and account for approximately 35 per cent of total net output.

Firms can grow in size by means of:

- **Organic growth** Firms expand by taking on more employees, investing in more machinery, buildings and so on.
- **Acquisitions or mergers** Firms expand by joining together to form a single, larger organisation.

The trend towards concentration of production into a smaller number of firms has been mainly due to the increase in the number of mergers. In recent years, most mergers have been conglomerate mergers, where firms in different industries have joined together, diversifying their product base. This avoids the risks inherent in limiting their operations to a narrow range of products in one industry – that is, the dangers of putting 'all their eggs in one basket'.

However, the diversification process can be taken too far if firms expand into many unrelated industries in which they have no expertise. The only answer may then be to sell some of their fringe activities and concentrate on those they define as core activities, a process which can prove very lucrative.

Overall, this trend towards larger firms can be attributed to the cost savings which result from an increase in the scale of production.

Scale of production

Large firms are able to produce their goods at a more competitive price than small firms because their fixed costs are spread over the larger number of units which are produced.

Once gained, this competitive edge becomes self-perpetuating, enabling large firms to expand their market share still further. Smaller firms cannot afford the initial outlay which makes these savings possible, and therefore are unable to operate as cost effectively. They can only survive by producing for a specialised area of the market. Rolls Royce does this in the car market where its 0.1 per cent market share is dwarfed by the big four UK manufacturers: Rover (31.6 per cent), Vauxhall (19.5 per cent), Ford (18.9 per cent) and Nissan (13.8 per cent).

As firms get bigger they gain the benefits of being able to spread costs and make savings by operating more efficiently. These are known as **economies of scale**. Apart from the **internal** economies of scale (see Table 4.1) possible within the firm, there are also **external** economies which can result from firms grouping together, such as:

- The presence of component suppliers nearby.

TABLE 4.1 *Internal economies of scale*

Type of economy	Enables large firms to:
Purchasing	Buy materials more cheaply by taking advantage of bulk discounts.
	Employ trained buyers who can negotiate the best deals.
Production	Use mass-production techniques to speed up and increase production.
	Afford to buy large, specialised, technically advanced machinery.
	Use specialised division of labour.
Risk-bearing	Afford to take more risks with launching a new product, as with a diversified range of products they always have others to fall back on if one fails.
	Afford to employ an R & D department.
Financial	Borrow more easily as they have greater reserves and are perceived as being more creditworthy by lenders.
	Obtain loans at more favourable rates of interest.
	Afford to use the services of accountants and other financial advisers.
Marketing	Afford to advertise extensively, as the additional cost per unit produced is small when spread over a large output.
	Afford to employ specialist sales and after-sales staff and run advertising departments.
Administrative	Sustain high overheads spread over greater output.
	Afford the higher salary packages necessary to recruit the best managers.
	Afford to install sophisticated computerised systems for controlling and monitoring the business.

- The use of one firm's end product or even its waste as raw material for another firm.
- The existence of a skilled, experienced workforce – perhaps trained at a specialised local college.

Of course, an increase in the scale of operations does not lead solely to benefits such as cost reductions and improvements in efficiency. It can also lead to **diseconomies of scale**, such as excessive **bureaucracy**. Companies can be stifled by the red tape involved in large company record-keeping, communications and committee decision making. Big, unwieldy firms often lose their capacity to innovate and become unable to respond to changes in the market.

To overcome these problems, the majority of large firms now split their organisations into smaller divisions, which function independently on a day-to-day basis yet remain within the overall control of the parent company. They therefore operate, in effect, as smaller firms.

Method of production

The decision as to which production method a firm should adopt is influenced by several factors:

- The nature and variety of the products.
- Market factors such as the size and frequency of orders.
- The stage of development reached by the firm.

At one end of the scale is **job production**, based on 'one-offs' or small orders, often of luxury goods. This can be carried out on a small scale, as with custom-made clothes, or on a large scale, as with shipbuilding and aircraft manufacture. This type of production is **labour intensive**, either because a skilled workforce is required due to the nature of the work, or because the volume of production is too low for any major investment in machinery to be justified. It is the method most often used by start-up businesses.

Once demand increases and the design of the product is capable of being simplified and replicated to a certain standard, then it becomes both economically worthwhile and technically feasible for **mass production** techniques to be employed. Mass production involves making large volumes of identical products to the same standard, at a low unit cost. Products can be mass produced in batches or as a continuous flow.

The second type, **batch production,** is a more efficient method than job production as the work process is divided into its component operations. Each operation is completed for the whole batch of items being produced before the next operation is carried out. Batch production accounts for 75 per cent to 85 per cent of total production in western countries.

The third type, **flow production**, is the most efficient method of all. Once the work on one operation is completed, the items are passed as a continuous flow to the next stage without having to wait for a batch to be completed. This is very **capital intensive** because an automated production line requires a heavy initial outlay. As labour costs per unit are minimised, however, variable costs per unit are kept low.

The degree of job specialisation involved in flow-production processes creates a highly defined division of labour. This can result in high productivity, though the boredom of the job may lead quality to slip. The modern approach is to avoid the repetition involved in a high division of labour. (See Table 4.2 on page 51 for more details about each method of production.)

CASE STUDY

Messier-Dowty – landing the world-leaders

Building aircraft is one of the world's largest manufacturing industries. With a single Boeing 747 ('jumbo jet') selling for $165 million (about £100

PRODUCTION

TABLE 4.2 *Characteristics of each method of production*

Characteristic	Job	Batch	Flow
Size of demand	Demand is small. Manufacture of a single complex product or small quantity. Selling aimed at particular customers or firms in specialised markets.	Demand increases. Manufacture of a product in stages. Each operation for a batch completed before the whole batch moves onto the next operation. Selling aimed at a wider market.	Demand is regular and long term. Manufacture of a simplified and standardised product in large volumes. Selling aimed at national or international markets.
Quantity of products	Single product or small quantity produced.	Batch or group of products produced, usually in small quantity, before next batch started.	Large quantities produced.
Variety of products	Very flexible system. Enables large variety of products to be manufactured, geared to customer specification.	Still fairly flexible. Products more standardised but can vary from batch to batch, so can still be geared to customers' needs.	Not flexible. A limited range of products manufactured. In large-scale operations a variety of production lines can be used to provide a wider range of products.
Type of workforce	Skilled workers needed with a high degree of technical expertise and the ability to adapt. Can be a large workforce if a technically complex project is involved.	Less skilled workers needed who are skilled in one operation rather than in a whole task. Skilled quality control and maintenance workers needed.	Unskilled workers used, who perform a limited operation which they repeat over and over again. Efficient planning and control system needed to manage production.
Worker satisfaction	Worker motivation enhanced. Each new job presents a different challenge, so they need to be adaptable. Workers gain satisfaction from being responsible for the complete product.	Less worker satisfaction as jobs are less skilled. Workers are not involved with product from start to finish.	Difficult for workers to get satisfaction from their jobs as they tend to perform mechanical, repetitive tasks, many of which have been automated in recent years. Workers are only involved in a small part of the job cycle.
Type of machinery used	Generally less technically complex machinery used. More emphasis on the technical expertise of the operator. Wide range of machines needed for different jobs.	Less machinery used than in job production, but more complex as emphasis is on capability of machines rather than on the skill of the workers. Machines need to be retooled for each batch.	Technically complex machinery needed to produce standardised products. High investment in machinery presumes steady market demand.
Layout of plant	By fixed position.	By process.	By product.
Costs of production	Variable production costs are high, particularly labour costs, but fixed costs are low.	Costs are lower than in job production. Planning needs to be efficient so that production runs are as large as possible to spread costs over many units.	Fixed costs are high initially to start up the production line but variable production costs per unit are lower than in other methods.
Problems	Expensive form of production. Difficult to organise if production is technically complex.	Workers and machines can stand idle if one operation for a batch takes longer than another.	The processes on a traditionally organised production line are interdependent, so if one section is disrupted by a strike or if a bottleneck occurs, the whole line has to stop.

million), the sums of money involved are staggering. To put this price into perspective, one jumbo sells for the same as 10,000 Ford Mondeos. Furthermore, whereas Britain is an also-ran in the world car production league, this country is in the top three world aircraft producers.

An understanding of Britain's role in the world industry can be gained by a visit to Messier-Dowty – the company responsible for 40 per cent of the world market for aircraft landing-gear. When a 100-ton plane comes in to land, the undercarriage slips out from under the plane, positioning the wheels ready for landing. The force with which the plane hits the ground is massive, but the shock absorbers in the landing-gear ensure a smooth, safe landing. The design skill and manufacturing know-how comes from Messier-Dowty – an Anglo-French joint venture with annual sales of over £250 million. Much of this turnover is generated from the production site in Gloucester – where huge pieces of aluminium or steel are engineered into complete aircraft undercarriages.

The production process starts with computer-produced work schedules based upon the company's own computer aided designs. They show exactly what materials and parts need to be ordered from suppliers, together with all the operations required within the factory.

Landing-gear is based upon a central rod serving as a huge shock absorber. This rod needs enormous strength and so it is machined from a single casting of pure steel or aluminium. For the Airbus A330, this single casting is a 5.6 ton block of steel. At the factory, this is hollowed out and sculpted into the shape shown in the accompanying photograph. This requires thousands of separate milling (cutting and shaping) operations.

Spindle profiling

Having produced the main fitting and the other metal parts (all to the highest possible standards), it is time to assemble the huge landing-gear and 'dress' it with the enormous quantity of complex wiring and tubing needed for the electronic control systems.

In many factories, the guide tells you proudly about this or that quality initiative. Being shown round the Messier-Dowty site by Mr Les George, the operations director, was different. When pressed to talk about quality, he said 'in our business, quality is a given . . . we don't operate to a 95 per cent or a 99 per cent standard; there is only one standard – 100 per cent'. Modern ideas such as 'right first time' and 'zero defects' have been common in the aircraft industry for many years. How else, after all, would such an inherently dangerous form of transport be so safe?

Where the Gloucester plant has been influenced by modern approaches is in lean production. The main plant for producing landing-gear for the Airbus 320 is organised into six production cells. A focus upon reducing production lead times has brought the time taken between order and delivery down from 51 weeks to 17.

Lean is also the word to describe the management hierarchy within the factory. Ten years ago there were nine layers of supervision and management. Now there are only four. Each cell leader is responsible for 25–30 staff, so there is no possibility for intrusive supervision. Members of staff must be responsible for their own actions and decisions, whether in terms of ensuring their machinery is well maintained or in keeping to time.

The future for Messier-Dowty looks very bright. The business has a three-pronged strategy:

1. To continue to provide top quality products to the number one client, Airbus Industrie. Future orders for the A320 are forecast to double within two years, and those for the massive A330/340 are also on a rising trend.
2. The second strategy is to offer a fully integrated landing-gear system and service for medium sized aircraft manufacturers such as Bombardier in Canada.
3. The third, and potentially the most important, is to offer a 'make to print' service to Boeing. In

PRODUCTION

Loading in transport

In-service

other words, Messier-Dowty is willing to produce landing-gear to the precise blueprints laid down by Boeing. Contracts won on this basis would draw only upon Messier-Dowty's production skills, not their design capability. Nevertheless, if that is the only way to win contracts from the world's biggest aircraft producer, Messier-Dowty is willing to try. After all, to grow from the current 40 per cent market share makes it almost essential to gain business from Boeing.

The essence of business strategy is that it requires a long-term vision and the willingness to plan for how to get there. Andrew Stevens, managing director of Messier-Dowty, Gloucester, has had a clear view on how to achieve the Boeing breakthrough. The starting point has been to push manufacturing costs down to (or below) the level of the main American rivals. This has been helped by the relatively low labour costs in Britain compared with America. The second approach has been to build up the company's factory in Montreal, Canada. For Boeing is much more likely to offer contracts to North American firms than 'outsiders'. Boeing regard Messier-Dowty of Canada as a home producer.

With a clear strategy and clear production, design and marketing strengths, it is hard to feel anything but optimism for the business. Les George and Andrew Stevens must feel the same way, because they are talking about actively stepping up the firm's graduate recruitment and training schemes – and that's always a good sign.

The modern approach to production

Today, most manufacturing companies focus upon two main strategies: **lean production** and **total quality management**, both of which have come from successful and influential Japanese companies such as Toyota and Sony. British firms had previously thought that the Japanese approach could only work with super-dedicated Japanese workers, but that view had to change when Sony, Nissan, Toyota and many others set up successful factories in Britain, using British workers.

Lean production

Prompted by shortages after defeat in the Second World War, Japanese companies had to be very resourceful in their approach to business. In the absence of any plastics industry in Japan, Sony's first tape recorders used tape made from paper, and Toyota, while in its early years as a car producer, had to find ways of manufacturing with the minimum possible machinery and materials. By 1950, Toyota had only produced 2,685 cars in its history, while a single American Ford factory made 7,000 cars a day.

The American mass production system used a series of huge machines, each dedicated to one task. One would press metal into the shape of a front bumper, another into a back bumper, another would produce the wing and so on. As reported by Jim Womack, Dan Jones and Dan Roos in their book, *The Machine That Changed The World*, 'The massive and expensive western press lines were designed to operate at about 12 strokes a minute to make a million or more of a given part in a year.' In order to compete, Toyota realised they would have to find ways of producing cheaply without the advantage of the Americans' huge scale of production.

The solution was to design machines that could be used for many different operations. The problem was the length of time taken to reset the machines. At first it took a whole day to change a stamping machine from producing one part to making another. By the late 1950s, however, Toyota engineers had reduced this time to just three minutes, and had so simplified the process that factory line workers could do it without needing help from engineers. This carried with it the advantage of flexibility. If buying habits changed in America, Ford could not react quickly, because each production line was dedicated to producing a particular product in a particular way. Toyota's multi-purpose machines could adapt quickly to a surge of demand for open-top cars or right-hand drive models.

JUST IN TIME

The same desire to minimise the use of resources also led to Toyota's most famous discovery – just in time (JIT). To reduce the space occupied, and money tied up, by high buffer stocks of materials and work in progress, Toyota devised a card ordering system known as kanban. The rule was that no components would be made, or supplies ordered, unless the instruction was given by the kanban. If an assembly worker fitted eight left-hand car doors, a kanban would be sent to the door production team which would produce another batch of eight. In theory these would arrive just in time before the assembly worker's remaining stock ran out.

At first, the new system caused chaos, as parts arrived late and suppliers complained about making frequent deliveries of small batches. Yet Toyota soon realised that the knife-edged nature of this system was its very strength. If a faulty batch of components to the door production team caused a halt to the final assembly line, the supplier was soon threatened with quality improvements or paying for the lost output. Existing with only an hour's worth of buffer stock ensured that every production, supply or quality fault would be acted on quickly, or else be clear for all to see. By 1990, Toyota was producing over four million cars a year, far outstripping any European or Japanese producer and rivalling the American giants, Ford and General Motors.

JIT also has enormous implications for managing the workforce. High stock levels were the management cushion against workforce indiscipline, be it absenteeism or strike action. Now a strike might shut the factory down within an hour or two. Accordingly, it becomes essential that management encourage cooperation instead of confrontation. Factory workers need to be treated as valued members of a complete team – trusted, trained and consulted.

As a result, JIT leads firms to rethink their approach to factory work. The traditional approach of splitting work into repetitive fragments results in an uncooperative workforce. So firms organise the workforce into teams, working together on large units of work instead of working in isolation on the same boring task.

From its origins at Toyota, this approach has spread widely throughout the west. In Britain, firms such as Rover, IBM and Rolls Royce have adopted and adapted JIT to suit their own needs. Rolls Royce has divided its car plant into 16 zones, each acting as a business within a business, responsible for purchasing, cost, quality and delivery. The engine assembly team, for example, has three hours to assemble each engine, and is then responsible for testing it. Rolls Royce's new approach has halved the break-even level from 2,800 cars per year to 1,400.

Total quality

Linked to lean production is the desire for zero defects, in other words a fault-free system. This is needed to avoid wasting time and money, rectifying faults and to ensure maximum customer satisfaction and therefore repeat purchase. The high cost of poor quality was shown by an analysis of British banks by the American quality consultant, Philip Crosby Inc. It showed that British banks waste more than 50 per cent of their operating costs because of error-prone procedures that result in problems such as lost documents.

The management of quality can be approached in three main ways:

- Total quality management (TQM) is the acceptance by every member of an organisation that quality is his or her primary duty, whether dealing with a colleague or a customer. This often requires a huge change in management and staff attitudes.
- The lean production approach is to focus the quality effort upon eliminating defects in every stage of the design, manufacturing and delivery.
- Quality assurance systems such as BS 5750 aim to provide guaranteed levels of quality; then customers can decide whether the promised quality level meets their requirements.

TOTAL QUALITY MANAGEMENT

The first European companies to adopt TQM methods were those facing the fiercest competition from Japan, such as Rank Xerox and Philips. Both started by adopting Japanese ideas such as quality circles, but found that quality improvements only became significant once senior management made quality a priority throughout the business. Philips started to measure quality in terms of defects per million, in imitation of the Japanese. This had real impact, because once departments were made aware of their quality shortfalls, they started to discuss how to improve. Defect levels fell by a factor of 100 and Philips' exports to Japan doubled in 10 years.

In a recent survey, the chief executives of 230 top European companies believed that their companies' gross profit margins could be boosted by 17 per cent and variable costs cut by 35 per cent if TQM practices were widely employed.

LEAN APPROACH TO QUALITY

Many firms suspect that TQM has become over-sold by management consultants, and that its attempt to change attitudes can radically backfire. So they approach the pursuit of better quality as part of the lean production process, often helped by the use of continuous improvement (or kaizen) groups. These meeting groups of shop-floor workers, supervisors and, often, engineers attempt to come up with new ideas regularly, to improve efficiency, quality and working conditions on the factory floor.

The traditional management approach was to send in consultants every five years to recommend a complete overhaul of production. Kaizen looks to a whole series of small changes recommended by the workforce, to provide continuous and therefore less threatening change. This approach has been helpful for the Japanese producer of excavators, Komatsu, in the north-east of England and for the motor spares company, Unipart.

BS 5750 – QUALITY ASSURANCE

The main criticism of BS 5750 is that it is not a way of improving quality, only of proving your level of quality. In other words, a producer could obtain the BS 5750 award for promising that its supplies will have a 10 per cent defect rate. This may be a harsh criticism as it at least gives the customer a clear basis for judging one supplier against another. In that way it encourages firms to work at improving quality standards.

Another criticism of BS 5750 (and its worldwide counterpart ISO 9002) is that it is overly bureaucratic. To gain the award you must be able to show the paperwork evidence for everything you do. In that way the customer can be sure that, no matter who is on holiday, the production process will be carried out in exactly the same way as usual.

Despite the doubts, British Airways are among many firms to have benefited from adopting BS 5750. The standards led to the discovery that, among other problems, baggage handlers were not trained to cope with new, automated unloading methods. Now workers are updated whenever changes occur. In the first year, complaints dropped by 65 per cent and the time spent fixing problems by 60 per cent.

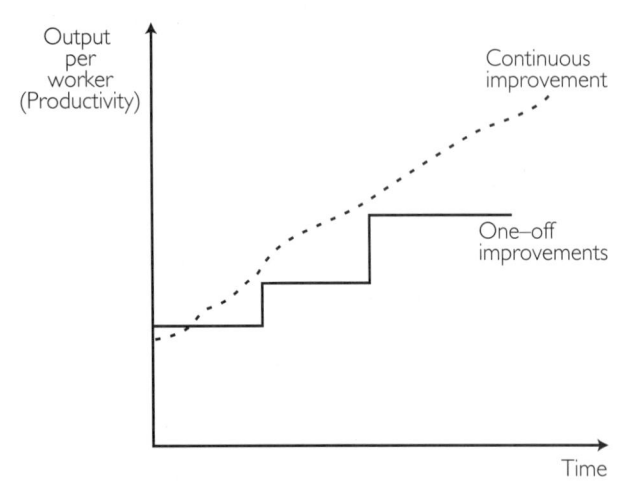

Kaizen: continuous improvement

CASE STUDY

Eurostar and the graduate engineer

Even though the Channel Tunnel started with teething problems, the Eurostar train service between London and Paris has been a great success. It has already grabbed a 40 per cent share of the London-Paris market, to the discomfort of British Airways and Air France. A great attraction of the Eurostar is its smooth, comfortable ride – ideal for tourists and business travellers. The train was designed and built jointly in France and Britain by GEC ALSTHOM.

Stephen Stretch, a young graduate engineer, made his own contribution. Based in Birmingham, he works for the British arm of GEC ALSTHOM, a joint venture owned equally by Britain's GEC and France's Alcatel Alsthom.

The modern approach to graduate recruitment is to provide challenges, not just training. When Stephen took a summer vacation job at GEC ALSTHOM, he was given the chance to spend some time at the Eurostar test facility. This tests the train's electrical power and control systems through a simulation of the complete London-Paris journey. Stephen was testing and fault finding the electrical systems as the train design was being developed.

Sponsored by GEC through his second and third years at Sheffield University, Stephen received a First Class Honours degree and was given a place on the GEC ALSTHOM graduate trainee scheme. The programme focuses as much on the personal skills of the trainees as on their product knowledge. Stephen's problem solving, teamwork and communication skills were developed by a tough outward bound course. This was followed by a series of projects to be completed during his 18 months of training in the main sections of the company. Stephen also took French lessons, which led to two weeks' training at a French GEC ALSTHOM site.

With the training completed successfully, Stephen is now an assistant electrical engineer. He is part of a team designing and developing the trains for a new rail link between Stockholm city centre and the neighbouring airport. The seven, four-carriage trains for this new line represent a multimillion pound contract that will take approximately four years to complete and employ many hundreds of people.

Stephen's role involves:

- Calculating and designing some of the electrical requirements for the trains.
- Meeting and discussing equipment requirements with suppliers.
- Monitoring the designs provided by electrical suppliers (including power supplies, lighting, heating systems and much more).
- Constantly looking for new and better ways to build a train.

PRODUCTION

For GEC ALSTHOM, the Swedish order is a relatively small one. Bigger contracts, such as the London Underground's Jubilee and Northern lines, involve hundreds of train carriages. Part of the job of engineers is to decide on the most efficient production method. Stephen expects that his trains will be produced in the traditional way – the so-called static build. In other words, each carriage is assembled in one place. For the huge London Underground orders, the company is making its first ever move towards flow production: each carriage will be assembled in stages, then moved on to the next production stage in the equivalent of a car production line.

The engineering decisions here, as at every stage in the Stockholm project, have convinced Stephen that he was right to choose the manufacturing industry as his career. He says that 'engineering means problem solving and it provides the opportunity to see exactly what you have achieved'. He feels part of the Eurostar success, just as he will one day get a special thrill from travelling by train from the airport to the centre of Stockholm.

ACTIVITY

Benchmarking the UK car components industry

	World class manufacturers	British average
Productivity index* (units per worker per hour)	95.0	53.7
Quality (defects per 100)	0.025	2.5
Rework (correcting mistakes, percentage)	1.5	4.1
Speed of stock turnover (times per year)	93.6	32.4
Employees in problem solving (percentage)	80	54

Source: Lean Production Benchmarking Project 1994 *100 = best

1. Look carefully at the comparisons between the world's best producers (all Japanese) and the average British ones. Jot down a brief conclusion about each of the five sets of data.
2. Discuss how the British firms might benefit from adopting a lean approach to production and quality.

Location of production

What factors do firms consider when deciding where to locate? The eventual choice is usually based on a combination of factors, including the presence of raw materials, markets, transport, labour, government grants and the characteristics of the site.

In theory, the decision should be made by weighing up the fixed and variable costs of operating on each available site and comparing them with the expected revenues. However, it is becoming recognised that decisions are not always made on such rational, financial grounds. One of the first Japanese firms to set up a factory in Britain was Nittan, a manufacturer of smoke detectors. When the Japanese managing director arrived to search for a site in 1970, he decided on Old Woking in Surrey because it was close to Heathrow airport, near to the company's bank in the City and had excellent golf courses nearby! Larger firms, investing many hundreds of millions, are more likely to apply more scientific criteria.

RAW MATERIALS

These can be minerals like iron and coal or, more commonly today, components, which may be the semi-processed or finished products of other firms. In the past, poor transport facilities made this a vital factor, so steelworks were established near coalfields. Supplies of materials still influence location today if the materials are:

- Bulk reducing, as in the sugar refining industry. Sugar loses seven eighths of its weight when processed, so it is uneconomic to transport bulky,

raw sugar beet for long distances. This is why the factories are located in the growing areas like East Anglia.
- Perishable, as in the fruit canning industry.

MARKETS

As the pull of raw materials has declined with the improvement of transport links, nearness to markets has become increasingly important. This is especially true of:

- Bulk increasing (weight gaining) processes such as bottling or canning drinks. Coca-Cola, for example, have bottling plants close to most centres of population. It is not worth transporting bottles over long distances when the water can be just as easily added to the syrup near to the marketplace.
- Perishable items such as bread, which must quickly reach the customer.

TRANSPORT

For firms with national and, even more, international markets, speed of access to motorways, ports and railways is of great importance. Not only because time is money, but also because customers expect deliveries to be made exactly when requested. Delays due to traffic jams are no longer acceptable in an era of just in time production. Today, more than 90 per cent of deliveries take place by road. Perhaps this will change in future, as the Channel Tunnel and ever-higher taxes on petrol encourage greater use of the railways.

LABOUR

There are two ways in which firms may look at their labour requirements. If the production process is labour intensive, low wage rates may be a key location factor. So the choice is likely to be an area of traditionally high unemployment. In many other cases, the firm will be more concerned to obtain (or keep) workers and managers with the right skills. Hence computer software companies tend to favour the Thames Valley area, while electronics manufacturers go to Scotland's 'Silicon Glen'.

CHARACTERISTICS OF THE SITE

Large plants like oil refineries and steel works require vast amounts of flat, cheap land. Nearness to water for cooling is often important. Over half of Scotland's whisky distilleries are sited around the Moray Firth, where the best water, which has drained through peat, is found.

For service businesses, the key site characteristics are passing traffic (on foot or by car), ease of parking and the availability of sites of the right size.

GOVERNMENT INTERVENTION

Successive governments have adopted regional policies in order to redistribute wealth and employment more evenly and halt migration to the south east. Expansion in the prosperous areas can be controlled by restricting planning permission for new houses or factories. At the same time relocation to the **Assisted Areas** has been encouraged by offering incentives such as a 15 per cent grant towards capital expenditure on plant machinery and buildings. More significant has been the government's use of **Regional Selective Assistance**. This has been used to attract foreign firms considering Britain among other possible European sites. In 1994, the Korean firm Samsung was persuaded to build its first European factory in Britain. It is hoped that if Samsung is as successful here as Japanese firms have been, then other Korean firms will come to Britain as well.

WHY DO FIRMS TEND TO REMAIN IN THE SAME LOCATION?

Once an industry has become established in an area, it will often stay even when the original location advantages have disappeared. This **industrial inertia** occurs for many reasons. The investment in fixed assets – buildings and machinery – may be great; even more important are the skills and knowledge of the labour force. To move away would be likely to cause the break-up of what is often a company's greatest asset – its people. In any case, completely new **green-field** sites are difficult and expensive to set up because of the additional infrastructure needed, such as the roads and services which have to be provided.

Many firms are loyal to the area in which they were founded, but others have become **footloose**, or willing to move anywhere if the incentives are great enough. Mercedes Benz have considered setting up a car plant outside Germany and Jaguar cars have considered America. In 1993, Timex was willing to close down its Dundee plant and move production overseas. The firm had been established in Dundee for 40 years, yet its American parent company felt no underlying loyalty to the area. See page 60 for an activity on selecting industrial locations.

The impact of automation

What constitutes efficient production? Most firms would say that to reduce costs and improve quality would be a sure-fire way of beating rivals and ensuring commercial success. Important as they are, though, to get these factors right is still only part of the answer. Increasingly, in the current climate of over-capacity, worldwide competition and rapid technological change, firms must also be able to compete on factors other than price or quality. They must offer a much wider range of products, by being able to adapt their production process quickly in response to changing market demands and by reducing lead times – the time taken to develop a new product until it is ready for full production.

The widespread automation of production processes which has been advocated in recent years is no longer seen as a universal solution for industry's problems.

There is no shortage of examples illustrating the benefits of automation. In addition, more advanced robots are continually being developed. For example, Ford developed the world's first 'seeing' robot. A magnet mounted on the robot's arm collects an engine part such as a crankshaft from storage. The robot identifies it by 'seeing' the part's shape and comparing it to information stored in a memory bank. The part is then placed with pinpoint accuracy on the production line.

Undisputed benefits such as these have unfortunately prompted business advisers in the last decade to advocate the wholesale adoption of automation. Many firms have been intimidated into spending vast sums of money on unnecessary technology by simplistic slogans such as 'automate or liquidate'.

However, unless the design and organisation of the production line are simplified and streamlined beforehand, automation will merely accentuate the existing problems, not solve them. Nothing less than the complete reorganisation of the whole production line will work, as the introduction of automation on its own merely speeds up an existing inefficient process and adds the purchase and upkeep of the machinery as an extra cost burden. When complete reorganisation does take place, though, extending from simplifying the original design of the product right through to changing the plant layout, as Vauxhall have done with their Astra production line, then the benefits can be substantial.

Car production at Vauxhall Motors

UNDERSTANDING INDUSTRY

ACTIVITY

Selecting locations of industries

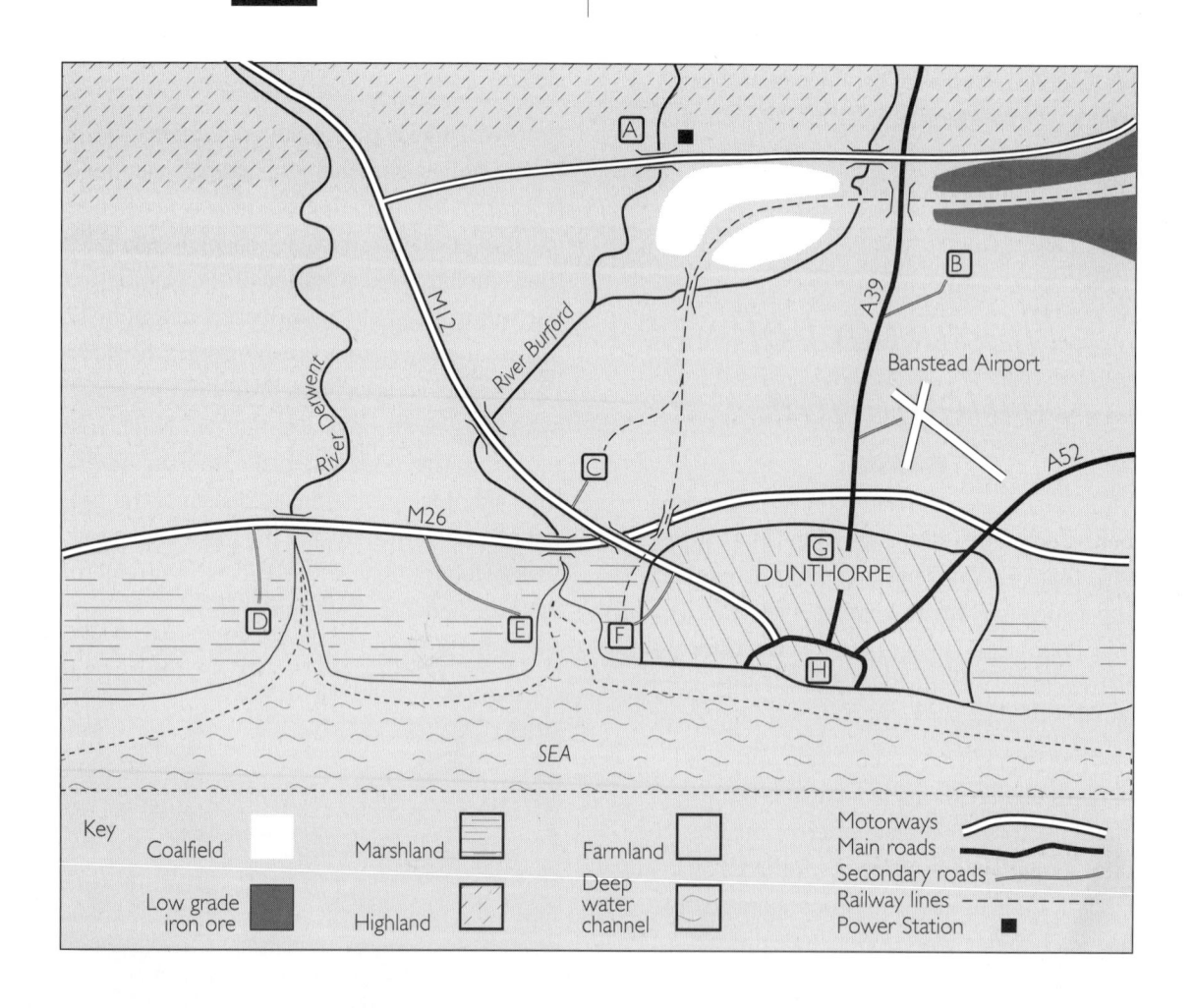

Key
- Coalfield
- Low grade iron ore
- Marshland
- Highland
- Farmland
- Deep water channel
- Motorways
- Main roads
- Secondary roads
- Railway lines
- Power Station

Decide which of the sites marked A–H would be the best location for each of the industries listed below, giving at least two reasons to explain your choice in each case.

- Shipbuilding
- Car assembly
- Oil refining
- Sugar-beet refining
- Jewellery manufacture
- Aluminium smelting
- Steel production
- Electronic engineering

New technology

THE IMPACT OF INFORMATION TECHNOLOGY (IT)

IT offers firms three main opportunities:

1 To increase employees' access to information.
2 To enable large quantities of data to be processed, stored, analysed and distributed – quickly.
3 To enable information to pass freely between organisations or between different branches of the same organisation, via on-line systems, electronic mail or the Internet.

It used to be thought that a major benefit would be the creation of 'the paperless office'. Few still believe that today. Computers can act as filing cabinets or internal mail systems, but they also generate large quantities of paper print-out.

1 Access to up-to-date information provides two main benefits within the workplace.

- First, it enables junior managers or shop-floor staff to make decisions based upon latest data. A novice employee at a travel agent can book a holiday; a sales manager can see how a revised sales forecast affects the firm's profit; and a retail manager can see how his store's results compare with others within the chain. In each case there is a potential benefit in improved efficiency and decision making.
- Second, information technology can provide quick feedback on performance, to show that, for example, 99 per cent of the morning's output within a particular section was fault free. This approach has a beneficial effect on employee motivation and the smooth running of a production system such as just in time.

2 The invention of computers was prompted by the need for better storage and analysis of numerate and written information, so this has always been a key function. During the 1960s and 1970s, large 'mainframe' computers provided a central point where an organisation's data could be sent for processing. The firm's sales figures, its accounts and its payroll would be handled in this way. The development of personal computers (PCs) in the 1980s gave an opportunity for more junior managers – and those away from head office – to store and analyse information about their own department or retail outlet. When, by the mid-1980s, these personal computers could be linked to each other and to the head office mainframe, a powerful method of communication was established. So, a store manager could have access to sales records of chocolate eggs for the pre-Easter period last year, together with a computer forecast of sales this year. The manager could then judge with more accuracy how many to order.

3 Direct lines of communication between computers present huge opportunities to companies, including:

- An increasing use of 'teleworkers', carrying out projects or analyses from home; this might mean a further increase in the use of part-time and freelance labour.
- Far greater efficiency in managing organisations with many branches; this is illustrated in the Marks & Spencer case study on page 62.
- Increasing the tendency for firms to become involved more closely with their suppliers, as with EDI (electronic data interchange) in which firms exchange data such as sales figures.

MANUFACTURING RESOURCE PLANNING (MRP II)

This is a complex computer software package that provides a universal planning system for the whole of a company's production processes. It is designed to translate sales forecasts (or actual orders) into purchasing requirements for raw materials and components, factory production schedules, individual work instructions and completion deadlines. Complex as this sounds, it only underestimates the real task. Most firms will have many different product lines and many different orders from a variety of customers. The MRP II system must coordinate and schedule all of these in order to use the factory and staff as efficiently as possible. If it is impossible to produce all the orders within the desired delivery deadlines, the computer will show the overtime requirement, or warn that customers must be alerted to delivery delays.

Once such a system is running effectively, it is easy to see that it not only replaces the planning role of production management, but is likely to lead to huge gains in efficiency. However, the process of setting up MRP II may be chaotic, unless the firm takes time to test every element of the computer programme before bringing the whole system on line.

A further benefit of MRP II is that because it creates a computer model of the entire workings of the firm, managers can 'consult' it. 'What if?' questions can be asked such as 'What are the cost, capacity and materials ordering implications of offering three for the price of two?' Using this facility makes it easy for managers to experiment in theory, before risking the firm's resources in practice.

CASE STUDY

Information technology at Marks & Spencer

When you buy something at Marks & Spencer, the till does a lot more than produce a receipt. An electronic message is sent instantly (on line) to M&S central computers to calculate what new stock is needed. This information is fed into suppliers' computers where it is used to organise the following day's deliveries.

This generates many benefits to customer and company alike. For the company, a key advantage is a reduced stock requirement. In the past, the only way to ensure enough supplies to meet changing customer demand was to have stocks of every product line in the warehouse of every store. The cost of those stocks at 350 M&S stores tied up a huge amount of capital. Today, the seven distribution depots know each night exactly what has been sold from each branch and can therefore supply exact replacements. This ensures that M&S food is very fresh, reducing wastage and improving quality.

Technology is also useful for non-food lines. When a new range of clothing goes into stores, the first few days' sales are computer-monitored, allowing production of faster-selling colours and sizes to be stepped up. Marks & Spencer suppliers have developed ways to react quickly. For instance, jumpers are knitted in advance, but dyed only when customer colour preferences are clear. This enables manufacturers to supply new stock within 48 hours and customers to find the exact item they want.

The most important customer benefit is probably the range of goods M&S can make available – regularly and reliably. The cost of holding stock used to make it impossible to hold a huge range of styles, sizes and colours of clothing and footwear. Today the precision and speed of information technology ensures that large numbers of lines can be stocked profitably without risking ending the season with a surplus of any one product. Stores receive deliveries that respond to their individual requirements, so if only one size is selling, only that one will be received. In the past, all lines were ordered in fixed size ratios (e.g. two pairs of size 12 shoes for every dozen size 9s).

Success with IT relies on far more than just buying clever systems. The way in which the technology is used is very important. In September 1993, Marks & Spencer decided to change the way their stores ordered new stocks of clothing. Previously, sales assistants checked daily on the amount sold of each product line. With larger outlets carrying 150,000 non-food lines, this daily stock count took a huge amount of staff time. The count, using hand-held terminals, also proved quite inaccurate. As every wrong order could mean a lost sale and a disappointed customer, action was needed.

The solution was to use the stores' existing technology in a different way. Instead of counting the amount of stock left, the electronic tills were used to count the sales made of each product line. The store's computer terminal would then calculate the correct order level based upon the day of the week, sales trends and seasonal factors. With the legwork being done by computer, sales assistants now had new roles. They could spend more time deciding on the right level of display stock for each product line.

Although there was no investment cost to this new system, a 12-week training programme was required. Yet this proved a minor cost when set against some considerable benefits. Size availability rose by 10 per cent, having a positive effect on sales and image. For Marks & Spencer, the computer has become central to the company's present and future.

The environment – can firms meet the clean technology challenge?

There was a time when green was simply another colour. But when the UK's Green Party leapt from nowhere to win a hefty 15 per cent of the votes cast in the 1989 Euro-Elections, even the most hardened sceptics were forced to concede that the depth of public support for environmental causes was not a passing fad. As concern mounted during the 1980s over issues such as global warming, acid rain, toxic waste and the destruction of the tropical rain forests, it became clear that a new breed of green consumer had emerged.

In the scramble to reflect the new green mood, some manufacturers began to make wildly exaggerated claims for their products. At one time, everything from lead-free petrol to fly-spray was labelled 'ozone friendly'. Inevitably, some of these firms were simply jumping on the bandwagon.

Nevertheless, there were an increasing number of companies who had begun to manufacture products or provide services which were genuinely 'green'. Many of the UK's leading companies have also shown that they are well prepared to meet the clean technology challenge in the 1990s and beyond.

ICI has developed a group of hydrogen-based gases which are designed to replace the chlorine-based CFCs as refrigerant gases. This is a particularly important development in view of the role that CFCs play in depleting the vital ozone layer which protects the earth from harmful ultraviolet rays – one atom of chlorine can wipe out a staggering 100,000 ozone molecules. On top of this, CFCs also contribute to global warming. In fact, as 'greenhouse gases' they have a potential impact 20,000 times greater than carbon dioxide, on a molecule by molecule basis, though carbon dioxide is actually implicated more strongly in global warming purely because it is released in greater quantities.

Another group of companies is concerned with developing methods to dispose of waste safely. Haden MacLellan converts toxic industrial paint sludge into dried powder to make paint and industrial filler for cars. Simon Engineering have developed a new method of sewage treatment which turns sewage sludge into an inert compost that is safe to use as a soil fertiliser. The process is likely to be widely adopted, especially in view of the announcement by the Government that it intends to outlaw the dumping of sewage sludge at sea from 1998.

Johnson Matthey is one of only four companies in the world to produce catalytic converters for cars. These clean up exhaust emissions by converting harmful gases into less harmful carbon dioxide, nitrogen and water vapour. It is a market that has boomed from 1993, when EC regulations made it compulsory for converters to be fitted to all new cars.

Nor have these environmental initiatives been confined purely to manufacturing. Amongst the major supermarket chains Tesco has been at the forefront of the green movement with its 'Tesco Cares' campaign. The label is used on products ranging from phosphate-free cleaning agents to recycled tissues. Tesco has also provided space for over 150 bottle banks and around 60 paper banks and is running trial schemes for the reclamation of aluminium and plastics. The company has pioneered a comprehensive labelling policy, sells a range of organic produce in many of its stores and abstains from animal testing on own-label goods. It sells lead-free petrol at all its filling stations and has also converted the company car fleet to run on lead-free petrol wherever possible. Other supermarket chains have since followed Tesco's lead and introduced similar measures in their stores.

In general, consumers have now come to expect that the products they buy should be ecologically sound. However, some of the products which have been widely regarded as environmentally friendly have recently come under attack. Critics point out that some recycled toilet papers are made of scarce top grade paper which ought instead to be used for high quality products such as stationery.

Ecobalance research can be useful in cases such as this. It involves weighing up the environmental impact of a product at every stage of its life from the extraction of raw materials needed for its manufacture through to its eventual disposal as waste. The analysis can sometimes yield unexpected findings. Ecobalance research carried out in Germany discovered that in terms of the balance between energy efficiency, manufacturing pollution and recycling, it was better to use plastic bags sparingly than to use recycled paper bags.

The whole environmental debate focuses increasingly on the crucial question of who should bear the cost of a cleaner environment – consumers, companies or governments? Some companies have spent considerable sums on making improvements where necessary, but in some cases environmental awareness has had to be balanced by commercial considerations.

Clearly, the solving of environmental problems poses many dilemmas. But an aspect of the debate that is often overlooked is that it can pay to be green. The market for environmentally friendly products and technologies is estimated to be worth between £100 billion and £150 billion. This is apart from the estimated £200 million which is invested in the shares of companies with a good record on ethical and environmental issues. Those with impeccable green credentials are also likely to fare better when recruiting young job applicants.

Personnel

IN ASSOCIATION WITH

STANDARD LIFE

Introduction: do people matter?

When Tom Peters and Robert Waterman were researching their book, *In Search of Excellence*, the conclusions they arrived at were not at all what they had expected. Rather than sophisticated systems of management and control being behind the success of their 'excellent' American companies, it was proven time and time again to be the employees' attitudes that made the difference. Do the firms with employees that perform consistently well have anything in common?

Although company styles vary, what is certain is that all successful firms possess the ability to tap the potential of their employees so that people identify strongly with company goals and are willing to channel all their energies and enthusiasm into achieving them. This degree of commitment is not achieved purely because they have concentrated on recruiting high fliers. In fact, quite 'ordinary' people produce exceptional performances in these progressive firms. Their employees appear, in general, to show commitment and feel that the company is a good one to work for. So how do these firms encourage such motivation?

Successful firms recruit carefully, train their employees well and recognise their achievements, adopt caring welfare policies, create climates which motivate people and have a cooperative company culture which minimises industrial conflict.

HOW TO STOP THE COMPANY STIFLING PEOPLE AND STRANGLING PROFITS

So reads the challenging subtitle of Robert Townsend's book, *Up the Organisation*.

In the 13 years prior to Townsend taking over as chairman, Avis Rent-a-Car never made a profit, yet three years later the sales had grown from $30 million to $75 million. The following excerpts of his views on different ways of treating people give some clues as to the reasons behind this remarkable turnaround.

On people

'Most people in big companies today are administered not led. They are treated as personnel not people. Get to know your people. What they do well, what they enjoy doing, what their weaknesses and strengths are and what they want and need to get from their job.'

Message to chief executives

'Certainly today, no meeting of the high and mighty is complete until someone polishes the conventional wisdom, "Our big trouble today is getting enough good people..."

This is crystal clear nonsense. Your people aren't lazy and incompetent. They just look that way. They're beaten by all the overlapping and interlocking policies, rules and systems encrusting your company.'

On promotion

'Most managements complain about the lack of able people and go outside to fill key positions. Nonsense. I use the rule of 50 per cent. Try to find somebody inside the company with a record of success (in any area) and with an appetite for the job. If they look like 50 per cent of what you need, give them the job. In six months they'll have grown the other 50 per cent and everybody will be satisfied.'

Recruiting the right people

Firms need to recruit carefully, so that they can find the right people for their requirements. If their recruitment procedures are inefficient, staff turnover will be high, with all the resulting waste of time, energy and administrative costs. Worse still, the people who are poor appointments might stay on and perform badly, blocking the career path of people who deserve to be promoted.

DO INTERVIEWS WORK?

How good are interviews at getting the right person for the job? A growing body of evidence suggests that traditional interviewing may be far less effective than people like to think.

Research has shown that interviewers tend to form an initial impression within the first five minutes or so of the candidate walking through the door, and from then on spend their time searching for additional information to substantiate their hunches. Worse still, research has also shown that a candidate rated best by one interviewer may be rated poorest by another. So a candidate's chances of success may largely depend on who interviews him or her on the day! There is also a danger of interviewers placing too much emphasis on one or two criteria they have identified as being important, and ignoring evidence relating to other qualities the candidate may possess.

As interviews are still the single most important method of selection and seem to be here to stay, it is vitally important to improve their effectiveness. To this end, many companies such as ICI, British Airways and National Westminster Bank are now using **situational interviewing** methods. This is where candidates are presented with a series of hypothetical events based on situations that might arise in the job they are applying for and are asked how they would respond. Their answers are then compared with what people who are already in the company and are known to be performing similar jobs effectively would do in those situations.

This technique has already proved highly successful in selecting people with management potential. Clearly, situational interviewing can prove invaluable for effective recruitment in that it lessens the danger of interviewers relying on their gut feelings.

CASE STUDY

Standard Life – recruiting tomorrow's managers

In 1995 over 6,000 university students applied for a place on the graduate trainee scheme run by the major insurance company, Standard Life. After many months of careful selection procedures, just 53 were recruited at a cost of £10,000 each! How and why was such a huge sum spent and how were the 53 chosen?

The process begins every September, with leaflets, brochures and application forms being distributed to all universities. In addition, Standard Life staff attend careers fairs at each of the 27 universities they regard most highly. The six-page application form is very demanding, with questions such as 'Describe a time when you felt under pressure. How did you respond?' The large spaces for answers are very off-putting, so only serious applicants apply.

The first filter applied to the 6,000 applicants is conducted not by Standard Life employees, but a firm of recruitment consultants. They look through the forms and reject those which fail to meet the required academic, character or personality criteria. Two thirds of applicants are rejected at this stage.

The 2,000 who pass this stage are invited to a 'behavioural' interview. This is carried out by staff trained to use a special type of interview devised by psychologists in America, who asked, 'What makes people successful?' and after careful research among successful sports and business people, identified common key characteristics. An interview procedure was then devised to pick out the right type of person. In Standard Life's case, the interview looks for eight main qualities:

- Problem-solving ability.
- Communication skills.
- Interpersonal skills.
- Focus (the ability to identify and concentrate on key issues).
- Creativity and courage (thinking of new approaches and sticking by them).
- Leadership.
- The ability to woo others to your point of view.
- Adaptability and flexibility.

The interviewer presents the recruit with a series of situations, problems or crises and asks for a response. It is designed to pick out the top 15–20 per cent from a group of talented people. In 1995, only 250 were shortlisted out of 2,000.

Those shortlisted are invited to a two-day selection process at an assessment centre. Usually held at Standard Life's Edinburgh headquarters, eight applicants are invited per session. Flown in the day before and put up overnight in a four-star hotel, the expenses-paid selection process also gives applicants a taste of executive life.

The two-day course starts at 8.30 a.m. The candidates are put through a series of demanding exercises, each designed to assess further the eight qualities already set out. Each applicant is given the responsibility to lead one session – perhaps a problem-solving exercise, perhaps a role play or a business game. Some candidates prove indecisive, others are unable to win people over to their own viewpoint. All end up revealing their personal leadership style: authoritarian, democratic or laissez-faire (see page 95). Ideally, Standard Life wants managers to have a mix of all three and the ability to alter the mixture to suit the situation. David Dimmock, the company's community and education liaison manager, says 'Too many are laissez-faire, just sitting back when they've finished briefing the team ... We'd want to see them involved: encouraging, coaching and team-building.'

Each exercise is observed by a Standard Life manager and a recruitment consultant. At the end, these two discuss each candidate's performance.

After a highly pressurised morning, the applicants will not be able to relax at lunch. Led into a boardroom, they sit down to an elegant meal with company directors and managers. Can they handle the situation? The small talk? The drink? After all, Standard Life are looking for high-flyers who, in less than a year, may be dealing with important customers. Are they up to the task?

If this is not daunting enough, there are still two more major hurdles. The first is a session in which the candidates are told about a problem requiring a group response but *without* the appointment of a leader. Who will speak first? Who will emerge as the leader? Some seize the opportunity, but over-reach themselves, causing the others to reject their leadership. Others might show clear thinking and quiet authority, only emerging as the leader towards the end of the exercise.

The final challenge is a personal interview with the manager directly responsible for the job being recruited. This checks that the two get on well together. The manager has access to the personality profile and the results of the two days' assessments.

Is it all worth nine months of effort and over £500,000? Certainly yes, if judged by the results achieved. In the past seven years over 99 per cent of the recruited trainees have completed the two year management trainee programme. Other large firms suffer quite a high drop-out rate as graduates become disillusioned, or because they cannot cope with the pressures of work. Even more important than the low drop-out rate is that, once trained, Standard Life's young managers have proved they possess the talent, dynamism and loyalty that the recruitment procedure set out to find.

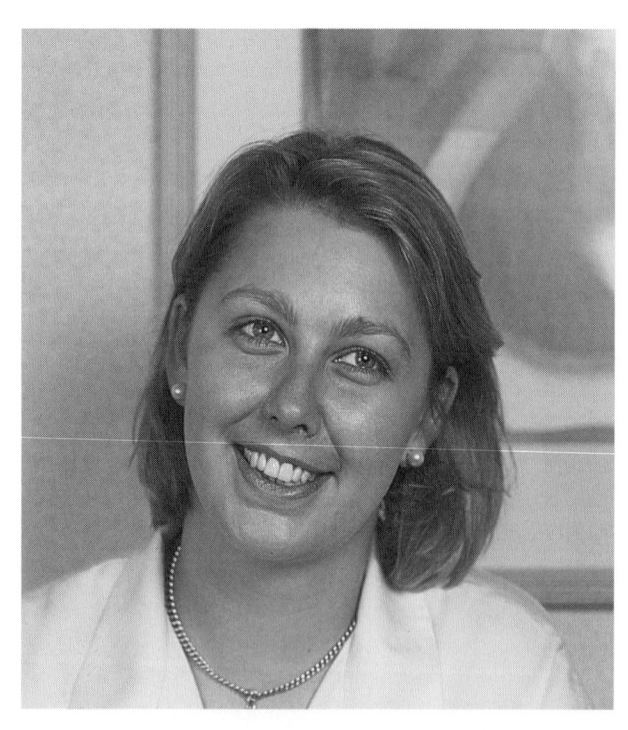

Sara Mills joined in 1993 and is now a business analyst in Standard Life's marketing division. She was offered the post before the end of her two-year training programme in general management. Her job involves anticipating customers' future needs to ensure that the company is developing the right products and services.

Karl Richmond joined Standard Life in 1993 after obtaining a First in Maths and Statistics at Warwick University. The company pays for him to study for professional qualifications, providing off-the-job as well as on-the-job training. Karl is currently working on quotes to buy out pension schemes.

Is appraisal necessary?

In most large firms, staff appraisal, where the employees individually discuss their progress with their immediate managers, is carried out once or twice a year. Appraisal is usually done in order to discuss how well employees are doing and how they can improve their work. The assessment of strengths and weaknesses is also useful in determining where further training may be needed and whether employees are ready for promotion. In some firms, the appraisal determines their salary increase for the year.

These advantages have prompted more and more firms to introduce appraisal schemes, sometimes based on the use of a standard appraisal form. Clearly, formal appraisal will only be useful in situations where employees do not see the criticism as being destructive and where the managers do not shy away from making unfavourable appraisals if necessary. In any case, formal appraisals should not be seen as a substitute for continuous feedback during the year.

Is training important?

It is claimed that each year in Germany two or three times more fitters, electricians and building craftsworkers become qualified than in the UK and five times as many clerical workers. As Brian Nickson of the Institute of Training and Development (ITD) points out, 'If companies are to keep up with new technology, become more competitive abroad, attract good quality staff and increase their profits, they must make a real commitment to training.'

How, then, can training help firms achieve these benefits? At a time when the pace of technological change is so rapid, workers must be retrained to learn the new skills needed and taught to be flexible enough to adapt to further changes in their working lives. Clearly, trained workers will produce a greater quantity and better quality of work than untrained workers. The existence of a good training programme within a company is likely both to attract good staff and to keep them, as people like to feel that they are improving their skills so that they can progress in their careers. On a practical level, training in health and safety is absolutely essential. It follows that an effective training programme which leads to improved performance for employees and boosts morale must also increase company profits.

Traditionally, training has been **on-the-job training**, the simplest form of which is learning by 'sitting next to Nellie'. This can be effective, though training by an experienced worker may be inefficient and could result in bad habits being learnt. However, the fact that most academic training for professional jobs, such as teaching, also requires a period of on-the-job training before the qualification is finally awarded, is a recognition of the importance of practical experience.

Off-the-job training, becoming increasingly popular with the decline of apprentice training, is when training is given by specialist instructors in the firms' own training schools or in colleges. The main advantage is that employees can learn faster by following a carefully planned training programme than by learning in the working environment.

In recent years, many firms have adopted **computer-based training (CBT)** methods, where trainees work through learning programs written specifically for the firm. Michelin Tyre Plc, for example, have found employees much prefer this type of training once they have overcome their initial fear of operating the equipment. The Royal Mail also found that 'by taking an active role in their own training and by learning at their own pace, people retain 40 per cent more information than they would with any other training method.'

What motivates people?

When people's needs are not met in their job, complaints and fatigue increase, productivity drops, absenteeism is likely to rise, and in extreme cases even violence and sabotage can occur. It is important, therefore, for firms to know what motivates people in order to ensure their needs are met. Various writers have tried to identify these motivating factors.

FW TAYLOR (1911)

Writing in the early part of the century, Taylor's methods were founded on the basis that 'what workmen want from their employers beyond anything else is high wages'. He argued that tasks, even simple ones like shovelling, could be broken down into smaller components and analysed, and then unnecessary or inefficient processes could be removed. After scientific study of the job, the correct output which workers should achieve in a day could be decided on. Workers who then met this productivity target should be paid much higher wages.

Though his principles later became widely adopted as the basis of **work study** methods, he was severely criticised, even in his own time, for seeing money as the main motivating factor and for reducing workers to the level of efficient machines. In all fairness, however, few employers have been willing to implement all his ideas fully, like having no limit to the amount highly productive workers can earn.

E MAYO (1933)

Mayo's research has been influential in revealing that the general ethos and values held by informal social groups at work are more important in determining productivity levels than are other changes.

In the famous Hawthorne experiment, a group of workers were segregated in order to observe the effect on output and morale of various changes to their working environment. As each improvement was introduced, such as incentive payments, rest pauses, shorter hours and refreshments, productivity rose. Then it was decided to return to the original conditions of a six-day, 48-hour week, with no incentives, no rest pauses and no refreshments. Expecting a fall in output, researchers were amazed when productivity soared to the highest levels ever reached!

Though it seemed a mystery then, Mayo's later explanation was that by this time a tightly knit social group had formed, who benefited from the attention shown by researchers and who worked to achieve the output levels they thought the researchers expected. The research has stimulated an increasing tendency for production to be organised in small groups and encouraged managers to realise the importance of praise, attention and good communications in getting workers to identify and work towards company goals.

AH MASLOW (1943)

Maslow argued that people seek to satisfy a hierarchy of needs, with lower-level needs being satisfied before higher-level needs (see the diagram on page 13). With increased living standards this century, lower-level needs such as those for physical survival and safety tend to have been satisfied. Firms who now wish to persuade their employees to work harder can only do so by offering them the opportunity to fulfil higher-level needs. These include the satisfaction of social needs (belonging to a group), esteem needs (being highly regarded) and the need for self-fulfilment (gaining satisfaction by being creative, for instance).

D MCGREGOR (1960)

Theories like Taylor's, which view employees as disliking work and which emphasise high wages and strict supervision as the best way of ensuring maximum productivity, are based on certain assumptions about what workers are like. McGregor called these assumptions *Theory X*. Instead, his own *Theory Y* is based on assumptions that people find work natural, that they exercise self-control in meeting objectives to which they are committed, that they will not only accept but actively seek responsibility and will want to take part in decision making.

The implications of McGregor's theories are far-reaching. Clearly, firms need to create Theory Y climates and working conditions so that workers can motivate themselves, with managers performing a supportive role rather than a traditional controlling role.

F HERZBERG (1966)

Herzberg developed his theory of incentives by asking a sample of employees what made them happy or unhappy at work. On this basis, he identified *hygiene* or *maintenance factors*, such as adequate pay and working conditions, as not being **motivators**. If these are inadequate, workers will fight to have them improved, but they do not actually encourage people to work harder. The *real* motivators were factors relating to the job itself, like the opportunity for achievement, recognition and advancement. The chance to exercise creativity and take on responsibility were also important.

Contrary to Taylor's early ideas, these later writers have argued that people are motivated by many needs and do not work for money alone. In fact, it can often be seen that people's whole identity stems from the work they do and the organisation they work for. The evidence that work is a psychological need is borne out by the effects of unemployment on people, many of whom report a loss of identity and esteem and a general feeling of alienation from society.

ACTIVITY

The needs fulfilled by different jobs

1. Identify which higher-order needs, such as the need for esteem and recognition, or for self-fulfilment through the chance to exercise creativity or take on responsibility, are likely to be fulfilled in the following jobs:
- Rock star
- Barrister
- Surgeon
- Cabinet minister
- First division footballer
- Train driver
- Airline pilot
- Music composer
- Fashion designer

2. Which needs would you expect your future job to fulfil?

" DISCUSSION POINT "

Do you think unemployed people suffer through not being able to fulfil any of these needs through a job?

CASE STUDY

Kalmar – production on a human scale

In the mid-1970s, the Kalmar car works in Sweden was hailed as Volvo's answer to the labour problems associated with traditional assembly line production methods, and still provides a classic example of production on a human scale. The high rates of absenteeism and high labour turnover being experienced generally were symptoms of the trend everywhere for production line jobs to become boring and repetitive as a result of increasingly specialised division of labour. Not surprisingly, workers found it almost impossible to take a pride in their jobs and in the finished product, when all they were doing was one small operation in the production process. Unlike Britain, Sweden suffers from a labour shortage, so Volvo faced great difficulties in recruiting labour. As jobs were freely available, workers were reluctant to choose assembly line work.

The unique design of its new plant to produce the Volvo 760 was, ironically, a step nearer to the way cars were originally made in the past, when they were made by teams of skilled workers in specialist workshops. Instead of the conventional production line organisation, teams of workers at Kalmar were made responsible for assembling one complete section of the car – for example, one team would assemble the whole steering system. The 15 to 20 operators who comprised each team could decide how the work was to be divided up between themselves and could control the pace of their 40-minute cycles. Changes such as these and the fact that teams could decide when to have their breaks went a long way towards breaking up the monotony of the work. Each team was also allocated their own area of the building, with their own entrance, changing room and coffee area.

The organisation of the work along these lines was designed to relieve boredom, increase job satisfaction, foster teamwork and enable workers to take a pride in the finished product.

As hoped, the problems management thought would be solved by the new system largely disappeared, though the initiative was not without its problems. The initial capital investment was far higher than for a traditional car plant and, although quality has improved, productivity is generally lower. However, there is no doubt that the human lessons learnt at Kalmar will act as a catalyst for change in traditionally organised assembly plants everywhere.

> ## DISCUSSION POINTS
>
> 1 Should companies organise production to ensure worker satisfaction or to gain high productivity?
> 2 Are the two aims in fact incompatible?
> 3 What factors might influence companies' eventual decision?

Do pay and incentives motivate?

Traditional payment systems based on **time rates** (i.e. the number of hours worked) are necessary for many jobs – where output cannot be measured, where quality is so important the job should not be hurried, or where the speed of work cannot be controlled by the workers. With this system, workers cannot earn more if they work harder.

The **payment by results** method is often used for production workers whose output can be measured. Here, workers can earn more if they work harder.

Much research since Herzberg has confirmed the importance of firms creating the right conditions where workers can satisfy their higher needs and thus work harder. Important though this is, many companies today also encourage motivation by operating **incentive schemes** which involve a merit award being paid for extra performance.

Merit awards should, however, not be regularly paid, but awarded on appraisal. Otherwise they become expected as a right, not a reward. As Robert Townsend also points out, in *Up the Organisation*, 'Rewarding outstanding performances is important. Much more neglected is the equally important need to make sure that the underachievers don't get rewarded. This is more painful, so it doesn't get done very often.'

An extension of the incentive principle is **profit sharing**, where employees get a bonus according to the profit made by the company, sometimes linked to the issue of shares. The John Lewis Partnership introduced a profit-sharing scheme as long ago as 1929. Apart from the motivating aspects of such schemes, they do also have the advantage of encouraging workers to identify with the company.

Does participation in decision making motivate?

Much research has been done which shows that where workers participate in decision making, motivation is enhanced through them becoming more involved and committed and feeling that their opinions matter. On a more basic level, it is recognised that when workers' opinions influence a particular course of action being taken, they are far more determined to go all out to make that course of action work, rather than if it is just someone else's decision handed down for them to carry out.

Worker participation can take place on different levels. At one end of the scale are **consultative committees**, found in many companies. Worker representatives elected to these committees can influence decisions concerning a wide range of everyday issues affecting the company. At the other end of the scale, in some companies **worker representatives** are appointed to the board and have a chance to influence major policy decisions. However, critics of this system argue that workers are not capable of making any long-term policy decisions.

Some European firms have avoided this problem by adopting a dual system. This consists of a top-level board which is equivalent to the traditional board of directors and makes overall policy decisions, and a second-level board, including worker representatives, which is responsible for day-to-day management.

The role of trade unions today

Trade unions were founded in response to the harsh working conditions in the factories and mines of the early Industrial Revolution. Workers realised that they had more power standing together than on their own. Therefore they grouped together to act collectively, electing representatives to bargain on behalf of all the union members. Later, these local workplace initiatives joined together to form national unions.

There are now 260 unions in the UK with just over 8.5 million members, about one third of the workforce. Although trade unions were founded by manual workers, almost half of members today work in services such as banking or retailing. Nearly 40 per cent of union members are women, so the stereotype of a union member as a male manual worker is becoming less accurate.

There are four main types of union:

- **General unions**, which represent workers in a range of industries, such as the GMB (General Municipal and Boilermakers' Union).
- **Craft unions**, which represent workers from a group of industries who share a particular skill, such as the National Union of Lock and Metal Workers.
- **Industrial unions**, representing workers in a particular industry, whatever their skill, such as the NUM (National Union of Mineworkers).
- **White collar unions**, which represent clerical workers such as the NUJ (National Union of Journalists).

Trade unions negotiate with employers by means of **collective bargaining** to improve pay, working conditions and job security. At the local level, the elected **shop stewards** take up many individual grievances with management. The most common complaints are about health and safety and about legal issues such as contracts of employment plus threats of redundancy or dismissal. In recent years there has been a marked increase in the use of unions' legal services, as workers have sought some protection from a harsh economic climate. In the year to April 1994, trade unions won a record £335 million in legal compensation for members who suffered injury or ill health because of their work.

When disputes cannot be resolved between union and management, there are two avenues that can be explored. The **Advisory Conciliation and Arbitration Service (ACAS)** was set up in 1975 to offer help and ways of resolving disputes between unions and employers. Conciliation means bringing both sides together and encouraging them to settle their differences, while arbitration means hearing the case put by each side then deciding on the appropriate outcome. In individual cases, **industrial tribunals** enable workplace disputes to be settled legally.

The influence of the law over the position of workers and unions has made it important to attempt to influence the government in its legislative programme. Most of the larger unions belong to the **Trades Union Congress (TUC)**, which represents the union movement in discussions with the British government or the European Union. The **Confederation of British Industry (CBI)** performs the same role on behalf of most large businesses in the country. In the past, these organisations needed only to influence the British government. Now the laws established by the European Union can outrank those within Britain, so issues such as the right to strike may be taken out of the hands of the British Parliament.

WHAT DO PEOPLE THINK OF TRADE UNIONS?

Trade union membership has fallen by nearly 40 per cent from its peak in 1979. There have been four main reasons for this:

- The rise in unemployment.
- The changing patterns in employment, from manufacturing to services and from full- to part-time or temporary work.
- The reduction in the strength of unions due to changes in the law.
- The damage to the image of unions caused by highly publicised strikes during the 1970s and early 1980s.

Yet there is now evidence of a shift in public attitudes. A 1993 Gallup survey found that 71 per cent of the adults polled considered unions 'a good thing'. The same survey found that 55 per cent believed the balance of power in industry had tilted too far in the direction of management compared with a mere 5 per cent who said the trade unions had the advantage. These positive findings were confirmed by the public support for the rail strikes of mid-1994.

Supporters of trade unions argue that they are essential for protecting the interests of employees who might otherwise get a raw deal from powerful employers. Yet critics believe that union wage claims can cause inflation and unemployment by pricing workers out of jobs. Another charge frequently levelled at unions is that they undermine the competitiveness of British industry because of opposition to technical progress and changing working practices. However, a survey by ACAS of 650 employers has shown that 'the presence of trade unions has not appeared to inhibit the introduction of new working practices'.

Among these new approaches have been the Japanese-inspired agreements between employers and unions involving single-union deals, multiskilled working and (sometimes) no-strike clauses. Originated by companies such as Toshiba UK in Plymouth and Nissan UK in Durham, these approaches involve a long-term commitment to workplace cooperation and investment. Their importance for attracting foreign investment to Britain cannot be overestimated.

In his 1994 book, *The Future of the Trade Unions*, Robert Taylor of the *Financial Times* concludes that it 'is a profound mistake' to believe that 'unions have become obsolete'. He sees them as 'allies of management in the negotiation of workplace change . . . where consensus is much more vital than competition in the achievement of corporate success'. In other words unions can succeed by working in partnership with employers.

ACTIVITY

Attitude battery towards the role of trade unions

On a copy of the table below, list the advantages and disadvantages of trade unions. Use the points mentioned in the text and any other points you can think of. You should have 10 statements in all.

	Statements	Agree strongly	Agree	Neither agree nor disagree	Disagree	Strongly disagree
Advantages						
Disadvantages						

Put a tick in the box which sums up your attitude towards each statement. What does your attitude battery reveal about your underlying attitudes to trade unions?

CASE STUDY

Mitsubishi Electric Europe (B.V.) – managing change

'Whatever Maslow or any other theorist says, I **know** that happy staff work better'. This statement by Neville Reyner, executive vice-president, Electronic Products Group of Mitsubishi Electric Europe, could be seen as unbusinesslike. Yet any director of a business that has grown tenfold in 10 years must be taken seriously. Especially when his own divisions of the business have an annual turnover of more than £120 million.

Mitsubishi Electric is less well known than its car-producing sister company, but it is a major force in consumer and industrial electronics. In Britain it produces televisions, videos, Apricot computers and air conditioning units. In total, the company employs over 2,000 people in Britain, with another 1,000 elsewhere in Europe (and some 900,000 worldwide).

The company's rapid growth since its 1978 origins in Britain threatened to make its sales and distribution centre less responsive and efficient. So the management response was to adopt a two-pronged approach:

- To work towards the international version of the BS 5750 quality assurance scheme (ISO 9002).
- To actively strive to stimulate workforce involvement by empowerment and the promotion of teamworking.

The move towards ISO 9002 was valuable in identifying weaknesses in the existing procedures within the business. For example, it emerged that if a customer sent a product back, up to six different people might be involved at the Mitsubishi depot. This maximised cost while minimising the chance of responding speedily to the customer's complaints or changed needs.

As inefficiencies emerged, it became clear that there would be consequences for Mitsubishi personnel. If just one person was responsible for a customer complaint instead of six, what would happen to those cut out of the new procedure? Mr Reyner's view is clear: that every effort should be made to avoid redundancies resulting from finding more efficient ways of working. 'Some companies can be too quick to cut staff. I believe in expanding our business so that new jobs emerge. Then we can retrain those whose own job is no longer needed.' Nevertheless, Mr Reyner is aware that problems may arise if employees do not want to be retrained.

Obtaining its ISO 9002 award took Mitsubishi over two years. Yet the focus of staff and management time upon quality yielded many spin-off benefits. It showed that involving the workforce in discussions and decisions about how the company operates could provide direct benefits from employee suggestions and indirect benefits from higher motivation. To capture the interest shown by staff in higher quality, the company built quality improvement teams (QIT) into its quality system.

Each product division of the business has a QIT consisting of representatives from engineering, marketing, sales and customer service. The team meets regularly to discuss any problems in meeting the standards set within the quality award. It can also look for ways of upgrading the quality targets set by Mitsubishi.

The process of empowerment proved easiest to establish in the electronics division that Mr Reyner set up in 1984. This was because the culture within this operation had always been democratic and based upon teamwork. The division introduced a system of customer focus teams ensuring regular meetings to agree how to provide total customer satisfaction. This process included regular meetings with large customers and came up with ideas such as using electronic data interchange (EDI) to establish a direct computer link to ensure faster, more efficient communication between Mitsubishi and its customers.

These customer focus teams have been so successful in providing total customer satisfaction in the UK that the idea has now been extended throughout Europe, Japan and the USA. Global customer focus teams are now being set up to ensure that improved relationships with customers are made on a multinational basis.

To what extent are Mitsubishi's approaches to personnel management the result of Japanese influence? On the face of it, a great deal, as Mitsubishi UK is headed by a Japanese and several of the senior executives are on five year secondments from Japan. In fact, much of the driving force has been from British managers, keen to keep abreast of modern management practices. Indeed, since the adoption of ISO 9002 in Britain, Mitsubishi divisions in Japan have decided to apply for this quality assurance certificate.

The main significance of Mitsubishi's Japanese parentage has been to ensure that long-term teambuilding approaches can be given the time needed to establish an upward flow of ideas and improvements. Hasty staff cutbacks during a tough year could undermine the whole approach to human relations within the company. Yet many British companies – even profitable ones – have done just that in recent years.

Mitsubishi Electric Europe has set itself the mission to 'become one of the leading corporate citizens of Europe, achieving sufficient profitability to ensure continuing success and investment'. So far they have achieved that balance between responsibility and success.

" DISCUSSION POINTS "

1. What advantages could a firm expect from involving staff in quality teams?
2. Why is it important that most Japanese firms offer staff a lifetime employment guarantee?

From personnel to human resource management

Flexibility and change have become the most commonly used words in personnel vocabulary. In some ways this represents progress. Yesterday's nine to five career is rapidly disappearing, to be replaced by more part-time opportunities and fixed-term contracts. Ten years ago, all the economists working at BP's Head Office were salaried, permanent staff. Today most work on two- or three-year contracts, renewable if performance is good enough. This makes life less certain, but may prevent employees slipping into a dull routine.

These changes have coincided with the transformation of many personnel departments into human resource departments. HRM (human resource management) has two main features:

- The acceptance that staff attitudes and skills represent a vital element in a firm's success or failure, therefore the management of human resources should form part of the overall strategy/business plan.
- The desire to analyse and develop people's individual talents, instead of treating 'the workforce' as a homogenous group, with the same needs and rewards.

Few would argue with the first of these features. The acceptance of the key role of employees in company success has helped make training a higher priority and put pressure on the government to improve the quality of academic and vocational education in Britain.

The second aspect of human resource management has caused more controversy, however. Supporters speak highly of the greater emphasis HRM has given to:

- Psychological testing during recruitment.
- The use of appraisal schemes to measure employees' achievements and to set new goals for the coming year; often the result of the appraisal will affect the employee's income through performance related pay (for instance an appraisal rating as excellent might lead to a salary increase of 10 per cent).
- Individualised training programmes to help each employee develop the skills needed to achieve their goals.
- Questioning whether full-time, permanent staff are always necessary and bringing in part-time, temporary or sub-contracted staff where this is more economic or suitable.
- More careful analysis of those to be made redundant; in the past redundancies were usually made on the basis of 'last in first out', in other words the newest staff would be the first to go; today HRM professionals analyse attendance records, appraisal reports and even conduct psychological tests to select those to be made redundant.

Critics, however, see these aspects of HRM as potentially damaging to workplace morale and therefore performance. Appraisal schemes can lead to accusations of favouritism, with 'yes-men' getting salary increases denied to others who are more productive, but more critical of their boss. Morale might also be damaged by cutting the permanent workforce in favour of temporary, more flexible staffing. The work of both Maslow and Herzberg shows that job security is a necessary underpinning of employee motivation.

Despite these doubts about HRM, the approach can be defended on the grounds that British firms need to become more competitive. If that requires a more active approach to the management of people, it must still be preferable to company failures and therefore redundancy for all the staff. There remains the possibility, however, that research will cast doubt on whether practices such as appraisal do lead to greater efficiency, in which case the critics will be proved right.

ACTIVITY

Stylair Ltd: role-play exercise in resolving conflict

GENERAL BACKGROUND

Stylair Ltd is a medium-sized private company based in Birmingham. No longer a small family firm, it now employs 430 workers and manufactures a range of electric hairdryers. In the last decade, the company has grown rapidly, profits having increased by 35 per cent each year. This rapid growth has been achieved by Stylair's strategy of supplying well-designed products aimed at the middle range of the market. In recent years, they have experienced considerable competition from other UK manufacturers and have tried to combat this by developing export markets and by keeping costs down.

During its growth, Stylair has experienced no industrial relations problems, though recently some of the workforce have been expressing a few grievances.

BACKGROUND TO THE DISPUTE

Stylair's managing director, Louisa Whittaker, keeps a regular eye on the levels of overtime worked. In her last meeting with the production manager, Mike Hutchings, she mentioned her concern that the level of overtime worked by the maintenance team of six men had been rather high during the last six months. She queried why so much overtime had been done and asked Mike to check that overtime was not being abused.

The following morning, Mike called George Collins, the maintenance supervisor, into his office and told him that the company wanted to clamp down on unnecessary overtime. From now on, overtime would not be allowed without Mike's personal authorisation. George replied that the maintenance men would not like this, as they had come to depend on a certain amount of overtime in their take-home pay. Besides, some machines could only be repaired outside normal working hours.

At lunch that day, George informed his men that management had decided that from now on overtime would no longer be worked. After a heated discussion in the works canteen, the men went back to work after lunch, still complaining angrily about the new ruling.

Ten days later, one of the machines broke down, in the midst of producing a large export order for an important new overseas customer. George allocated Mandy Johnson and Dave Hopkins to fix the machine urgently. At the end of the day Mike found out from George that Mandy and Dave had gone home at 5 p.m., leaving the machine half repaired, in spite of George having asked them to work on and finish it. When Mike insisted that he wanted the machine repaired straight away, otherwise the important export order would not be ready for shipment on the agreed date, George told him that Mandy and Dave were not prepared to work overtime because of the company's new 'overtime ban'.

At this point, Mike decided he ought to inform Louisa Whittaker of the problem. When Louisa heard what had happened, she asked to see everyone concerned, first thing the next morning, in her office.

THE BRIEF

In groups of five, you will be asked to act out the situation in Louisa Whittaker's office the next day. When you have decided which role you are going to play and have read all the following descriptions of the characters, you will need to act out your role, bringing out your side of the story, in relation to the other people involved. The group's eventual aim is to resolve the dispute.

ROLE DESCRIPTIONS

Louisa Whittaker, managing director

Age 54, married with two children. Bought the company 15 years ago, when it was struggling, with the redundancy money from her previous job as marketing manager with a well-known company. Highly respected by the workers, though they see less of her nowadays as the company has expanded.

PERSONNEL

Mike Hutchings, production manager

Age 39, unmarried. Loyal, works long hours and is ambitious. Aims to be a director of the firm one day and is keen to show he has a firm grip of things. Has worked his way up from the shop floor.

George Collins, maintenance supervisor

Age 56, married with three children. Has been with the firm since it started. Was a supervisor when Mike started as a trainee with the firm. A steady, reliable employee. Prefers the way things were done in the old days and is looking forward to his retirement.

Mandy Johnson, mechanic

Age 34, married. Been with the firm two and a half years. Good at her job but does not go looking for extra work. A bit of a loner, she never goes out with the others on Fridays for a drink after work. Can get 'in a huff' at times.

Dave Hopkins, mechanic

Age 28, married with two young children. Has been with the firm 12 years, since he joined as an apprentice at 16. He likes it there and is a good worker. Enjoys going out with the others on Friday nights and gets on well with everyone.

" DISCUSSION POINTS "

1. Why might Louisa Whittaker have been concerned about overtime levels?
2. How far can the dispute be said to have arisen through poor communications in the organisation:
   a) downwards from the management to the shop floor?
   b) upwards from the shop floor to the management?
3. Why is there a need for different communication channels in the firm now, compared to when it was a small firm?
4. To what extent might the situation have been aggravated by possible personality clashes between the people involved?
5. Taking each person in turn, describe how far you think he was responsible for the dispute which arose.
6. How was the dispute eventually resolved in each of your groups?
7. What might have happened if the dispute had not ended at this stage?
8. How might the presence of a trade union have:
   a) helped
   b) hindered
   the resolution of this dispute?
9. In what ways is this situation:
   a) typical
   b) untypical
   of the way disputes can happen?

Finance

IN ASSOCIATION WITH

RAILTRACK

When running a business there are two main financial priorities: generating enough cash to pay the bills, and enough profit to satisfy the shareholders and to finance growth. So, are cash and profit not the same thing? Surprisingly, they are not. To help explain the difference, cash flow will be analysed in detail, followed by profit.

Cash flow

Cash flow is the difference between the flows of cash into and out of a business over a period of time. For example, if a firm starts up by spending £40,000 of cash on premises and materials in its first month, but receives only £500 from customers, its month 1 cash flow is minus £39,500.

Cash flow can be looked at in two ways:

- As a way of predicting the future state of a firm's bank balance (a cash-flow forecast).
- As a record of how a firm has obtained and used cash over the recent past (a cash-flow statement).

This chapter will look at cash-flow forecasting only. This is especially important when starting a new business, as few firms start with capital to spare. If a sales forecast proves too optimistic (and this is a common problem) or if production proves slower than expected, the firm may struggle to keep paying its bills. For an example of the key role of cash-flow forecasting, take the case of Clare Kilby:

Clare decided, fresh from catering college, to use £4,000 of savings to start a high quality, premium-priced catering service. 'Crystal Cuisine' would offer to plan, cook, deliver and serve superb and beautifully presented food to important business meetings or exclusive dinner parties. This would require a large, well-equipped kitchen, a van and a high initial outlay on publicity. Having completed the cash-flow forecast shown opposite, Clare was able to persuade a friend to come in as a partner (investing £2,000) and a bank to lend £5,000 for a good, second-hand van.

A cash-flow forecast shows two key things about money: *when* and *how much*, in the case of both incoming and outgoing funds. For example, Clare found a kitchen available for hire at £1,200 per month. She planned to move in at the start of January and expected to need £600 of extra kitchen equipment. As she only intended to start advertising in February, cash inflows would start in that month.

FINANCE

	January	February	March	April	May–Dec
Crystal Cuisine – Year 1 cash-flow forecast				
(all figures in £s)				
Start-up capital	11,000				
CASH INFLOW	–	500	4,000	5,000	52,000
CASH OUTFLOW					
Start-up costs	600	7,300	–		
Running costs	1,200	1,400	2,600	3,100	26,000
Wages	400	600	1,000	1,200	13,000
NET CASH FLOW	(2,200)	(8,800)	400	700	13,000
CUMULATIVE CASH	+8,800	0	+400	+1,100	+14,100

Crystal Cuisine – Year 1 cash-flow forecast

This forecast convinced Clare's bank to grant her an overdraft facility of up to £1,000, in case February's zero balance slipped into the red. She was able to start up her business and – after a month or two of struggle – it has become a great success.

Even when a business is up and running, forecasting cash-flows is important. Most firms have periods in the year when cash is especially tight. For example, bookshops often make a quarter of their year's sales in just one month – December. So, in the autumn they have to plough a lot of cash into buying stock to build up the stock of books that will be sold for Christmas.

If a firm entered a period of **negative cash flow** without having forecast it or discussed the situation with their bankers, one of two things would probably happen. One is that the firm may be unable to pay bills to suppliers of raw materials, packaging, electricity or even labour costs (i.e. unable to pay staff their wages). This situation would be hard to

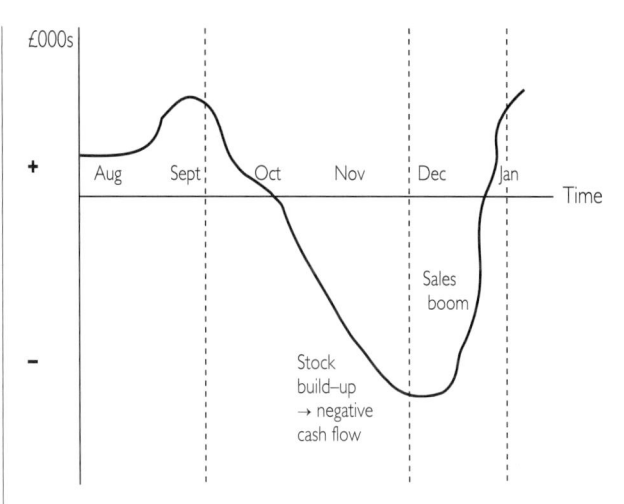

Cash-flow graph for a bookshop

sustain for long. The other possibility is that the firm may write out cheques to pay the bills, either going into an unauthorised overdraft (which banks charge very heavily for) or finding that the bank refuses to honour them (so the cheques 'bounce').

By making a cash-flow forecast, a firm is able to adjust its actions to avoid calamity or to maximise potential benefits. For example, if it expects to go severely into the red during the autumn, it could take various actions to prevent this happening, such as:

- Negotiating with suppliers to delay cash payments until the new year.
- Postponing cash outgoings, such as replacing company vans or equipment, until the new year.
- Working much harder at the careful organisation required to delay the ordering and arrival of stock so that it arrives just in time to meet customer demand.

On the other hand, perhaps the cash-flow forecast shows a four-month period of really high cash balances, such as in a bookshop during and after Christmas. If a firm is confident that it will have plenty of surplus cash for a few months, it can open an interest-paying deposit account or use the cash to make a short-term investment. Either approach may provide a useful boost to a firm's profit.

Profit and loss

Cash flow is straightforward enough to understand, but why is profit any different? The answer is that whereas cash flow is a simple record of *when* sums of money flow into or out of a business, the calculation of profit is based upon a series of quite complex concepts. So, a firm that has recently declared a £60,000 profit may, in fact, be desperate for cash because its customers are stalling payment or because a large loan is due to be repaid.

Unlike cash flow, profit measures revenue earned and costs generated in a theoretical way. It is a bit like the difference between actual football results and Fantasy League™ results. Actual results equate to cash-flow: cash in = goals scored; cash outflow = goals against. It is easy to know who won and who lost. The calculation of profit is like Fantasy League™ schemes, however, where you have to make assumptions about what it is worth to have made the pass to the person who scores. You might even deduct a point because a booking could lead to a suspension later on (in accounting, this would be known as a provision). In other words, calculating profit involves taking a wider view of the situation and taking into account many other factors.

This book does not need or want to go into full details about the calculation of profit. However it will be useful to provide some indication of the ways in which the calculation of profit is different from the calculation of cash flows. Table 6.1 shows how different, everyday financial events are recorded in a firm's accounts.

TABLE 6.1

Financial event	*Cash flow*	*Profit*	*Notes to profit calculation*
Sale to a customer	When cash arrives	When product is delivered	Cash may arrive months later
£40,000 invested by new shareholders	When cash arrives	Not recorded	The £40,000 is extra capital, not profit made by the firm
£20,000 of supplies bought on credit	No record (until later, when cash is paid)	When supplies are delivered	Cash is paid later, but profit records the transaction straight away
A £50,000 bank loan is repaid	When cash leaves	Not recorded	£50,000 less capital, but no loss has been made on the firm's trading

The important message here is that profit is not the same as cash. To be successful in business, it is vital to realise that a manager needs to forecast both its cash flows and its profit. The latter can be forecast or recorded through the profit and loss account.

A profit and loss account (often known as the P & L) shows the various deductions that are made from a firm's revenue, ending up with the figure that is left for reinvestment in the business. This, the 'bottom line', is crucial as it shows how much the firm is making to help it grow in the future. Without reinvested profit a firm will stand still or decline.

Below is a simplified version of the 1995 accounts for Denby Pottery:

Denby Group plc Accounts for year end October 30th

	1995 (£000s)	1994 (£000s)
Sales turnover	25,795	21,915
Cost of sales	13,314	11,125
Overheads	7,540	6,240
Interest charges	179	420
Pre-tax profit	4,762	4,130
Taxation	1,571	1,364
Dividends	1,153	924
Retained profit	2,038	1,842

Raising finance

In order to start a business, capital must be raised. Start-up capital usually comes mainly from the founders of the business or their family, for unless the founders are willing to put their own funds at risk, who else would be silly enough to do so? In addition, whereas interest on bank loans has to be paid even when times are bad, owners' capital does not receive a fixed rate of return. This enhances flexibility in the early years of trading.

At this initial stage, entrepreneurs willing to put in their own capital could also turn to several possible sources of extra investment funds. The first destination is likely to be a visit to their bank manager. The bank will not invest share capital into a new firm, but may be willing to provide loans to supplement the start-up funds. This loan capital will only be provided, though, if the firm demonstrates the ability to repay it – with a plausible cash-flow forecast, perhaps. Security such as property may be needed to back up the loan, but is not as important as evidence that the loan can be repaid.

If the bank is worried about the security of its loans, but still believes the business has a good chance of succeeding, it could offer to lend via the government's Loan Guarantee Scheme. This scheme guarantees the bank that if the business fails, the government will repay from 70 to 85 per cent of what is owed. This limits the bank's risk and so makes it more willing to provide the loan. The only downside to the Loan Guarantee Scheme is that the borrower has to pay between 0.5 and 1.5 per cent extra every year to the government.

What if someone has a great business idea – perhaps an invention – but has too little capital to make the bank even consider lending? There are still some possibilities. One is to convince a Venture Capital provider that your idea and your own track record make you worth backing. This will not be easy, because although Venture Capital houses accept a relatively high level of risk, they pride themselves upon the care they take over each application. As their careful checks are expensive to carry out, Venture Capital houses are rarely interested in investments of below £200,000. Also, they insist upon a share stake in the business (perhaps 30 per cent of the shares) so that they can share in the high profits made by the occasional Body Shop.

Once a firm is up and running, statistics show that reinvested profit is by far the biggest source of extra capital to finance growth. Indeed, according to Stephen Pegge, senior product manager for TSB, 75 per cent of small firms have no overdraft at all at any one time. In addition to reinvested profit, there are many other ways in which a firm can find short-, medium- or long-term finance (see Tables 6.2, 6.3 and 6.4).

Short-term finance can be used to:

- Bridge temporary finance gaps when customers pay late or a sudden, rush order requires a large sum to buy raw materials.
- Get through periods when cash-flow is poor for seasonal reasons.
- Cover temporary needs for extra funds due to unexpected problems or opportunities.

Medium-term finance can be used to:

- Finance the purchase of assets with a two to five year life, such as vehicles and computers.
- Replace an overdraft which is difficult to clear and is proving expensive.
- Finance a change in strategy, such as to switch marketing focus from Britain to the whole of Europe.

TABLE 6.2 *Types of short-term finance*

Source of finance	Advantages	Disadvantages
Bank overdraft	Simple to arrange. Flexible, as amounts borrowed can vary up to the limit arranged. Relatively cheap, as interest is charged only on the actual amount borrowed, for the number of days overdrawn.	Interest charged is between 2.5 per cent and 4 per cent over bank base lending rate, so can work out expensive over long periods. If limit is exceeded the overdraft facility can be withdrawn and immediate repayment demanded.
Trade credit	Improves the flow of money as suppliers often give as long as three months to pay invoices. A free form of credit.	The prompt payment discount which many firms offer is lost if the trade credit is used. If payment is made after the credit period, suppliers may refuse to send goods in future, or may insist on cash in advance.
Debt factoring	Capital tied up in money owed by customers is released. The factoring company takes over the debt and advances up to 80 per cent of the amount owed straight away. This improves the firm's cash flow. The factoring company then sends out invoices and chases up the debtor, paying the remainder of the debt to the firm when the customer settles up – less their charge.	Factoring companies can charge as much as 5 per cent of the bill for their service. They tend only to be interested in handling bills from firms with sales of over £1 million a year.

Long-term finance can be used to:

- Provide start-up capital to finance the business for its whole life span.
- Finance the purchase of assets with a longer life, such as buildings.
- Provide expansion capital for large projects, such as building a new factory or taking over another business.

TABLE 6.3 *Types of medium-term finance (two to five years)*

Source of finance	Advantages	Disadvantages
Bank term loan	Financial planning is made easier as repayments are made in regular instalments and the interest rate is often fixed.	Small businesses generally pay higher rates as they are seen as presenting a higher risk.
Leasing	When vehicles and equipment are leased or rented from a leasing company, the firm is able to use equipment which it could not otherwise afford to buy outright. Working capital can then be used for other purposes. Leased equipment can be changed when it becomes obsolete, unlike purchased equipment which has to be kept for longer to recover the initial investment.	The vehicles and equipment which are leased are not owned by the firm. The rental charges add up over a period of time, to the point where the firm has effectively paid for the goods even though the goods cannot be classed as company assets, because they are still owned by the company renting them out.
Hire purchase	After an initial down-payment for the vehicle or equipment, goods are purchased in instalments over a period of 2 years. This means the cost is spread and is more manageable than an up-front payment for outright purchase. Unlike leased goods those bought on hire purchase are owned after the last repayment is made.	Goods remain the property of the finance house until full repayment has been made, so if any payments are missed the finance house can repossess the goods. A more expensive form of borrowing than bank loans.

ACTIVITY

Choosing the most appropriate source of finance

For each of the following descriptions, state which source of finance you think it is most appropriate to use. Explain your decision in each case.

1 A firm that wishes to finance a major purchase of land for a new factory.

2 A successful firm where the owners are willing to dilute financial control in order to expand, by giving up part of their equity.

3 A firm that has borrowed as much as it can but cannot pay its expenses until slow-paying customers pay their bills.

4 A firm that has to decide between paying a bill from

TABLE 6.4 *Types of long-term finance (over 5 years)*

Source of finance	Advantages	Disadvantages
Owners' savings (in the case of a sole trader or partnership)	Owners use their own capital (from a second mortgage, life insurance policy, savings etc.) to inject capital into the business, which reduces the amount borrowed on which interest has to be paid. Owners retain more control than if financial control is diluted by the sale of shares.	Owners' capital is tied up and cannot easily be taken out of business. Owners' capital is at risk if business fails – they are liable to lose their own home and other possessions.
Sale of shares (in the case of a private limited company or public limited company)	The main advantage of issuing shares is that the shareholders have **limited liability** if the business fails. Personal possessions are not at risk and their liability is limited to the actual capital invested. Capital is raised by issuing shares (which are a proportion of what the company is worth) to investors, who are encouraged to buy by the promise of receiving **dividends** or profits on their shares. Shares can be sold as **preference shares** which offer a fixed return and have priority when dividends are paid over ordinary shareholders. **Ordinary shares** offer a variable return as profits change from year to year, according to how well the company has done.	The administrative cost of issuing shares is high. It is difficult to estimate the market price of shares, though this problem can be avoided if they are issued by **tender**, where investors state how much they are willing to pay for them. The price of shares can go up or down and shareholders may have to sell at a lower price than they bought at. A listing or **quotation** on the Stock Exchange is needed so a company's shares can be bought or sold on the exchange. This is difficult to obtain as financial requirements are stringent in order to safeguard the interests of people buying and selling shares.
Reinvested profits	Capital can be raised by the company reinvesting or ploughing back the profits made at the end of the year, after expenses and dividends to shareholders have been paid.	Profits may be scarce or non-existent, especially in times of recession. Expansion may be slow and limited for companies relying on self-financed growth.
Mortgage loans	Capital is often supplied by pension or insurance funds for a loan over 25–30 years for buildings or land, with the asset as security.	The loans are usually only given when large sums are required.
Venture capital loans	Capital is supplied by venture capital firms who accept a certain degree of risk as being inevitable. Most venture capitalists also provide help in the form of back-up management and financial expertise. The government's **Enterprise Investment Scheme** offers incentives to private investors willing to invest in unquoted companies.	Most venture capitalists are only interested in loans for more than £50,000 and some only consider ventures where more than £250,000 is involved, as the administration costs are not worthwhile on smaller projects. They charge a negotiation fee for arranging the finance. They generally expect a non-controlling **equity stake** of 20–40 per cent in the firm's capital, as a return for their investment.
Government loans	Capital can be raised for eligible companies from local authorities, government enterprise agencies and regional selective assistance. Capital can also be raised from the EU.	The vetting procedures needed to minimise risk can cause long delays in obtaining the grants.
Debenture loans	Individuals can supply capital to a company in the form of long-term loans called **debentures** which have to be repaid on an agreed date. These repayments take priority over payments to all other shareholders.	Generally the company has to offer some security for the loan, which can be sold if the company cannot meet the repayments. In the case of a fixed debenture this is a specific asset such as a building, and in the case of a floating debenture it can be any asset owned by the company.

FINANCE

British Telecom or a bill from a supplier, both of which were received two weeks ago.

5 An established firm, quoted on the Stock Exchange, which wishes to raise money from the public to be repaid after a specific period of time.

6 A firm that wishes to spread the cost of high capital outlay on equipment and has borrowed the maximum possible from the bank.

7 A firm which will create many new jobs and is being set up in a depressed area.

8 A successful, well-run, private limited company which has expanded as far as possible on self-financed growth. **9** A firm that has bills from suppliers which are due for payment now, though money owed by customers will not come in for a few weeks.

10 A small firm started by an entrepreneur who intends to trade on a small scale initially and who wishes to retain full control of the business.

11 A firm whose owners intend to expand at a steady rate without diluting financial control and without borrowing too much.

12 A firm in a high-technology industry which does not wish to purchase all the expensive equipment it needs.

13 A firm that wishes to raise finance to invest in buildings and equipment.

CASE STUDY

Price Waterhouse – financing the future

What do the huge Dartford (Thames) Road Bridge, the University of Greenwich student halls of residence and the Royal Berkshire hospital's new wing have in common? All were financed in a completely new way – the Private Finance Initiative (the PFI).

The PFI is a way of bringing private sector finance and expertise to bear upon public sector projects. This has the potential to allow projects to proceed that would not otherwise do so and perhaps to identify proposals that are ill considered and therefore should not go ahead at all.

In the past, if a hospital wanted a new wing, it would put its case to the local health authority and – if turned down – could do nothing more about it. Now the NHS Trust that runs the hospital can arrange a joint venture in which the private sector provides the capital and takes much of the risk, whilst the Trust contracts to pay for patients using the wing.

A good example of the way the PFI works is the current plan to construct a completely new hospital in Durham. The area's existing hospital is thought too old to be capable of providing modern, efficient, high quality healthcare. The NHS Trust began investigating how best to replace it. A new specification was discussed with staff, costings were undertaken and an architect briefed. Then the Government suggested considering the Private Finance Initiative.

The Trust began by hiring Price Waterhouse, one of the leading accountancy and management consultancy practices. Price Waterhouse's role was threefold:

- To advise the Trust how to attract a strong field of bidders for the contract.
- To organise the bidding procedure.
- To help short-list and select the winning bidder.

Having considered the matter with care, the Trust decided that it required not only capital to finance the hospital-building, but also ongoing management of the site. So the winning bidder would not only build the hospital, it would also run the catering, cleaning, laundry, security and maintenance of the site. That would allow the Trust to concentrate its management skills on the key staff – the doctors, nurses and technicians. So, in years to come, although patients will get the same access to free NHS healthcare, only the medical staff will be employed directly by the NHS Trust.

The first step after bringing in Price Waterhouse was to brief the company fully on the Trust's plans and forecasts. Then Price Waterhouse advertised the contract to invite bids. There were 25 expressions of interest, though only 15 bids were submitted. Some were individual firms; far more were groups of firms with complementary skills (such as a construction company, a bank and a service business). Price Waterhouse and the Trust managers decided on a short list of five.

Each of the five had to show how they would meet the detailed requirements put forward by the hospital's medical staff. For example the medical staff specified which hospital wards should be closest to the operating theatres, where the intensive care unit should be and so on. The bidders hired architects to show how the building would look and function. Several had highly original ideas within proposals that had cost as much as £750,000 to put together; just two were short-listed. At the time of writing, the final decision between the two had not been made.

As shown by the diagram below, the financial implications of the PFI are very considerable. It shows a conventional hospital-building exercise, in which a heavy drain on cash flow is followed by income generated from the sums paid per patient by the NHS. This not only causes the problem of how to finance the cash outflow/investment, but also leaves the hospital open to great risks. Will the local demand for healthcare in five years' time be high enough to generate the funding levels needed to pay the interest and capital on the sum borrowed? If not, brand new hospital wards may be kept closed to save money.

The diagram opposite shows the PFI alternative from the hospital's point of view. The investment outlays are paid by the private sector investors, so the financial implications relate solely to the period when the hospital is open. Then, as long as the expected NHS funding per patient is as high as the staffing plus PFI cost per patient, the Trust should be able to recover its initial costs quite quickly.

Despite the attractions of this apparent financing miracle, Ian Wooton at Price Waterhouse is convinced that the major long-term benefit to the public sector will be learning private sector management methods. Price Waterhouse staff, with their experience in accounting, auditing and management consultancy, certainly expect to contribute some useful new ideas to the management of any project, but the only new aspect for them is working with the public sector.

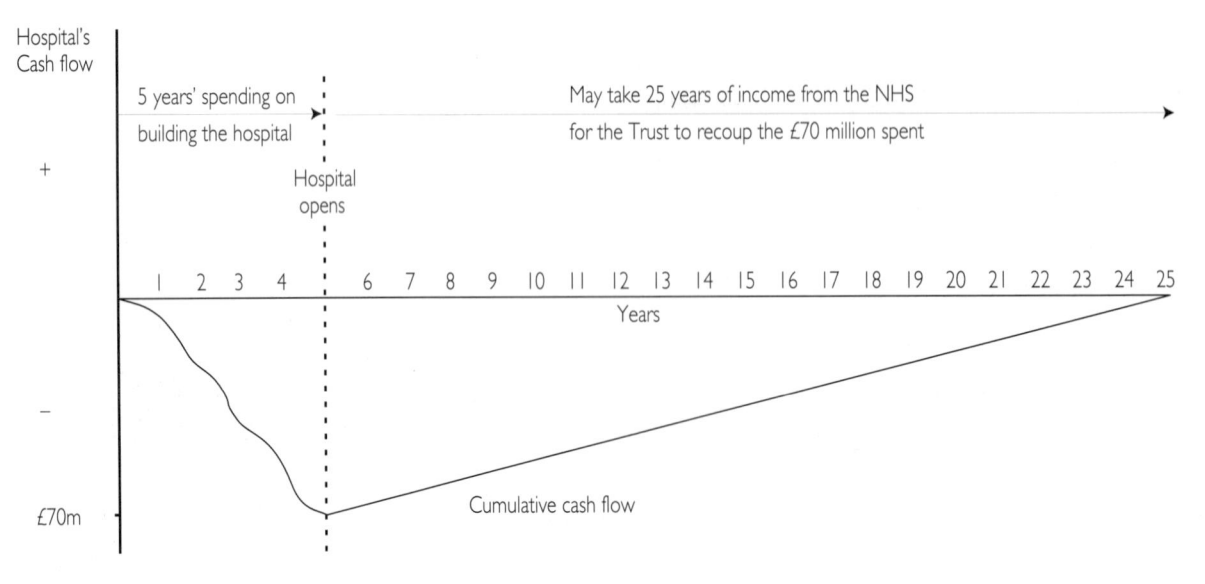

The traditional way to fund the building of a new hospital

FINANCE

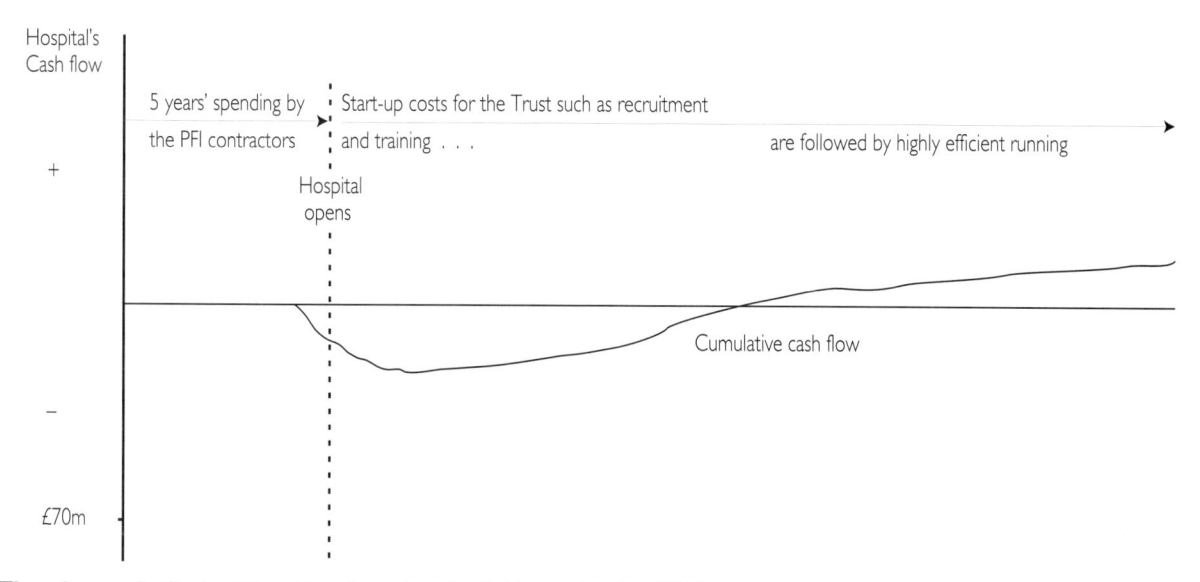

The planned effect of funding hospital-building with the PFI

> ## ❝ DISCUSSION POINTS ❞
>
> 1. *Why might the government be unwilling to put more money into financing projects such as hospital- or bridge-building?*
> 2. *How might the accounting and management consultancy skills of an organisation such as Price Waterhouse help the public sector enterprise make its choice of the right contractor?*
> 3. *Does it matter to the user how a project was financed? If so, in what ways?*

What of the private sector companies themselves? What do they hope to get out of financing a public sector project? There may be prestige; there may be good publicity; but the major attraction is the hope of making sufficient profit to justify the risks involved. As with the Channel Tunnel, private sector finance by no means guarantees profit. Price Waterhouse has no doubt, though, that commercial banks and businesses have the expertise to ensure that the vast majority of Private Finance Initiatives will be profitable for both the private and the public sector.

Break-even analysis

When considering whether to start up a business, nothing could be more important than an idea of how large a profit or how big a loss you might make. This can be shown by use of a break-even chart.

A **break-even chart** shows revenues and costs at all possible levels of output. From this, it is easy to see the *profit* at any level of output, as the profit is the difference between revenue and cost.

To construct a break-even chart, it is necessary to break costs down into two parts: fixed and variable. **Fixed costs** are those that do not vary as output varies, such as rent, salaries and interest charges. In other words, even in a month when sales are awful, these costs are as high as ever. **Variable costs**, by contrast, do vary in relation to output. In other words, if sales slump by 50 per cent, these costs will slump by the same proportion. Examples include raw material purchases, components and packaging costs.

CONSTRUCTING A BREAK-EVEN CHART

A break-even chart is a line graph showing total revenue and costs at all possible levels of output/demand, i.e. at every point from an output of nil through to the maximum the firm can produce.

This enables the reader to see at a glance the profit at any output level that interests them (by looking at the vertical difference between revenue and costs).

For example: A firm selling 40,000 widgets per year has fixed costs of £50,000, variable costs of £1 per unit and a factory capable of producing 60,000 units. The widgets are priced at £3 each.

Quantity	Revenue (£)	Variable costs (£)	Fixed costs (£)	Total cost (£)
0	0	0	50,000	50,000
30,000	90,000	30,000	50,000	80,000
60,000	180,000	60,000	50,000	110,000

From this information a break-even chart can be drawn as follows, with £s on the vertical axis and output on the horizontal.

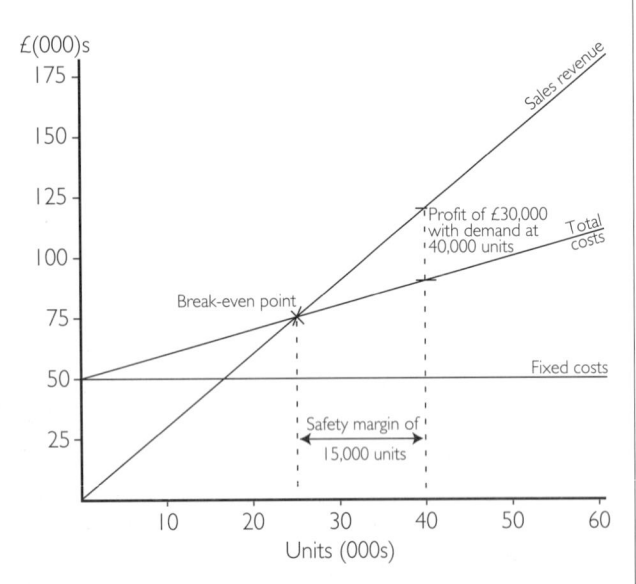

Break-even chart for a firm selling widgets

The chart can be used to show various things:

1 **The break-even point.** This is usually indicated by a vertical line down to cut the horizontal axis, i.e. to indicate the output level at which all costs are covered; beyond this output level the firm starts to make profits. In this case the break-even point is 25,000 units.
2 **The safety margin.** This is the amount by which demand and therefore output can fall before the firm starts making losses. As sales are currently 40,000 units, the firm can afford demand to fall by 15,000 units before output goes below the break-even point.
3 **Profit or loss at a particular level of output.** Here, the company's profit is the difference between revenue and costs at 40,000 units. As marked on the graph, this comes to £30,000.

ACTIVITY

Quik Kalc Ltd: analysing break-even points

You work in the financial department of Quik Kalc Ltd, a rapidly expanding firm which manufactures calculators, aimed at the 'volume' end of the market. Mr Singh, the senior accountant, has asked you to work out the exact level of output at which the firm breaks even or just recovers its costs. Quik Kalc's fixed costs are £4,000. Each calculator costs £2 to make in terms of variable costs (labour and materials)

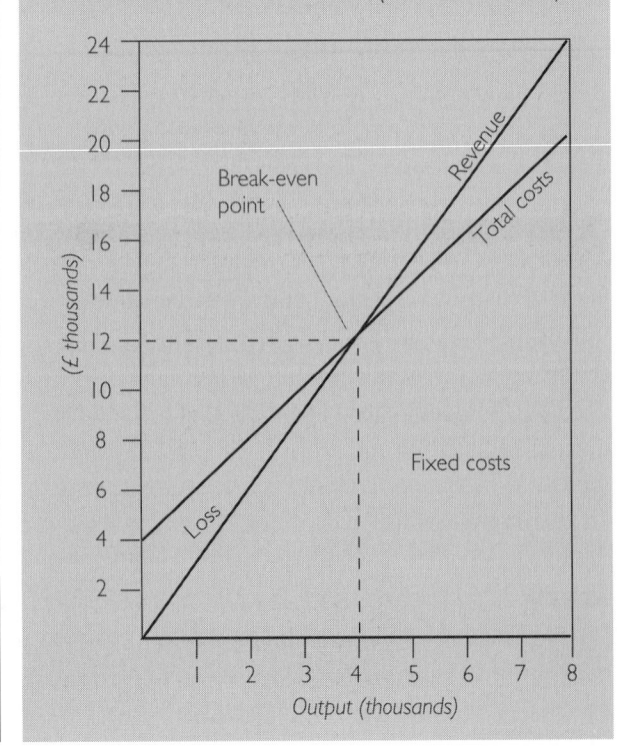

FINANCE

and sells for £3. In order to work out the **break-even point**, you will need to use these figures when you fill in your copy of the table below to show the costs and revenue at different output levels.

Output (£)	Fixed costs (£)	Variable costs (£) (Multiply by output level)	Total costs (£) (Add fixed and variable costs)	Revenue (Multiply price by output)
0	4,000	0	4,000	0
1,000	4,000	2,000	6,000	3,000
2,000				
3,000				
4,000				
5,000				
6,000				
7,000				
8,000				

The results from the table you have filled in have been plotted on the previous page. You will see that the break-even point occurs when Quik Kalc produces 4,000 calculators. This can also be worked out by a simple calculation. One of their calculators costs £2 to make in terms of variable costs and sells for £3, so each calculator sold makes a contribution of £1 towards fixed costs. As the fixed costs are £4,000, this means 4,000 calculators have to be sold before the break-even point is reached. If Quik Kalc sells any more than 4,000 it makes a profit and if it sells any fewer it makes a loss. The greater the output, the greater the profit, though eventually a stage will be reached when the fixed costs will have to rise to cater for the increased production.

ACTIVITY

Analysing the factors affecting break-even points

Use the simple calculation method described above to work out the new break-even point (if any) in the following situations. (Figures remain the same unless otherwise stated.)

1 Quik Kalc begins to experience fierce competition and has to reduce the selling price of each calculator to £2.50.

2 Demand increases in the months before Christmas and Quik Kalc raises the selling price to £4 per calculator.

3 A shortage of raw materials encourages suppliers to put up their prices by £1 so the variable costs are now £3 per calculator.

4 A severe recession forces Quik Kalc to reduce the selling price to £2.

5 Explain why the break-even point changed in questions 1 and 2.

6 Why was it not possible to break even in questions 3 and 4?

Working capital

Once a business is up and running, a key aspect of good financial management is to keep a tight control of **working capital**. Working capital is the finance available for the day-to-day running of the business. It is sometimes known as circulating capital, because of the way it flows around the business (see the diagram on page 92).

Although this cycle appears neat and tidy, it can quite easily get out of control, especially if a sales boom is keeping the directors of a small firm so busy that they cannot make time to monitor the working capital. For instance, customers may not pay unless they are chased. This may mean that the firm has too little cash to pay for raw materials, leaving the factory idle and customers frustrated.

The key to good management of working capital is to have efficient systems. For instance, if stock levels are computer-monitored using laser scanning, the firm should know exactly what it holds in its stores. This ensures that extra materials will only be ordered when they are really needed, rather than just in case they are needed.

In addition to careful stock control, at least one employee should be responsible for credit control. This entails checking the creditworthiness of customers and then ensuring that they pay on time. If the firm lacks the market power to press customers to pay, the job of obtaining payment may be done better by a debt factor. This is a business which charges a fee for organising the collection of the sums owed by customers (see Table 6.2).

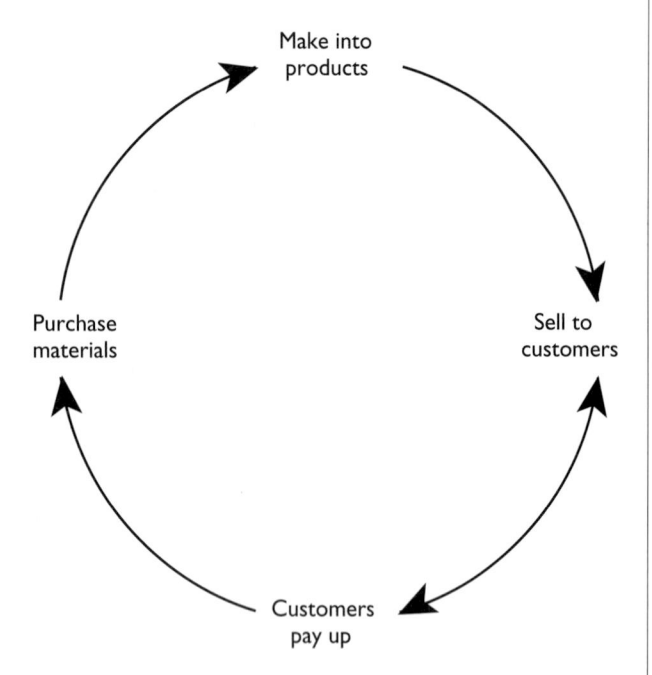

[Diagram: Purchase materials → Make into products → Sell to customers → Customers pay up → (cycle)]

Another key component to controlling working capital is to set budgets that are monitored closely. **Budgets** are usually agreed before the start of a financial year, and represent the maximum a manager can spend on an item. For example, a brand manager may be given a budget of £620,000 for a year's advertising and promotions. The manager will have to decide how to split the money up between the months of the year; then the accounts department will send a statement each month showing how much has actually been spent compared with the budgeted level. This comparison is known as **the variance**.

By ensuring that managers know each month whether they are under- or over-spending, the budget and variance statement makes it quite easy for staff to cut back to avoid over-spending. Variance figures can also highlight where and why an under- or over-spend has occurred. A typical example is shown in Table 6.5 below. Note that the variance column is calculated in relation to profit. Therefore revenue which is *lower* than forecast is a negative variance (in brackets), as are fixed costs which are *higher* than forecast.

TABLE 6.5 *A budget and variance statement*

	January			February		
	Budget	Actual	Variance	Budget	Actual	Variance
Revenue	85	80	(5)	95	86	(9)
Materials	36	34	2	42	39	3
Fixed costs	42	44	(2)	45	45	–
Profit	7	2	(5)	8	2	(6)
Year to date (Profit)	7	2	(5)	15	4	(11)

Note: All figures in £000s.

The figures in Table 6.5 show that although the firm's profit is much lower than forecast, the fault does not seem to lie with costs. The main cause of the profit shortfall is the lower than expected sales revenue. Having established this, the firm can decide whether the cause was outside the firm's control (such as a recession seizing the economy) or whether the business itself has made some poor decisions.

Conclusion

Financing and running a business – even if small – requires a great deal of knowledge and attention. If the planning is careful and the monitoring is constant, few firms get into financial trouble.

Yet even the best plans will go wrong sometimes, such as when a sudden consumer scare halts the purchase of a company's products. An unexpected collapse in revenue would wreck the calm planning of most companies. In this situation, as in many others, a close relationship with the company's bank manager can be useful. Together, a new strategy can be worked out.

CASE STUDY

Railtrack – building long-term profitability

In May 1996 Railtrack became the latest enterprise to be privatised. Formerly part of the state-owned British Rail, Railtrack was floated on the stockmarket as the owner and operator of Britain's railway network. With over £4,500 million of long-term assets and £2,500 million of annual turnover, this new company is a major undertaking.

As with most privatisations, staff were offered shares in the new company. Ninety per cent took up the offer of free shares (only available to those with six months service). Substantial proportions of the 11,500 workforce also took advantage of a series of other offers. Sixty per cent invested the maximum of £250 to 'buy one get two free', while 30 per cent took up the 'sharesave scheme' which enables staff to invest regularly in a tax-free, discount share offer. These schemes were seen by the company as a way of encouraging long-term staff participation and cooperation.

A unique feature of Railtrack's employee share schemes is its 'performance share scheme'. To explain it requires a brief account of the company itself, and the role of the Rail Regulator. The latter is appointed by the government to oversee the efficiency and value for money provided by the rail companies.

Railtrack receives its income from the train operating companies such as Stagecoach. To stimulate improvements in the reliability and punctuality of rail travel, the Rail Regulator approved a system of financial incentives and penalties. Every late train incurs a penalty per minute. If punctuality improves, the companies receive a bonus and enjoy higher profits. If punctuality deteriorates or even stays the same, increasing penalties will be due. In Railtrack's case, achieving the tough, five year performance targets set by the Regulator would avoid a negative impact upon profit of around £46 million.

Spurred on by this, Railtrack set out to provide a share-based incentive scheme to encourage staff to help the company meet the target. In year one of the scheme (1996/97) the performance targets were set to encourage improvements worth £15 million to the company. The achievement of this would trigger payments worth £450 to every employee. In addition, staff in each region (Zone) achieving its share of the performance improvement would receive a further £300. So the annual bonus could be a maximum of £750 worth of shares. That would mean Railtrack spending over half the £15 million on shares for its staff.

Performance award (share bonus)

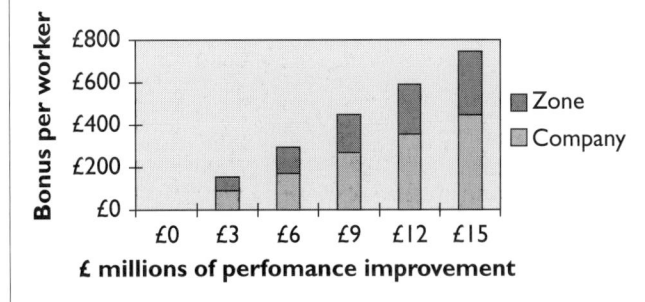

[Bar chart showing Bonus per worker (£0 to £800) vs £ millions of performance improvement (£0, £3, £6, £9, £12, £15), with stacked bars showing Zone and Company components]

Two features of this scheme are noteworthy. First, it has been structured so that every employee receives the same bonus. Usually firms provide bonuses in relation to earnings, so the shopfloor worker's £750 is dwarfed by the director's bonus. The fairness of Railtrack's performance share scheme should encourage good industrial relations. Second, the share issue is tied in with the government's profit sharing scheme, which ensures that the bonus is tax-free, as long as the shares are held for three years. To staff, 'tax-free' is clearly attractive; to management, it is also appealing that staff have to hold the shares for at least three years. This should help to encourage a sense of involvement with the company's fortunes. In turn, this could help the long term interests of the company – and its wider shareholders.

❝ DISCUSSION POINTS ❞

1 Within a few years there will be many Railtrack employees with £5,000 or more in company shares. What effects may that have on the customer, the railway traveller?

2 What financial benefits may Railtrack and its shareholders receive from the employee share schemes outlined in the text?

Management

IN ASSOCIATION WITH

Dixons

Introduction: doing the right things

A good definition of a manager is 'An individual who is accountable for more work than he/she can do themselves and who gets some of it done through other people' (W Brown and E Jacques). This definition includes managers who function at all levels, from operational manager right up to the chief executive at the top of the organisation. The **span of control**, however, or number of employees whose work is directed by managers at different levels, will obviously vary.

Successful managers have invariably learnt the difference between efficiency and effectiveness. Managers who have the ability to 'do things right' will merely be efficient, but to be really effective a manager must 'do the right things' – in other words, produce results. Peter Drucker, in his book, *The Effective Executive*, describes five practices which are necessary for effectiveness.

Effective executives:

- **Know where their time goes.** 'They systematically manage the small amount of their time that they can control.'
- **Focus on outward contribution.** 'They start with the question "What results are expected of me?", rather than starting with what work needs to be done.'
- **Build on strengths.** This includes building on 'their own strengths, the strengths of their superiors, colleagues and subordinates and on the strengths in the situation – that is, on what they *can* do.'
- **Concentrate on a few major areas.** 'They force themselves to set priorities.'
- **Make effective decisions.** 'They make judgements after taking into account a variety of opposing viewpoints. The decisions they make are few but fundamental.'

What does a manager do?

The earliest attempt at isolating what a manager's job involves was made by Henri Fayol, whose writings were first published in English in 1947. Based on his own management experience in the French mining industry, he arrived at a definition of the role of a manager – which was to:

- **Forecast and plan** – examine the future and draw up a plan of action.
- **Organise** – build up the organisation's structure so that plans can be carried out effectively.
- **Command** – obtain the best possible performance from personnel.
- **Coordinate** – make sure each department's efforts harmonise with other departments.
- **Control** – make sure everything works according to plan.

Later on, in 1973, Henry Mintzberg's approach was more concerned with what managers *actually* do, as opposed to what they ought to do. On the basis of studies of managers' work activity, he showed in *The Nature of Managerial Work* that managers perform a wide variety of roles.

These 10 roles can be grouped into three broad areas:

- **Interpersonal** – the relationships a manager has to have with others.
- **Informational** – the collecting and passing on of information.
- **Decisional** – the making of different kinds of decisions.

Of course, Mintzberg recognised that these roles can be combined in a number of different ways according to the manager's own personality, the situation he or she is in, the kind of job he or she does and the general environment.

ACTIVITY

Classification of a manager's roles

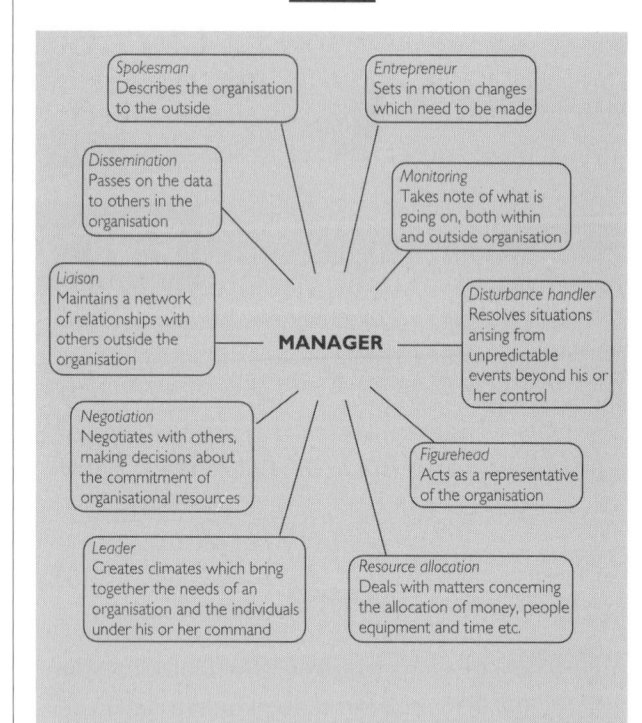

Spokesman – Describes the organisation to the outside

Dissemination – Passes on the data to others in the organisation

Liaison – Maintains a network of relationships with others outside the organisation

Negotiation – Negotiates with others, making decisions about the commitment of organisational resources

Leader – Creates climates which bring together the needs of an organisation and the individuals under his or her command

Entrepreneur – Sets in motion changes which need to be made

Monitoring – Takes note of what is going on, both within and outside organisation

Disturbance handler – Resolves situations arising from unpredictable events beyond his or her control

Figurehead – Acts as a representative of the organisation

Resource allocation – Deals with matters concerning the allocation of money, people equipment and time etc.

MANAGER

Using Mintzberg's descriptions of the 10 roles performed by a manager, select which roles should be grouped under the three broad areas of activity that he recognised and list each under the appropriate heading on a copy of the table below.

| Interpersonal | Informational | Decisional |

❝ DISCUSSION POINTS ❞

1. How many of the roles does your headteacher probably carry out?
2. Are some roles more important than others?

What qualities do managers need?

In 1988, a report called 'What Makes a Manager?' was published by the Institute of Manpower Studies (IMS), which looked at how 40 leading UK employers defined managerial skills. The report, reviewed by Michael Syrett in *Director* magazine, found that the qualities these employers looked for most often were the ability to communicate, leadership, judgement, initiative, organisational skills and motivation. Other attributes less frequently mentioned by employers, but still regarded as important, were planning, innovation, good appearance, interpersonal skills, maturity and numeracy.

One of the co-authors of the report, Wendy Hirsh, says that, 'The need for managers to deal with change was apparent in the frequent mention of adaptability, the capacity to deal with stress and the need for personal energy.' She added that, 'Employers also tend to look for "macho" managers with rather assertive personalities. Where sensitivity is needed, it tends to be expressed in terms of skills, for example the ability to work in teams, rather than in personality.'

In the next activity, you will be asked within groups of five to rank these management qualities yourselves and decide which *you* think are most important.

ACTIVITY

Ranking of management attributes

On your individual copy of the table below, rank each management attribute in order of importance from 1 to 16 and write the ranking in column 1. Rank the attribute you rate as being most important as 1, through to the least important as 16. Collect the rankings of the other members of your group and add them to your table. Add the figures across and fill in the column for the group's total ranking. the **lowest** total (nearest to 5) is the most important attribute, the next lowest the second most important attribute, and so on. What do your results reveal?

Management qualities identified by IMS report	Group member 1	Group member 2	Group member 3	Group member 4	Group member 5	Group's total ranking for each quality	Final order of importance for each quality
Communication							
Leadership							
Judgement							
Initiative							
Organisational skills							
Motivation							
Planning							
Innovation							
Good appearance							
Interpersonal skills							
Maturity							
Numeracy							
Adaptability							
Stress handling							
Personal energy							
Assertiveness							

1 a) Did you generally agree or disagree as a group?

   b) Were there any attributes you all agreed or disagreed on?

2 Was anyone's ranking vastly different to the others?

3 Are there any attributes that you think are important which are not on the list?

> **DISCUSSION POINT**
>
> *Why would the attributes which are regarded as important vary from company to company?*

Is there a typical manager?

Your answers to the activity ranking managers' qualities probably showed some agreement within your group about the most important qualities needed by managers. Does this mean, then, that there is a 'typical' manager?

The need for management to become a chartered profession was clearly stated by John Banham when he was CBI chief, at an annual conference of the Institute of Personnel Management. 'There is a misguided belief that management is nothing but applied common sense and the realm of the gifted amateur', he said, adding that, 'If we want to attract the most talented people into our business, management must become a profession with its own qualifications.' In other words, we need to have chartered managers as we have chartered accountants and chartered surveyors.

The concept of a chartered manager does, however, presume the existence of a universally accepted set of skills and knowledge. Certainly, the IMS report showed a great degree of consensus among the UK companies surveyed as to the qualities they looked for in managers. However, as Wendy Hirsh points out, the same terms can vary in meaning according to the company culture and job role of the manager. 'Good decision making in one company means taking innovative decisions, in another it means analysing hard data and minimising commercial risk.' The implication, therefore, is that skills gained in one company, which are closely related to the way things are done there, are not easily transferable to another company which is run on very different lines.

In any case, as John Kotter of Harvard Business School points out in his book, *The Leadership Factor*, 'Figuring out the right thing to do in an environment of uncertainty caused by intense competitive activity and then getting others, often many others, to accept a new way of doing things demands skills and approaches that most managers simply did not need in the relatively calm 1950s, 1960s and early 1970s. It demands something more than technical expertise, administrative ability and traditional (especially bureaucratic) management. Operating in the new environment also requires leadership.'

What makes a leader?

Ask anyone about their idea of a leader and they would probably describe political figures such as Churchill, Martin Luther King and Mrs Thatcher or business leaders such as Richard Branson or Anita Roddick; leaders with such personal charisma they drew people to them like magnets and whose supporters wholeheartedly gave of their time, effort and commitment in following their leaders' goals. Famous examples such as these, which influence popular conceptions of what leaders are like, encourage most people to think that they could never aspire to being leaders themselves.

Yet most definitions view the essence of leadership as being the ability to motivate groups to achieve certain goals, without the use of any force or coercion. On this basis, many more people can be seen to function as leaders, though not perhaps with the same verve and dash as the truly inspirational figures. In fact, as firms today fight for survival in intensely competitive world markets, the need for leaders at all levels, not just at executive level, has never been greater.

Sir Michael Edwardes, the former chairman of BL (now Rover) cars, is quoted in Berry Ritchie and Walter Goldsmith's *The New Elite* describing the qualities he thinks good leaders have in common. 'They have this driving force inside them and people follow them because they inspire trust. They create confidence that they know what they are doing. The good leader is someone who is followed, rather than someone who obviously leads. People make the leader.'

Clearly leaders' influence stems from their acceptance by the group, and though this influence may often be reinforced by the power and authority conferred by their position within the organisation, acceptance is nevertheless not dependent on their formal status. In fact, any leaders who try and rely on their rank to command authority will never have more than a tenuous hold on their group. Respect must be earned, as it will not be automatically accorded by virtue of a person's job title or rank. Groups may reject a leader they do not respect, and if this happens they are likely to do the minimum required and may even work towards sabotaging the leader's efforts. Strong leadership is therefore essential if groups are to work productively.

In an interview with George Bickerstaffe of *Director* magazine, John Adair, the UK's leading authority on the subject, defines leadership as the control and integration of three elements – the task, the team and the individuals on the team. The role of the leader is therefore to motivate the individuals to come together as a team to complete the task in hand.

66 DISCUSSION POINTS 99

1. What are some of the characteristics of a good leader?
2. Can you think of any examples of strong, 'natural' leaders?
3. Do you agree with the old saying that 'leaders are born, not made'?

What do Britain's top executives earn?

TABLE 7.1 *Executives' salaries over £500,000*

Company	Chairman or chief executive	Highest paid director
Glaxo Holdings	Sir Paul Girolami	£1,440,000
Hanson	Derek Bonham	£1,360,000
Tomkins	Greg Hutchings	£1,235,000
SmithKline Beecham	Robert Bauman	£1,015,000
Tesco	Sir Ian Maclaurin	£967,000
Cable and Wireless	Lord Young	£863,410
BOC	Patrick Rich	£786,393
Guinness	Sir Anthony Tennant	£777,000
Marks & Spencer (UK)	Sir Richard Greenbury	£721,126
Unilever	Sir Michael Perry	£695,102
British Airways	Sir Colin Marshall	£665,000
Boots	Sir James Blyth	£620,000
Bass	Ian Prosser	£615,000
Ladbroke	John Jackson	£585,000
British Telecom	Sir Iain Vallance	£560,000
British Petroleum	David Simon	£530,000
Carlton Communications	Michael Green	£530,000
ICI	Sir Denys Henderson	£526,000
Vodafone Group	Gerry Whent	£515,144
GEC	Lord Weinstock	£514,000

Source: 'How much do other people earn?' by Eleanor Mills, *The Observer*, 16 January, 1994
Note: The top director's salary is not necessarily that of the chairman or chief executive. Highest paid directors' salaries exclude pension payments and share options.

> **DISCUSSION POINTS**

1. Can any person's abilities be worth over £514,000 a year?
2. What impact can a good top executive have on a firm's fortunes?
3. Are high salaries needed to attract and keep top executives?
4. What other benefits might top executives get?

Leaders or managers?

Leadership and management are very different roles and require very different people, according to Professor Abraham Zaleznik of Harvard Business School. Managers are essentially *administrators*, he believes, who motivate people to meet the company's objectives. Leaders, on the other hand, are *visionaries*, challenging existing practices and capable of motivating people to create and follow *new* objectives.

This does not imply that one role is more valuable than the other. The chief executive at the top obviously needs to exhibit leadership in the sense of having a clear long-term vision of where the company is going, yet may not always be good at administration. Managers at the operating level, however, tend to be better at administration and managing resources.

In any case, managers today, whether they are **line managers**, responsible for the running of a particular department or section, or **staff managers**, responsible overall for an administrative function like personnel, need increasingly to demonstrate leadership in order to motivate their groups towards greater performance.

As John Adair points out in the *Director* interview referred to above, people's expectations are changing. 'People now look for a much higher level of leadership than before. They expect to be consulted; to be listened to; to be informed; to be kept in the picture; to be partners in the enterprise. Good leaders create that sense of being a team, of involvement and commitment.'

So how many of you could make good leaders? 'There's a lot talked today about charisma,' says John Adair, 'but the old definition of genius as 90 per cent perspiration and 10 per cent inspiration also holds true for leadership.' In other words, there is no substitute for hard work, energy and enthusiasm.

What does one of Britain's top chief executives look for in picking good people? Richard Giordano, non-executive chairman of The BOC Group, is quoted in *The New Elite* as stressing that 'You pick people by looking back at their records first of all . . . The second element I have learned the hard way. Make certain you pick people with a good set of personal qualities. I've had people who were probably intellectually below the salt. I've chosen employees who have been excessively defensive, bordering on dishonesty. They can't stand to see their mistakes in the light of day and have covered them up. I've had people who were just not articulate – brainy and all that, but hell on wheels to communicate with . . . Then there are some who just don't want to work!'

CASE STUDY

Dixons – managing a service revolution

The importance of leadership can be seen clearly in the recent change of business strategy at Dixons, Britain's biggest electrical retailer. For most of the past 50 years, its leader has been Sir Stanley Kalms.

In 1948 Sir Stanley joined a one-store family business called Dixons. Today he is chairman of Dixons Group

Plc, with its annual turnover of over £2,000 million and over 15,000 employees. This remarkable growth stemmed from many causes. At the strategic level, the key was focus upon the pursuit of clear, demanding profit targets. In terms of day-to-day operations, success rested largely upon the firm's deal-making skills – both with suppliers and with customers. The company's sales success was based on financial incentives to store staff (through commission) and a training focus on clinching a sale.

By the late 1980s, however, there was increasing evidence that this might not be enough. Customers were looking for more than just the right products at the right price. They wanted better, quicker and more responsive service. As Peter Cox, Dixons personnel director, says: 'Products are so complex nowadays. Customers want advice from well-informed staff and expect support following their purchase – preferably from the person they dealt with in the store'.

The prime mover in making service a top priority was Sir Stanley. In 1995 he set up a new executive committee called the Quality Standards Committee, in which he takes a keen interest. This sent out a message to all staff about its importance. Customer service would be the focal point of the company's strategy for the year 2000.

The new strategy would be three-pronged: investment in new service initiatives such as next-day delivery (including Sundays); a change in staff attitudes in favour of a greater customer focus; and partnerships with suppliers to identify and deliver the product quality improvements sought by customers. Within the stores, the need was to encourage staff to take an interest in all their customers' needs. This led to a service strategy called 'My Customer, My Responsibility' (MCMR). This would not be a simple task. The Dixons growth story had been rooted in staff focus on selling. Might a shift in emphasis undermine the company's turnover and profits? Or might sales staff only pay lip-service to their responsibility for customer service?

Peter Cox was sure that the answer was not just to retrain staff. A few days' training could not be expected to change attitudes. More important was to ensure that all 15,000 employees received a consistent message about the importance of service and their personal responsibility for providing it.

To help provide the consistent message, a Quality Standards director was appointed in September 1995 – answerable directly to the chairman. John Pluthero sees his job 'as being the customer champion'. John is clear that this is no less businesslike a job than any other in the company, because 'we didn't come to it from a moral point of view, we just want to be better than the competition'. So John has built on the change in staff attitude brought about by 'my customer my responsibility' with service initiatives such as Sunday delivery and 'service excellence week'. This helps turn Sir Stanley's aims into customer reality, with the likely long-term benefit of more loyal customers.

Yet would even these initiatives be enough? Customer service demands change constantly, so the company needs to spot new trends before the competition. And how can the company make sure that the customers from all its stores are equally happy with the service they receive?

A long-term solution is to provide a system for measuring service success. Dixons already had a measurement system called 'complaints against turnover' (CAT). This was calculated by dividing the number of customer complaints by the store's sales turnover. The lower the number, the better. This made it possible to produce a monthly league table of performance.

Customer complaints were not the only issue. A customer might leave a store feeling dissatisfied with the service, yet do nothing more than walk across the road to a competitor. So the hunt was on for a new way of measuring service performance. If successful, this would provide an incentive for store managers and sales staff to improve customers' experience of going into and – even more – buying from a Dixons outlet.

Head Office initiatives are all very well, but do they really affect what happens at local level? Not always, to be sure. In this case, though, the consistent messages from the company's leadership have ensured action. To Joe Earle, manager of the Curry's Superstore at Slough, the 'My Customer, My Responsibility' initiative has been important for its message to staff, rather than the systems it has introduced. It has encouraged individuals to take more personal responsibility for what they do and focused attention on service rather than sales. 'Take this customer complaint, for example', he continues. 'It was the only one we had last week, but my area manager has phoned this morning to ask about it. That would never have happened in the past.' He also cites service initiatives such as same-day delivery and installation. 'We used to just deliver a cooker to someone's door. They had to install it. That's all changed, which is great for the customers.'

Joe Earle with a member of staff and a customer

> Julie Smith makes sales of over £1 million a year at Curry's, Slough. Her reward is a 1 per cent commission, but her motivation is 'to provide the standard of service I expect when I go anywhere'. Recently a customer phoned to ask about the length of the electrical lead and waste pipe on a dishwasher. Others would say they didn't know. Julie unfurled the items, measured them and phoned the customer back. The sale was made.

Joe Earle is also clear that the changes will help, not hinder, long-term profitability. He has no doubt that top-class service is the basis of high sales. At the Slough Superstore, 'my top salesperson gets the most customer praise – service and sales go hand in hand.'

Successful leadership, then, requires three elements: a clear vision of what is required; selecting the right people with enough power to deliver the vision; and providing the resources to finance a plan that turns the vision into practical changes which staff believe in.

ACTIVITY

1 You have £300 and want to buy a new midi sound system. Identify the factors you would consider before deciding what to buy and where to buy it. List six of each and then place them in order of priority.

2 Imagine you are the manager of a PC World Superstore. How would you make sure that your sales staff give excellent customer service? Try to think of at least eight methods.

What should management training include?

According to a report published in 1987, 'The Making of Managers', whose principal author was Professor Charles Handy, the extent of management training in the UK lags far behind that of its four main competitors.

The USA invests vast amounts in training; Japan has a compulsory system whereby managers have to go through a systematic process of self-education; in France, employers are required by law to spend a minimum annual sum on training for each employee; and the Germans go through a long preparatory training and normally do not even start their managerial careers until they are at least 27 years old.

What should a good management training programme include? Sir Trevor Holdsworth, the former chairman of GKN, has reservations about some of the courses at management training centres being too academic. He is quoted in *The New Elite* as arguing (jokingly) that the best management training course would be one confined to three disciplines: chess, bridge and poker. 'Chess represents strategic thinking in a wider form, while bridge is working with a partner and poker is taking a calculated risk and having the nerve to see it through. All the elements of business management are captured in those three games.'

Apart from the courses run at business schools and management training centres, many UK companies do in fact offer their own training courses.

How do management styles vary?

The degree to which a manager gives responsibility for decision making can be ranked along a scale, as shown in the diagram below.

High

Tells — manager makes decision and informs the group

Sells — manager makes decision and explains it to the group

Consults — manager listens to suggestions, then makes decision

Shares — manager defines limits and lets the group make decision

Delegates — manager allows groups members to operate within defined limits

Low

Scale of management styles

Source: Tannebaum and Schmidt, *Harvard Business Review*.

At either end of the scale are the two styles of management – autocratic and democratic.
- **Autocratic** managers set objectives for the group, demonstrate their own authority, and expect orders to be obeyed blindly and without question. Communication is downward, so group members do not have the necessary information to make their own decisions. Such managers see workers as replaceable production units who can only be motivated by fear or by appeals to their self-interest in terms of money.

- **Democratic** managers, on the other hand, encourage group members to set their own objectives and delegate authority wherever possible, giving reasons for any orders or instructions they give out. Participation in decision making is encouraged and group members are given the necessary information to form these opinions, which the manager takes into account when making a final decision. This managerial style is based on workers being seen as human beings, who can be trusted to put their hearts into the task.

Research has shown that this last style results in the highest productivity, greatest feelings of involvement and job satisfaction and the best relations, though it does mean managers have to be good communicators and have to take time for the necessary consultation with workers.

However, a job-centred autocratic management style can also achieve high productivity, though groups managed like this tend to show dissatisfaction with their work and output is generally of lower quality. Such groups also experience greater conflict with management and suffer from a high turnover.

In any case, much research has also shown that managers do not adopt one style in all situations. The style adopted varies according to the manager's own personality, ability and experience and the personalities, skill and experience of the group members. The size of workforce, kind of job done and time available for completion are also influential. The nature of the organisation and the management style which have traditionally been used are important factors too.

ACTIVITY

Comparison of management styles

1 Decide which type of management style would be most appropriate in the following situations:

a) A group of unskilled workers engaged in completing a complex task.

b) A group of inexperienced workers meeting a tight time deadline.

c) A new manager appointed to run a division of a large firm, where consultative committees have traditionally existed.

d) A group of skilled workers making high-quality products.

e) A group of skilled employees in a small family firm.

f) A large factory with hundreds of employees, when a fire breaks out.

g) A new manager taking over an ailing company who needs to cut production costs, reduce staff and introduce financial controls.

h) A group of inexperienced workers who believe management is paid to make decisions.

2 Why could you make a case for either style being appropriate in the situations in g) and h)?

" DISCUSSION POINTS "

1 Can one management style work best in most situations?

2 Which styles have been adopted by successful leaders that you can think of?

Management structures

Most companies have traditionally been organised on a **pyramid structure**, where employees at each level in the hierarchy are at a certain rank and have a particular role to fulfil in the organisation. In this kind of structure, there is a clearly defined **chain of command**. Orders tend to move downwards and the main flow of information is upwards.

At ICI a very steep pyramid existed, where it was calculated that there were as many as 16 layers of management between the shop floor and the chairman. As part of his recovery strategy for ICI, Sir John Harvey-Jones pruned out many of these layers in order to revitalise the management structure.

Some companies are now organised instead on a **matrix structure**, where the authority for decision making is shifted down the organisation so that it lies with the heads of sections or of subsidiary companies, giving them more autonomy. Even a business organised on a traditional pyramid structure may use the matrix approach at times, when complex problems need to be solved quickly. For example, a team of people spanning different areas like production, personnel, finance and marketing, drawn from all levels in the organisation, may meet together to investigate a problem like poor quality control. A matrix structure such as this improves communication, speeds up decision making and encourages motivation through allowing employees greater opportunities for involvement and participation.

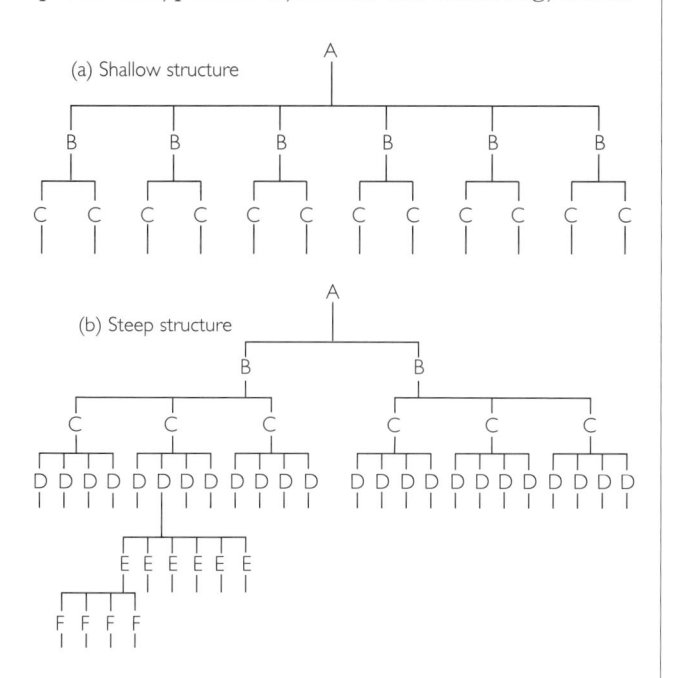

Pyramid organisational structure

CASE STUDY

Leadership to win at Allied Domecq – the managing director's view

'I started in a small firm – a *really* small firm. When I asked the boss for an office, he gave me a hammer and nails. I came in at the weekend to build it! ... It helps me appreciate working here.' Via a career at Mars and Bulmer's, Chris Banks is now the managing director of URM Agencies, a division of the huge drinks company, Allied Domecq. He heads a business with 150 staff and annual sales of £200 million.

His view is that 'leadership can be about process as much as personality ... It's easy to behave in a Victorian, top-down way – especially when the pressure's on – but the key is coaching and questioning.' In other words the good leader provides the facilities and the encouragement to get the best out of people, while always asking for advice and ideas. (Top-down is a term used to describe company structures where all decisions are made by senior management without input from other staff, and is looked at in practice below.)

Chris Banks, managing director of URM Agencies

Yet can it be that simple? That easy to learn? By no means, as there are also important issues of personality. Chris Banks believes that a leader must show 'passion for success', though he 'likes to be seen as a calm influence – controlled, even when others are panicking'. Charisma is not enough, because workers would soon lose patience with charismatic chaos. Yet self-confidence is vital for leaders, both to enable them to cope with crisis and to allow others to take credit for their successes. A leader should challenge others to set themselves really stretching goals and then help provide the confidence to reach them.

Mr Banks believes that the key to his role is successful delegation. His approach is to ensure that staff know enough about the issues to be able to set their own objectives. He likes to meet with each project team monthly to discuss progress: 'Providing support and resources without interference, and then rewarding success.'

He cites a recent reorganisation of the salesforce. Instead of top-down decisions on how this should be achieved, the sales team were brought together for two days of brainstorming and discussion. By the end they had decided on the new salesforce structure, and presented their views to senior management. So instead of a management decision causing grumbling and a muted response, the salesforce were fully committed to their new ways of working. The result has been very encouraging.

Another aspect of Chris Banks' style is 'the big tick'. He considers it vital that staff should feel secure and valued. So instead of fearing a stab in the back he wants his team 'to walk around with a big tick on their backs'.

So what does he do to ensure that all staff are consulted and involved? Does he employ quality circles or joint consultation committees? Not a bit of it. He thinks formal procedures for consultation are doomed to be dull talking shops. He does a lot of 'corridor checks', popping his head round doors to ask how people are getting on. As all staff work within teams, there are many opportunities for discussion. He likes to tap in and out of all the teams. Overall, his views on communication are simple: deformalise. 'If you want to keep a secret, display it on the noticeboard . . . and if you want everyone to hear about something, use the grapevine.'

He wants a company 'where people come up to me and say: "I've been thinking. . ."'.

How well has this leadership approach worked? In two years URM Agencies has become the fastest growing drinks agency in the UK. For 10 years its Teacher's brand of whisky had seen sales declines. It is now the fastest growing in the whisky market.

> **DISCUSSION POINTS**
>
> 1. How well do the views of Chris Banks fit into either the autocratic or the democratic leadership styles outlined on pages 103–4?
> 2. Which of the leadership characteristics set out by Mr Banks could be acquired by training and/or experience, and which would you have to be born with?

Who makes decisions?

How is authority for decision making actually allocated in different organisations? In organisations with a **centralised management structure**, the majority of decisions are made by a few people. Those with a **decentralised management structure**, on the other hand, may give responsibility for decision making to senior managers in different divisions concerned with different product groups. Such a shifting or **delegation** of responsibility for decision making downwards through the organisation encourages greater motivation, because of the autonomy gained.

A spectacular example of a company trying to shake itself free of head office bureaucracy occurred when Bob Horton, the former chairman of BP, was first appointed to the post. Within a week he announced that more than 1,000 jobs would be cut from BP's massive headquarters in the City. With them went an elaborate hierarchical structure and about 70 committees, all supposedly needed to manage or coordinate the global business, but which were actually stifling initiative and action in the operating units.

Peters and Waterman highlighted the fact that the successful American companies they studied invariably split their operations into small, independent units. Each unit is allowed maximum freedom to operate except in certain key areas, which management feel are so important that they need centralised control over them.

In their description of 23 successful British companies which they identified as standing out from the crowd, Walter Goldsmith and David Clutterbuck, in their book, *The Winning Streak*, found decentralised management structures were the norm. The only exceptions were the retailing chains and the Trust House Forte hotel chain, where a greater degree of central control is required to maintain uniform standards.

In describing the situation at Clarks, who operate in the shoe making industry, Goldsmith and Clutterbuck point out that 'The revelation came during the Second World War, when the company had to give up its main factory for the production of torpedoes. The mass production halls were dispersed into numerous smaller buildings in the surrounding area. Productivity rose 250 per cent. Since then, Clarks has retained all its production in relatively small, semi-autonomous units.'

These authors also observe that the basic philospohy behind the success of the Racal Electronics Group is their policy of establishing small individual companies, with less than 500 employees, each responsible for the design, development and marketing of its own products. According to Sir Ernest Harrison, the former chairman of Racal Electronics, 'A small business has one product and a small team of people, who can be so intense in their interest that they get the best product and the best effort out of the people who work for them. . . . Everyone knows the costs, everyone knows the boss and everyone knows the customers.'

ACTIVITY

Decentralised management structure

Using the table below to help you, draw up a similar table listing the advantages and disadvantages of a decentralised management structure.

	Centralised management structure
Advantages	Senior management provided with information from all parts of the organisation, so are in a good position to make decisions.
	Senior management can be expected to make better decisions than more junior staff with less experience.
	Less time spent in coordinating activities of different divisions or departments.
	Managers can ensure uniform standards are met.
	Succeeds well in an organisation with an autocratic management structure.
Disadvantages	Senior management may be inundated with more information than they can absorb or have the time deal with.
	Junior and middle managers have fewer opportunities to gain experience, as decision making is restricted to senior management.
	Decisions may take longer to make as information is relayed to managers through people at different levels in the organisation.

More expensive because of the administrative systems which need to be set up when the organisation is controlled from the centre.

Senior management may lose touch with operating conditions through being several layers of management removed from 'grass roots'.

CASE STUDY

Virgin – effective management in action

Pick up any newspaper or magazine and there's a good chance you'll come across a picture of Richard Branson sporting his irrepressible toothy grin and trademark woolly jumper. Airline owner, daredevil stunt man and entrepreneur extraordinaire, few businessmen have captured the public imagination as completely as the larger-than-life chairman of Virgin. The press have elevated him to the status of folk hero, reporting his hot-air balloon and speedboat exploits with relish and devoting endless column inches to each new business venture.

Branson's earliest business venture was in fact as the publisher of a student magazine when he was still a 16-year-old schoolboy. However, the real break came when, in a bid to raise cash for the financially-strapped magazine, he hit on the idea of selling discounted records by mail order. The initial advertisement produced a flood of responses and he was soon able to open his first Oxford Street record shop in 1971. The purchase of a recording studio in 1972 proved a huge success when the first album released – Tubular Bells by Mike Oldfield – went on to sell five million copies. At the age of 23, Branson had made his first million. In the years since, artists like Janet Jackson, Culture Club, the Human League, Phil Collins and Paula Abdul helped to turn the music division into one of the most successful record labels in the world. Branson later pulled off the deal of a lifetime when the sale of Virgin Music to Thorn EMI in 1992 netted the company a cool £560 million.

In the space of 25 years Branson has built a major entertainment empire with a turnover of £1.4 billion and 7,500 employees in 150 operating companies. Virgin interests around the world, as they are now, consist of five holding companies: Travel, Retail, Communications, Hotels and Investments. The two major divisions are Virgin Travel, which is dominated by the airline, and Virgin Retail which operates music and entertainment stores, including the Megastores chain. So what are the management principles governing the company whose growth has been almost entirely self-generated, with only a handful of acquisitions and partnership deals?

Branson's management philosophy rests squarely on the 'small is beautiful' principle put forward by the economist EF Schumacher. According to Schumacher, it is only when a large organisation is broken down into many small autonomous units, that the proper balance between freedom, which promotes creativity, and order, which gets things done, can be maintained. As Branson says, 'Once people stop knowing the other people in the building, it's time to break up a company into smaller units. The ideal size is around 50 to 60 people. By keeping a company small, you give more people a chance.'

In line with this philosophy, the highly decentralised management structure that has evolved at Virgin is a classic example of 'empowerment', with managers being given the freedom to organise the day-to-day running of their companies as they see fit. As one manager points out, 'He'll sometimes disagree with you but then says, "Go ahead, you're the boss".' The fact that many of the top executives have been with the company since it started is perhaps the best proof that managers appreciate being given the room to follow their own judgement.

Staff turnover is also low. So what factors explain this loyalty? 'We're an entertainment company so things are done slightly differently to other companies', admits Branson. 'We don't have a clock-in, clock-out mentality. Because of this climate, people are quite willing to work long hours.' Based on the principle that people feel more motivated when they have a stake in the company's future, 85 per cent of promotions are internal appointments. Other key factors include the use of incentive payment schemes and the fact that employees have the option of buying shares in the company. In fact, well over a dozen of the top managers at Virgin are now millionaires in their own right.

Branson has clearly fostered a winning management style at Virgin, delegating authority to his managers whilst leaving himself free to do what he does best – coming up with ideas for new ventures and getting them off the ground.

ACTIVITY

Jinx Games Ltd: 'all in a day's work!'

BACKGROUND TO THE COMPANY

Jinx Games Ltd is a manufacturer of board games, located in the small town of Daleford in the Pennines. The company employs 40 people, has a turnover of £1.8 million and is

UNDERSTANDING INDUSTRY

regarded locally as a reputable and well-run firm. Sales are seasonal and the firm gets especially busy in the run-up to Christmas. The company gets orders steadily from small toy shops round the country, but their biggest orders tend to be from the major department stores in the cities.

The firm was started eight years ago by Helen Robinson, who is the managing director. On this particular Friday in September, Helen arrives in the office at 10.30 a.m., after a meeting with one of the suppliers, to find on her desk a list of phone messages from her secretary together with a letter which arrived this morning. She also has a list of things written down in her diary to deal with today.

DECIDING PRIORITIES

Put yourself in the position of Helen Robinson. Having read the phone messages, letter and diary entries, decide how **urgent** and how **important** each situation is.

1. Make a list of the order in which you have to deal with each situation. (Plan the possible combinations in rough first.)

2. By the side of each item on your list, state which managerial role you are carrying out in dealing with each situation. (Refer back to the diagram of roles identified by Mintzberg on p.92.)

DALEFORD FOOTBALL CLUB
127 The Links
DALEFORD
OF7 2AL

Mrs Helen Robinson   September 9th
Jinx Games Ltd.
DALEFORD
DF3 4BH

Dear Mrs Robinson,
   We will be holding our annual disco at the end of next month at 8.30 p.m. on October 28th.
   As you have very kindly sponsored us this year, we wondered if you would come along and present the cups to the winning players?
I look forward to hearing from you.

Yours sincerely,

Kenneth Jameson

Kenneth Jameson
(Club Secretary)

PHONE MESSAGE

1. Factory foreman rang. Would like an interview to discuss his prospects in the company. Has had another job offer and needs to give them an answer by next weekend.

2. Finance controller rang. Customer owing £20,000 gone into receivership. He thinks another consignment of goods is to be dispatched today.

3. Reporter from 'Derbyshire Business Review' rang. Would like an interview for an article in next week's issue.

4. Buyer from Jarrods department store rang. Goods due to be delivered a week ago not arrived yet.

ACTION REQUIRED   Friday September 13th

1. Write memo informing everyone the company Christmas 'do' will this year be held at 'Marco and Luigis' on December 15th.

2. Arrange to see 'Platt and Margate' insurance brokers to update insurance policies which will run out at the end of the month.

3. Look at budget figures to decide where the money for advertising the new game to be launched in two months time is to be drawn from.

4. Ring 'Apollo Computers' to arrange for a representative to visit and discuss the computerisation of the company accounts system.

5. Arrange meeting with Sales Manager to review last month's sales figures.

Small business

IN ASSOCIATION WITH

Introduction: the small firms revival

How small is small? Definitions vary, from the 'under 24 employees' stated by the Small Business Research Trust, to the measure adopted by the Department of Employment, which classifies small firms in manufacturing as being those with fewer than 200 employees. However, an accepted formula seems to be that described in the 1981 Companies Act. This defines a small firm as being one which during any accounting year does not exceed *two* of the following criteria: a turnover of £1.4 million, total assets of £0.7 million, a workforce of 50 employees.

The 1993 *Size Analysis of UK Businesses* showed that 89 per cent of all manufacturing firms are small firms of under 50 employees, accounting for 24 per cent of manufacturing employment. In fact, 66 per cent of all manufacturing firms were very small firms of under nine employees. Only 3 per cent of manufacturing firms have more than 200 employees!

In the post-war period of economic growth, small businesses were widely regarded as being inefficient. Only large firms could afford to adopt all the latest technological developments and improve their productivity by making huge economies of scale. The impact of such attitudes was confirmed by the government-commissioned Bolton Report, published in 1971, which concluded that, 'The small firms sector is in a state of long-term decline.' However, the report argued that small firms (which they defined as having fewer than 200 employees) fulfilled an important role in the economy, by creating jobs and stimulating competition and innovation. Some of the measures recommended by the report, such as the setting up of a Small Firms Service, were later adopted.

Since 1971, there has been a dramatic increase in the numbers of small firms. Why is this so? What advantages do small firms offer over larger firms? The UK's SMEs (small and medium enterprises) are estimated to have accounted for two-thirds of private sector employment and 75–100 per cent of net job creation in recent times, whereas during the 1980s the larges companies reduced their collective workforce by over 1.3 million. Unlike large firms, which are tending to shed jobs, small firms are creating jobs and thus stimulating economic growth.

In addition, their small scale of operations means that they do not face the same problems as larger firms, many of which are associated with production-line work. Due to their closeness to the market, they also tend to be more in touch with market trends. They can be more flexible in responding to changing market demands, because they are owner managed and so decisions can be taken quickly. They generally tend to be more innovative and, because they often provide highly specialised products and services, are seen as being important in providing consumers with a greater choice.

Apart from the advantages inherent in their small size, there are various economic, social and political factors which have encouraged the small firms revival.

Why do some industries have many small firms?

Richard Scase and Robert Goffee, in their book, *The Real World of the Small Business Owner*, describe four conditions which encourage small manufacturing firms to grow up. These include:

- **Labour intensiveness**. The textile, footwear and printing and publishing industries provide many opportunities for small firms. They are all traditional industries that depend on most work being done by hand rather than by machine.
- **Subcontracting**. The engineering industry sustains large numbers of small firms, who survive by supplying the specialised goods and services which large firms subcontract out.

TABLE 8.1 *Why are there more small firms today?*

Service industries	As the service sector of the economy has increased dramatically in recent years, more opportunities have been created for small firms. Service firms, being labour intensive, can be started with very little capital outlay, unlike manufacturing firms which need heavy initial outlays on plant and equipment.
Standards of living	More small firms are starting up as general standards of living have risen. These have exploited new markets catering for the specialised products and services demanded by consumers with higher disposable incomes.
Redundancies and unemployment	Many of the workers made redundant as a result of their firms closing down or cutting back have decided to start up small firms, especially if they live in areas where their chances of finding another job are slim. Similarly, many unemployed people have decided to set up their own businesses, as an alternative to the dole queues.
Opportunities for subcontracting	Large firms prefer to subcontract out limited production runs or specialised services where the work is not profitable for their scale of operations. This creates opportunities for small firms to survive in the **sheltered market** created. Opportunities increase in times of fierce competition, which causes large firms to concentrate even more on their core or principal activities.
Government encouragement	Small firms are widely recognised as creating jobs, stimulating economic growth and avoiding many of the labour problems larger firms face. As a result, most governments have actively encouraged the formation of small firms in recent decades.

- **Technological innovation**. The plastics, instrument engineering and electronic engineering industries are all areas where small firms have grown up making the innovative products which have been developed.
- **Market variability**. The furniture and clothing industries and the manufacture of various domestic items are all consumer goods industries which offer **market niches** for new businesses, catering for particular fashions or specialised items.

Of these factors, Scase and Goffee conclude that 'labour intensiveness is perhaps the most important since the initial capital requirements for start up purposes tend to be low'.

ACTIVITY

Percentage of employees in small firms found in each manufacturing industry

On your copy of the table below, write down the percentage of small firms in each manufacturing industry. Which industries have the highest concentration of small firms?

Manufacturing industries (standard industrial classification)	Total number of employees in small firms (under 50 employees)	Total number of employees in each industrial sector	Percentage of employees in small firms within each industrial sector
Chemical industry and production of synthetic fibres	28,967	258,582	
Manufacture of metal goods	112,109	288,845	
Mechanical engineering	180,627	524,627	
Manufacture of office machinery and data processing equipment	9,401	53,990	
Electrical and electronic engineering	70,991	450,029	
Manufacture of motor vehicles and parts	19,312	223,749	
Manufacture of other transport equipment	15,091	240,475	
Instrument engineering	20,848	77,919	
Food, drink and tobacco manufacturing industries	75,350	520,297	
Textile industry	32,651	169,985	
Manufacture of leather and leather goods	6,902	15,034	
Footwear and clothing	66,683	228,878	
Timber and wooden furniture industries	83,790	179,111	
Manufacture of paper and paper products, printing and publishing	151,967	432,945	
Processing of rubber and plastics	56,330	222,495	

Source: Central Statistical Office, *Size Analysis of UK Businesses* 1993, Table 7a.

Why do people set up in business?

Becoming an **entrepreneur** involves undertaking a risk in a commercial venture. What factors motivate the ever increasing flood of people to risk going it alone? The 'Enterprise in Britain' study of almost 6,000 small business owners and self-employed people showed that the age at which most people start up is between 30 and 40, when they have the work experience, access to capital (with mortgages easier and children growing up) and necessary motivation (if promotion does not materialise).

Dissatisfaction with being an employee is undoubtedly the trigger for many, especially if there is no challenge or job satisfaction left in their present jobs and prospects of promotion are limited. Running a business can provide an attractive alternative to being stuck on the company ladder, with the opportunity to make decisions, take on responsibility and enjoy what is for many entrepreneurs the main benefit – the ability to control their own destiny. Some employees may decide in time to put their skills and abilities to use making profits for themselves, rather than for the organisation they have been with. Those who are at a disadvantage in the labour market because of discrimination, such as ethnic minority groups, also find business start-ups attractive.

Similarly, according to Robert Goffee and Richard Scase in their book *Women in Charge*, a growing number of women are starting their own businesses to avoid the frustration of limited career prospects. 'To a large extent this is because senior male managers continue to query their ability to occupy top corporate positions. Some are concerned about the supposed psychological and emotional qualities of women, others are anxious about their organisational "commitment". As a result, there may be a reluctance to train or promote women. By starting their own business women can achieve the material success and personal ambitions denied them in large organisations.'

People may also be tempted to become entrepreneurs through deciding to develop an innovative idea for a product or service that they have come up with, but which their present company does not regard as commercially viable. David Oates, in his book *The Complete Entrepreneur*, quotes the case of Robert Mann, who stumbled on an idea for a fire protection product he was sure would sell well. The product was based on a material which is inset as a thin strip in vulnerable areas such as door frames. If a fire occurs the material expands under the heat, sealing off the gap in the frames and preventing the fire spreading. The chemical group he was working for at the time thought the product was too specialised and was unlikely to generate a big enough sales volume to justify the necessary investment. However, the firm agreed to support him by supplying him with the raw material at a good price and also helped him with credit. Within just five years, Mann's company was exporting worldwide and had a turnover of £400,000.

In some cases, people have become entrepreneurs because they have discovered a gap or niche in a particular market through wanting to use a product or service, finding it does not exist and then deciding to manufacture or supply it themselves. Others seek to provide an existing product or service for a gap which they have identified in a local or regional market. Less often than is commonly thought, small businesses are founded by those who manage to invent a completely new product or service, thus stimulating a new demand. Sometimes entrepreneurs can discover a useful product which is not widely available and set up a company themselves to market it more extensively.

Changing personal circumstances, such as being made redundant, can often be a powerful spur, with the redundancy lump sum providing some of the finance needed. However, evidence suggests that businesses started by individuals who have been pushed into start-ups by negative reasons have a lower growth rate than businesses started by those who have become entrepreneurs for positive reasons, such as identifying a gap in the market or coming up with an idea for a new product.

The trend towards increasing numbers of **management buy-outs** in recent years shows no sign of slowing down. This is where the managers buy out the company they are working for, or a division of it, and then run it as an independent concern. The impetus for taking this step is often the threat of closure. Buy-outs have tended to be very successful, on the whole, largely because the management team who already have experience of running the company stays in place. Finance is easier to obtain for such ventures because they are already a going concern, so constitute less risk for investors than completely new start-ups.

Whatever the motivating factors, with the 'enterprise culture' that exists in Britain today and the degree of help and advice available, conditions for starting up a small business have never been more favourable. The first step for any new entrepreneur is to prepare a detailed business plan on all aspects of the proposed venture, in order to assess whether the idea is commercially viable.

ACTIVITY

Factors considered by a bank manager when assessing a business plan

The questions that follow are adapted from Barclays Small Business pack for small firms.

Which of the following factors do you think a bank manager would assess most carefully in a business plan?

- Background of entrepreneur
- Background of business
- Products or services
- Markets and sales
- Financial considerations
- When will break-even point be reached?
- Has the entrepreneur any relevant experience in this field?
- Have the strengths which make the business competitive in the market been identified?
- Can the repayments be met on the amount borrowed?
- What will happen if the key personnel are unable to work?
- Has a target market been identified?
- Are premises adequate for future needs?
- How much of his/her own capital is the entrepreneur prepared to put in?
- What are the entrepreneur's business objectives, and how practical are they?
- Have the core or principal products or services been identified?
- Is the level of projected sales realistic?
- Who are the key suppliers and how much trade credit will they allow?
- Is the choice of premises suitable, in terms of size, location and cost, for the type of business?
- What percentage does each product or service contribute to turnover?
- How will prices be calculated?
- Does the cash-flow forecast include a reasonable margin of error?
- Is the market declining, static or increasing, and why?
- How detailed is the breakdown of expenditure?
- Who are the major competitors?
- Is the cash-flow forecast realistic and detailed enough?
- Has the entrepreneur any recognised business training?
- Has any market research been carried out?

UNDERSTANDING INDUSTRY

- Has the entrepreneur already got any firm orders?
- What methods of marketing will be used?
- What insurance cover will be taken out?
- Does the planned expenditure take into account future growth?
- Is the general character of the entrepreneur suitable for running a business?
- Can the business obtain any grants?

CASE STUDY

Richer pickings – a sound success

Who is the busiest retailer in Britain? Marks & Spencer? Sainsbury's perhaps, or Tesco? Wrong on all three counts. The answer is Richer Sounds, a little known, privately owned, cut price retailer of hi-fi equipment with 13 shops in the UK. In last year's *Guinness Book of Records*, Richer Sounds warranted an entry for the highest sales per square foot of any retailer in the UK – £17,553 – for its store on London Bridge Walk in the City.

It is profitable too. In 1994, Richer Sounds made profits of more than £1.8 million on sales of £20 million. By contrast, Dixons made virtually nothing on retail sales. The man behind the company's success is founder, chairman and 100 per cent shareholder Julian Richer, a 35-year-old Londoner. In simple terms, the company sells discounted hi-fi equipment from tiny basic shops with low overheads. Stock turnover is rapid and the company's small size gives it flexibility to take advantage of deals offered by manufacturers on end-of-line or surplus equipment. The technique has enabled Richer Sounds to secure itself a lucrative niche in a £4 billion audio visual market dominated by independents.

Suppliers are keen to do business with this quirky retailing operation. 'People like Dixons and Comet have so many stores (900 and 300 respectively) that unless you've got 5,000 of a model it's not worth their while putting it into their distribution system', says Clyde Roberts, sales and marketing director of Akai. 'With Richer, you can do a deal on 30.'

Kevin Harrington, regional sales manager with Sony, agrees. 'With a small management team they can make decisions quickly.' Marketing is a key weapon. Richer Sounds advertises regularly in national newspapers ('We buy late space at a discount,' Richer says) and in alternative magazines such as *Private Eye* and *Viz*.

The shops are like walk-in warehouses. And prices are cheap. Low prices are possible because fixed costs (rents and rates) are kept to a minimum – 2 per cent of turnover. The shops are tiny and in secondary locations, so that rents are low. Shop fittings are basic – no carpets and no fancy lighting.

Good service is another priority. At Richer Sounds staff are trained not to be pushy. First time hi-fi buyers get a call to check that they are happy with the equipment. Customer receipts include a freephone number they can dial if they have a problem. Richer's own name and office number are supplied too.

The emphasis is on fun. If it is raining, customers are given a free umbrella. In summer they get an ice lolly. Other seasonal gifts include mince pies at Christmas and hot cross buns at Easter. 'We have a laugh,' Richer says. 'We don't take ourselves seriously, but we do take our customers seriously.'

Richer's treatment of his staff – or 'colleagues' as he calls them – is reminiscent of Marks & Spencer (where his parents met as young employees). Fifteen per cent of profits are distributed to staff in a profit-share scheme. A further 1 per cent goes to a staff hardship fund for use in case of crisis, and 4 per cent goes to charity. Harley Street advice is available free of charge. Incentives are unusual: in addition to the standard 'carrot' of company cars – the best two performing branches each month get free use of a Bentley for four weeks. 'I think it's great, but my insurance broker is not so sure', Richer jokes.

With 19 shops, good profits and a burgeoning reputation, Richer seems well placed to expand his niche. But, aware that this year's fastest growers are often next year's receiverships, he says he is not going to open shops on every high street. 'I'd like to cover every major conurbation and that would mean about 25 or 30 shops,' he says. 'But I'm not in a hurry. Things that are built slowly last longer.'

ACTIVITY

The lending quiz – how would a bank rate your business plan?

On your copy of the questions below, tick the answer which you think is most appropriate for each question. When you have finished, add up the scores given for each answer on the scoring sheet, to determine **your** credit rating.

1. You are writing your own business plan to apply for a bank loan to start up a small business. Do you:

   a) include a short paragraph outlining your background and career so far?

   b) include a detailed profile of yourself giving full details of your previous relevant experience, work achievements, training and education?

   c) leave out any details about yourself as this is less relevant than the sales projections and cash flow forecasts you have included?

2. You are able to raise as personal finance, through a variety of sources, a percentage of the start-up finance required. Do you contribute:

   a) 10 per cent?

   b) 20 per cent?

   c) 40 per cent?

3. You are assessing the likely size and nature of potential demand for your products. Do you:

   a) carry out an informal survey amongst friends and family?

   b) commission a well-known, reputable market research agency to carry out a detailed survey?

   c) obtain any previously published survey results for similar products and carry out some field research for a small sample?

4. You are deciding how to plan the marketing most efficiently. Do you:

   a) carry out test marketing in order to decide how to use adverts, leaflets etc. in a logical sequence?

   b) commission a well-known and reputable advertising agency to test-market your products?

   c) avoid wasting scarce start-up resources on test marketing, as you already know what products you want to sell and how you need to market them?

5. You are deciding which bank to approach for start-up finance. Do you:

   a) approach a new bank as you think it is going to be more receptive than your own, giving them a complete set of bank statements for the last three years, showing satisfactory account behaviour?

   b) approach your own bank with which you have banked satisfactorily for five years?

QUIZ SCORING SHEET

Add up your scores:

1. a) 4 marks
   b) 8 marks
   c) 2 marks

2. a) 2 marks

3. a) 2 marks
   b) 2 marks
   c) 6 marks

4. a) 4 marks

5. a) 4 marks
   b) 6 marks

MY SCORE:

| b) 4 marks | b) 2 marks | MAX SCORE: 36 |
| c) 8 marks | c) 8 marks | |

CREDIT RATING

Final score

30 or more — Your loan application is certain to be approved as it is well prepared and thorough.

24–29 — Your loan application is likely to be approved though some areas will need a bit more attention to detail.

18–23 — You need to go away and prepare a more carefully thought-out business plan if you wish the application to go through.

Under 18 — You need to think again about whether there is any point in your going into business on your own.

Phil's business plan

'Phil Davies, isn't it? Good to see you. I'm John Woodford, the manager of this branch. Do take a seat. I understand from the business plan which you sent me that you would like a Barclays Business Starter loan of £10,000, to set up a small business.'

'Yes, that's right. I want to set up a business making a range of small leather gifts. You see, I've had a lot of experience in the leather trade and I'm sure I can make a go of it if I work hard enough.'

'Fine. But I think it would perhaps be helpful if we could go through the plan now, as there are some areas which you might want to consider in more detail before the loan application is assessed by the bank. I see that you've been with Classic Leather Goods for the last 12 years, as assistant production manager. Are you still with them?'

'No, actually I leave at the end of this month. I decided it was time I went, having just been passed over for promotion for the second time. I was ready for a change anyway. Who needs all that aggravation? I just want to be my own boss from now on, with no one telling me how I should do my job or breathing down my neck all the time.'

'I see, but do you have any capital to invest in the business?'

'Well, there's quite a lot, almost a thousand I think, in my savings account, though I want to use that to tide me over in the first few months. Anyway, the profits will be rolling in soon from all the different products I plan to make, so after a year or so I'll be fine.'

'You mentioned making a lot of different products. Are there any products you would concentrate on making, which would form the core of your business?'

'Not really. I thought originally I would just make wallets, purses and credit-card holders, but then I decided to make a complete range of gifts – everything from leather photograph frames to desk sets. After all, people always want something a bit out of the ordinary, don't they?'

'Oh, have you done some market research, then?'

'There wasn't much point really. Classic Leather always seemed to make good profits, and anyway people always need to buy presents, especially around Christmas time.'

'That's certainly true. But even if the overall size of market demand is good, why should consumers choose your products rather than anyone else's? Do your products have any strengths or special features which will make them stand out from the crowd?'

'Well, I thought that as a small business I could afford to charge lower prices, because my expenses and running costs will be lower, so that way I can undercut the competition because my products will be cheaper.'

'The trouble is, you can come unstuck trying to compete solely on the basis of price with firms who produce in volume, because they can cut their costs right down by making economies of scale. It would be far better if you could compete with the big firms by offering better quality products, or specialise by making something they don't. During your time at Classic Leather, perhaps you noticed a gap in the market which is not being catered for as yet?'

'No, I can't say I have. I thought I would stick to making the same sort of gifts, just sell them more cheaply. I can get the materials I need quite a bit cheaper if I pay cash in advance. I haven't actually got any firm orders yet, but once I get going, I won't have any trouble meeting those sales projections figures. After all, good products sell themselves, don't they? I'm certainly not going to waste any money on marketing to begin with. The main thing is for me to spend time going round all the stores and gift shops with my samples. Later on, I might get a few leaflets printed up or put some ads in a trade magazine.'

'Though of course your cash-flow forecasts do depend on meeting the level of sales you predict. Does your planned expenditure include a margin of safety, in case you don't manage to sell as much as you hoped?'

'Oh, I'm sure there'll be absolutely no problem in selling the amounts I quoted. Anyway, so long as the business ticks over, I'll be quite happy – I'm not bothered about making millions!'

'Well, you will certainly need to look carefully at whether the business will generate enough profit to cover your own salary, which has to meet your mortgage and other commitments, before you decide whether or not to proceed with this venture.'

'I see. But surely if you're prepared to work hard and your products are much cheaper than everyone else's, you can't go wrong, can you?'

ACTIVITY

Assessing Phil's business plan

1 Using the list in the previous activity as a guide, state all the ways in which you would consider Phil's approach and business plan inadequate, if you were the bank manager.

2 Are there any areas in which you would rate Phil well?

3 In pairs, role play how 'you' think the conversation should have gone.

Raising the finance to start up

Most entrepreneurs struggle hard to raise the start-up capital needed for all the one-off purchases like machinery or premises, together with the working capital needed to pay for everyday running costs such as a stock of materials, wages, overheads and so on. Though preoccupied with survival and trying to keep their heads above water, their thoughts might occasionally stray to the day when their business takes off to the point where it starts to make millions and becomes a major household name. Just a pipe dream? Perhaps, yet the dream does become a reality for some.

The founding of Apple, the US-based computer firm, illustrates the kind of rags-to-riches success story which inspires many hard-pressed entrepreneurs to keep going when they might otherwise be tempted to give up. In common with the majority of small business start-ups, Apple began life on a shoestring budget.

The company was founded in 1977 by Steve Jobs and his partner Steve Wozniak. They began working from a garage, having sold some of their belongings to raise their start-up capital of $1,300. A shop owner liked their design drawings for the second version of their computer so much that he placed an order for 50 computers straight away. But this large order created problems because it meant they could not afford to buy the electronic parts they needed. In fact, they eventually obtained the $20,000's worth of parts needed from a supplier on a 30-day-trade credit basis – and managed to pay it all back in 29 days with the cash they got from the sale of the 50 computers.

However, things might well have gone wrong. If they had not been able to manufacture and deliver the computers within 30 days, or if the customer had been late paying them, the story might have been very different. In the event, the company went from strength to strength. Within the next four years, sales multiplied 430 times, according to one estimate.

Entrepreneurs generally have some of their own capital to invest, from savings, for instance, or a second mortgage on their home. Just how easy is it for small businesses to borrow money today? The high street clearing banks are by far the most important source of initial finance. They tend to have a reputation for being conservative, preferring safe rather than speculative investments – mainly because they are, after all, responsible to their own depositors, whose savings they are investing.

Most advances are based on the concept of shared risk, where only about 50 or 60 per cent of the capital required is lent. Investors want to see the entrepreneur put in the rest, partly as a gesture of good faith (if you are unwilling to risk your own money, why should they risk theirs?), and partly because they would expect even greater effort and commitment if some of the entrepreneur's own capital was at stake. This principle is also adopted in the government's **Enterprise Allowance Scheme**, where people who have been unemployed are given £40 a week for a year when they start up a business, conditional on them already having or being able to borrow £1,000 themselves.

Lenders also require security to recover their loan should the business fail, the **collateral** often being provided in the form of the entrepreneur's own home. The government's **Loan Guarantee Scheme** is useful because it enables a loan to be granted in situations where it might otherwise not be; for instance, where inadequate security or the lack of an established track record makes the proposition unattractive to lenders. The government guarantees 70 per cent (85 per cent in some inner city areas) of a loan made by banks or financial institutions, up to a maximum of £100,000, thus enabling small businesses to provide the security lenders require. The small firm pays a 2.5 per cent premium to the government for the guarantee, which adds to the cost of borrowing. The scheme is now administered by the Training and Enterprise Councils (TECs).

In addition, small businesses can obtain finance through schemes such as LINC. Run by 14 Enterprise Agencies, this is a nationwide business introduction service which functions essentially as a 'marriage service'. Details of the small firms seeking capital are published in a monthly bulletin and investors can contact the firms which interest them via the box numbers given. Small firms can also raise finance through the European Investment Bank (EIB), which advances funds to banks and financial institutions which then lend on to small businesses. In the UK, this loan arrangement is carried out by Barclays Bank and 3i.

CASE STUDY

Braebourne Ltd – turning water into gold

'On day one we borrowed a van and went down to fill 30 bottles in a spring in Devon. It took us two months to sell them!' Six years later, on 19 September 1996, William Record went down to the Savoy Hotel to pick up his prize at the 1996 Venturer of the Year Award. In the meantime, his business had grown to generate a profit of over a quarter of a million pounds a year.

SMALL BUSINESS

William Record

It was while studying economics at Southampton University (he received a 2.1) that William Record started thinking about starting up on his own. 'Working for a huge company wasn't appealing' he says. Advice from his father pointed him towards rental businesses, because of their steady cash flow. 'My first thought was renting tropical plants to London offices . . . but the 1989 recession was starting . . . so it seemed unwise . . . then I came across water coolers.'

When he completed his degree he started researching the market for bottled water: 'I went through all the Mintel reports . . . we drank 2–3 litres per head compared with 25–30 in the U.S. . . . the growth rate in Britain was about 25 per cent a year . . . and there were more than 10 million water coolers in the States.' His mind was made up – the business would be renting water coolers to offices, delivering 22 litre bottles of natural mineral water to the customer with speedy and efficient service. He drew up a business plan, decided on the company and brand name 'Braebourne', and started up with £10,000 of share capital and a £25,000 loan from Lloyds Bank in February 1990.

Having collected the bottles of water from Devon, he and a friend started phoning everyone they knew, hoping for custom. They were offering a free 10 day trial with a free bottle of water. Selling proved very difficult. They tried visiting offices directly, but that proved a waste of time. Telephone selling ('telesales') using Business Directory numbers proved the best approach. Although it took two months to persuade the first 30 customers to try the free offer, 60 per cent of them converted into regular renters. Slowly, the business was starting to take off.

By early May, though, William realised the business was running out of cash. Every sales success was at a huge cost in wasted telephone calls and mailings. And every sale meant buying a water cooler for cash, then paying extra to deliver and install it. These cash outflows should have been offset by cash in from sales, but the free offer together with slow payments from customers caused the company's cash to drain away at an alarming rate.

Looking back, William thanks his father for the fact that 'from day one we had excellent management accounts, so we always knew where we were month by month'. As a result the cash crisis was anticipated. William hired an accountant to help draw up a revised, very full business plan, then went round the banks in search of capital. Remarkably, NatWest Bank gave Braebourne an overdraft of £80,000.

Shortly afterwards, William struck oil. The summer of 1990 was a beauty. Suddenly, instead of Braebourne staff phoning out, it was the incoming calls that had to be coped with. Demand soared as high as the temperatures. This, again, caused cash problems as more and more coolers had to be bought and staff hired. Even the water was running out! The demand was so high that the original Devon spring could not cope. So a new, larger spring was found in the Cotswolds. Braebourne coped with the summer only with the help of family loans to the tune of £30,000.

company's strong growth prospects. Braebourne's capital was restructured, with the share capital increased to £50,000, of which £12,500 was to be held by 3i. In addition, 3i provided £106,000 of medium-term loans – an act of faith which encouraged NatWest to increase the overdraft to £100,000. From that day onwards, the involvement of 3i meant an end to the cash flow crises. When extra finance was needed, discussions with 3i led to further capital being made available. Today (February 1997) William feels confident that 'borrowing £1 million wouldn't be a problem'.

Since the frantic days of 1990 Braebourne has made huge progress. While the industry has been growing at 35 per cent a year, Braebourne has grown at 65 per cent to make it the third largest water cooler supplier in the U.K. In the year to January 1997 it made over £500,000 profit on net assets of £750,000. William has considered floating the business on the AIM stock market, but decided instead to keep the business growing until it is large enough for a full stock market listing.

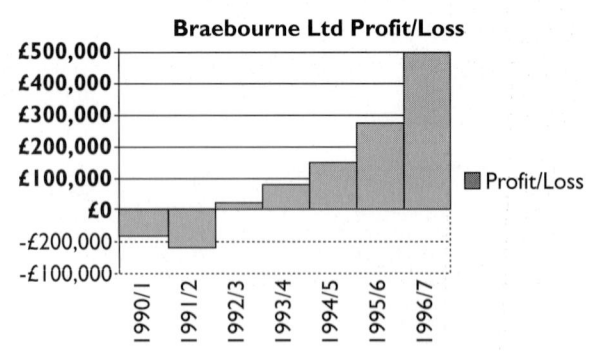

The key factor in the long-term future of the business was soon to be settled. What would happen when summer turned to autumn? Would the phone start to ring with customers cancelling their rentals? Fortunately, then and today, Braebourne's customer retention rate is 90 per cent. In other words the company loses only 10 per cent of customers per year. Bearing in mind that half of those are because of non-payment (i.e. Braebourne sack the customer) and some are due to office moves, the rate of loss due to customer disenchantment is very low indeed.

By Christmas 1990, the company's cash problems were heading for a new crisis. William recalls: 'We were really up against it . . . we considered leasing instead of buying coolers . . . and tried but failed to borrow money through the government's Loan Guarantee Scheme . . . then we went round the venture capital houses . . . they all turned us down because we were too small – we only wanted £100,000!'. Eventually 3i were persuaded of the

Despite the rapid growth, William has not seen a need to spread outside London and the South East. His principle is that every customer should be no more than an hour's drive from a Braebourne depot. So customer service is rapid and reliable and costs are kept down. Today there are three Braebourne depots, in the south, west and north of London. He believes his market share in London is about 12 per cent, so there is still plenty of growth potential.

So what has William learnt from the whole process? Looking back he feels that his main weakness was in marketing: 'If I'd done a marketing degree I'd have approached the whole thing more scientifically'.

Today he has a team of eight telesales staff and two marketing graduates to provide accurate market research information and a fully costed marketing strategy. The company will spend £600,000 in 1997 on marketing, including advertisements on the London Underground, mailshots to personnel managers and to managing directors and a series of attractive brochures.

Another lesson has been focus. In 1993, slow sales in the winter encouraged William to start up a coffee machine rental business. In fact it proved a slow, relatively unprofitable distraction from the rapidly growing water market. Far more sensible has been the introduction in Autumn 1996 of water cooling machines which have an extra tap which delivers the water at just below boiling point. This provides a quick, easy way of making a cup of tea or coffee with mineral water – appealing and convenient for staff, and a great way of stimulating water sales in the winter.

The most important lesson to be learnt from William Record, though, is the fun he had on route to becoming successful. He recalls that: 'Starting your own business is like the first day of the summer holidays . . . It's exciting!'. He has also enjoyed the process of learning – from his own mistakes or from the people he has employed. There is no question of him sitting back and counting his money. William is already planning where Braebourne will be in three years' time.

An example of Braebourne's advertising on the London Underground

ACTIVITY

Ranking of ingredients of success in new ventures

On your individual copy of the table below, rank each ingredient of success in new ventures in order of importance from 1 to 10, and write the ranking in column 1. Rank the ingredient you rate as being most important as 1, through to the least important as 10. Collect the rankings of other members in your group and add them to your table. Add the figures across and fill in the column for the group's total ranking. The **lowest** total (nearest to 5) is the most important ingredient, the next lowest the second most important, and so on. What do your results reveal?

1 Did you generally agree or disagree, as a group?

2 Were there any ingredients of success that you all agreed or disagreed on?

3 Are there any factors that you think are important which are not on the list?

Ingredients of success in new ventures	Group member 1	Group member 2	Group member 3	Group member 4	Total ranking for group	Final order of importance
Having relevant experience of the industry.						
Identifying an unexploited gap in the market.						
Creating a new need by offering an innovative product or service.						
Catering for a specialised part of the market, rather than for the majority market.						
Directing marketing at the target market.						
Keeping overheads low in the early stages.						
Having enough cash to meet requirements for working capital						
Ensuring interest charges and loan repayments can be funded from profits.						
Applying for any grants available and seeking advice from outside agencies						
Diversifying early on to avoid overdependence on a few products.						

Raising the finance for growth

Research has shown that business start-ups are usually financed by a combination of personal finance, bank loans and overdrafts, obtained mainly from the high street banks. Business expansion, on the other hand, tends to be financed by reinvested profit. However, if a company continues expanding the profits which are ploughed back into the company may not be sufficient to fuel continued growth. An injection of **equity capital** may then be required. Equity is risk capital: the proprietor's own funds in the case of a sole trader or partnership, and share capital in the case of a limited company. Further equity can provide the funds required to pay for extra factory space and machinery, or for the higher wages and overheads resulting from expansion.

How easy is it to find risk capital, once a decision has been made that an injection of equity is needed? Unfortunately, major investors prefer to invest their money in large public companies quoted on the Stock Exchange, which offer a lower risk than small businesses.

A worry about investing in a small firm is that success might lead to excessive expansion. A common cause of company failure is overtrading, meaning expanding so rapidly that cash outflows outstrip inflows, leaving the firm vulnerable to a shock such as a large bad debt.

Derwent Valley Foods Limited (Phileas Fogg) nearly went into liquidation in 1984. It doubled its factory size and hired new workers to cope with demand. This caused a major cash drain made worse by the failure of the accounting system to keep up with the increased level of business. Derwent asked the bank for an extra £200,000 overdraft, but the bank manager had lost confidence in the Derwent directors and refused. For several weeks the directors feared liquidation. Fortunately the regional director of the bank had attended Prince Charles's opening of the factory extension, and was willing to listen. Backed by 3i (Investors in Industry) and the Derwent directors, the extra overdraft was granted in November 1984.

In recognition of the problems of business expansion, the government's Enterprise Investment Scheme has been set up to encourage investment in small firms. Under the scheme, individuals are encouraged to invest between £500 and £100,000 in eligible companies (which are not quoted on the Stock Exchange). The incentives for them are that they can claim 20 per cent tax relief on their investment and pay no capital gains tax on any profit made. The investment must be maintained for at least five years.

Venture capitalists accept that a certain degree of risk is inevitable (as much as a one-in-three failure rate for start-ups). They tend not to be interested in investing below £50,000. They usually hold between 20 and 40 per cent of the company's shares and aim to recoup their investment when the company goes public, by selling the shareholding. The world's largest source of private investment capital is 3i Group plc. They have helped over 11,000 firms since 1945 and currently have investments in over 3,500 companies.

CASE STUDY

Denby Pottery – a management buy-out success

Wedgwood, Denby and Royal Doulton are internationally famous for traditional English china and pottery. All three were established around two centuries ago, yet all have had dramatic, even traumatic, changes of ownership during the last 15 years.

For Denby, the drama started in 1987 when the company became one of many firms taken over by

Coloroll plc. This fast growing, ambitious company allowed local Denby management to run the business and were keen to provide capital for investment. Yet the onset of recession in 1989 dragged Coloroll down, leaving Denby's fate in the hands of the receiver. A receiver's task is to raise as much as possible from asset sales, in order to repay creditors, so the directors knew that their business would soon be sold off.

The directors responded by proposing a management buy-out. They found experienced advisers who recommended 3i as financial backers. After 3i had checked the assets, trading position and cash-flow forecasts, the final issue was the personality fit. Could the 3i team work with the Denby managers? The answer was a resounding yes, so an agreement was reached.

Now the management buy-out (MBO) team could put together a detailed plan and offer to the receiver. A number of other companies were bidding to buy the business, so the Denby directors were pessimistic about their chance of success. Yet on 24 July 1990, the MBO team's bid of £5.3 million won the receiver's approval.

Denby was now an independent but potentially vulnerable small firm with large debts to its bankers. The four directors owned 60 per cent of the shares, with the remainder held by 3i.

The directors faced three main problems:

- The product range had become too large and diverse, making it hard for customers to develop a clear image of the Denby look and leading to short, uneconomic production runs.
- As Denby offered big profit margins to retailers, it had become common for Denby tableware to be displayed 'on sale, 33 per cent off' at many shops, threatening to cheapen Denby's image.
- In the 1970s, half of Denby's sales had been for export, but by 1990 this share had fallen to just 10 per cent, and the overseas distribution channels had withered away.

Denby was fortunate to have a managing director, Stephen Riley, whose career background was in marketing. Within the buy-out team he was responsible for marketing and product design and in a position to focus the business on these three problems.

The design team was encouraged to look for distinctive products of broad, international appeal, building on Denby's production strength of deep, rich glazes. This was to pay off with successful new product launches in each of the following years, culminating in 1994's award winning launch of Greenwich tableware. By 1995, 65 per cent of sales were stemming from products launched since the management buy-out.

Managing director, Stephen Riley, in the design studio at Denby Pottery

To tackle the image problem of retail discounting, Denby discussed the position with each of the major retail chains (such as Debenhams and House of Fraser). A three-year programme was agreed whereby the retailers accepted lower discounts in return for Denby's promise to invest in new, distinctive products. These would then be launched without promotional pricing.

The third element of the marketing strategy was to build export sales. The problem here would be the cost. Setting up a sales and distribution network in America, for example, might prove a hugely expensive flop. After an unsuccessful push in

Greenwich tableware

California, Denby decided to target the smaller, more receptive department store chains of middle America. This proved very successful, making it ever easier to find new US outlets willing to stock Denby. Sales in America more than doubled in 1994 alone and by 1995 Denby had more than one thousand American stockists. Europe is also being targeted, with France the stepping stone.

In addition to these strategic moves, the directors decided on two further marketing initiatives. Denby began to advertise regularly in magazines to emphasise the slogan 'Distinctively Denby'. There was also a substantial development of the factory shop into a varied and attractive Visitors Centre, including a full factory tour. This now has more than 250,000 visitors a year, and has turned from a promotional device into a profit centre in its own right.

With sales on a strongly upward path, the directors' attention needed to turn to production. How could the firm ensure sufficient output to meet customer demand? Raw materials presented no problem, as the pottery is built into the side of the hill where the clay was found nearly two centuries ago. More staff could, and would, be hired, but the kilns were already in operation 24 hours a day, so extra capital investment was required.

Two new tunnel kilns were installed at a cost of £580,000, each capable of firing pottery at the 1,200 degrees centigrade required for Denby's glazing process. A further £7 million was spent on up-to-date machinery such as a Japanese plate-making machine that uses a microwave drying process to speed up production. Happily, this huge investment has not been at the cost of jobs. With production volume more than doubling between 1990 and 1995, 200 more jobs have been created.

By 1994, with substantial progress on all fronts, the directors decided to float Denby on the stock market. This would raise extra capital for the business and enable the buy-out team to sell some shares. In May 1994, the shares were offered to the public at 130p, which placed a market value of £43 million on the business. This made all four directors multimillionaires, and gave 3i a substantial profit on its investment. On 2 June 1994 shares in The Denby Group Plc began trading on the London Stock Exchange.

TABLE 8.2 *Denby's financial progress 1990–94*

	1990/91*	1992	1993	1994
Sales turnover (£000)	12,550	12,484	17,563	21,915
Operating profit (£000)	1,371	1,588	3,243	4,550
Profit margin (profit as percentage of sales)	10.9	12.7	18.5	20.8
Pre-tax profit (£000)	724	1,261	2,755	4,130

*14.5 months

Looking back, Stephen Riley can see that the four were lucky to have had the opportunity to buy out a run-down but profitable company, largely financed by borrowed money. Hindsight makes the directors' success look easy. In fact, the four pushed ahead with the MBO to save their own jobs and families, and those of their staff. It was not obvious in the midst of the 1990 recession that the new Denby would necessarily survive, let alone thrive.

Now, with the original shareholders still owning 40 per cent of the shares, and the team's sights set on a trebling of export sales by the year 2000, the future for Denby's 680 staff looks secure.

CASE STUDY

The Body Shop – from little acorns...

'I look at what the cosmetics trade is doing and walk in the opposite direction' says Anita Roddick, displaying the kind of unconventional stance that has enabled her to transform The Body Shop from a tiny start-up venture into a multinational operation within the space of a few short years. From the first shop in Brighton, which was financed by a bank loan of £4,000, Anita Roddick has seen the company she founded in 1976 become something of a retailing legend with a turnover of £195.4 million in 1994. When The Body Shop went public and was floated on the **Unlisted Securities Market (USM)** in 1984, it was valued at £4.75 million. Eight years later the company had out-performed all expectations to achieve a market valuation of £500 million. The exotic-sounding lotions and potions such as Jojoba Moisture Cream, Apricot Lip Balm and Peppermint Foot Lotion are now available in 45 countries worldwide. As their products have gone on sale in over 1,200 shops from New York to Tokyo, the level of overseas profits has led some City analysts to predict that the company's true potential for growth may yet lie ahead.

It was whilst working for the United Nations in the mid-1960s that Anita Roddick first became aware of the effectiveness of natural ingredients. In Sri Lanka she saw how women used pineapple juice as a skin cleanser (later discovering that natural enzymes in the juice help to remove the dead skin cells) and watched the Polynesians using untreated cocoa butter to soften their skins. Back in England she tracked down a herbalist who shared her interest in natural ingredients and together they concocted 25 recipes.

She admits that the reason the products were originally sold in five sizes was because it made the shop look full. Similarly, the use of information cards on the shelves came about because the products were so unusual she realised she ought to explain what each one contained and what it was good for. In fact, the characteristic design features of the shop interiors, which have since come to symbolise The Body Shop style, all resulted from the need to improvise through lack of money. For example, green paint was first used in the Brighton shop because it hid the damp patches!

From the outset, Anita Roddick had a mission – to make The Body Shop the 'most honest cosmetics company in the world'. In an industry that calculatingly chooses the most perfect faces and figures as images for men and women to aspire to, The Body Shop prides itself on 'promoting health rather than glamour and reality rather than the dubious promise of instant rejuvenation'. For this reason, the company refuses to make any extravagant claims for its products, other than simply stating their main uses. The atmosphere in the shops mirrors this low-key approach to selling. Sales staff are helpful and knowledgeable, but are trained not to be pushy. Packaging is noticeably plain and functional. Given that the company does not believe in traditional cosmetics industry advertising for its products, the phenomenal sales record might, at first sight, seem difficult to explain.

In reality, the very absence of advertising hype and of high-pressure sales techniques sets the company apart from its rivals. In the same way, policies such as using products that have not been tested on animals, recycling waste paper, minimising packaging and offering a refill service, all **differentiate** The Body Shop products from those of competitors. In addition, there cannot be many companies who have made as much effort to make consumers aware of important environmental issues, and fewer still who have made as firm a commitment to sourcing raw materials from the developing world.

Clearly, then, there are a number of factors underlying the rapid rate of expansion; the quality and unique nature of the products themselves, the attractiveness of the shops and the strong environmental concern. Less often cited as a contributory factor, but one which has proved significant in the company's growth, is the fact that most of the shops are operated under a **franchise system**. This is where **franchisees** purchase individual shops and the right to sell The Body Shop products, though the company still retains tight control of products, displays, staff training as well as the general operating style of the shops. For example, franchisees are encouraged to adopt a local community project, to which, it is hoped, each employee will devote at least half a day a month during working hours.

The franchise route was chosen initially because the company did not have the capital to expand quickly enough. It was a good decision, as the franchise system provides two benefits: the shops are run as separate enterprises so individual franchisees have an incentive to increase profits; the company does not have a high fixed cost investment in shop buildings and is therefore insulated from the interest rate increases that crippled other retailers during the recent recession. In fact, as far as The Body Shop is concerned, the pace of expansion shows no sign of slackening – every three days a new branch of The Body Shop opens somewhere in the world!

It is perhaps inevitable that this degree of success would attract competition. Yet despite hosts of imitators, The Body Shop continues to lead the field. 'Business is not just about the profit and loss sheet', Anita Roddick is fond of stating. In building a thriving business from scratch in the space of a few short years, she has confounded the sceptics by proving that it is possible for a company to be financially successful as well as socially responsible.

A Body Shop franchise

Business integration

IN ASSOCIATION WITH

Unilever

Pulling together for international success

The job of the designer, the production manager, the marketing executive or the human resources manager are each stimulating and challenging. More demanding still are the jobs requiring a deep understanding of the *whole* enterprise. For business success can only come if the different departments work together towards a common goal. The people who identify the company objectives and coordinate the departments' efforts at achieving them are the subject of the final chapter of this book.

To achieve continuing success in any business requires three factors above all others:

- Clear ambitions/goals.
- A well considered strategy for achieving those objectives.
- The resources and organisation to make the strategy work.

A good example is Newcastle FC. Until Sir John Hall took over, the club enjoyed great support, but very little success. Sir John made the inspired appointment of Kevin Keegan (who had no managerial experience) and an important partnership began. The success of the club since then has relied upon many of the themes of this book:

- Good financial management.
- Clearly focused marketing, including good product development, well-run outlets and excellent distribution; sales of Newcastle kits and souvenirs have become a multimillion pound business.
- Charismatic leadership from Kevin Keegan, then Kenny Dalglish.
- Recruitment and training policies that many a multinational company would envy!

More important than any single one of these has been the effective way they have been brought together in an evident sense of common purpose – a mission to succeed. Sir John Hall's passion to bring success to the North-East is as evident (and as powerful) as Anita Roddick's passion for ethical standards in business.

Powerful a force though mission can be, for most businesses there is limited scope for rousing staff passions for the company's benefit. The huge Anglo-Dutch company Unilever is a case in point. Making a range of products from detergents to ice cream provides many challenging jobs, but provokes fewer passions. The keys to running such a business successfully are thoroughness, intelligence and vision, rather than missionary zeal.

A case in point is Unilever's approach to one of Europe's most dynamic and competitive consumer markets – 'personal products' such as fragrances, deodorants and shampoos. Unilever owns a remarkable array of brands such as Elizabeth Arden, Calvin Klein, Sunsilk, Fabergé, Impulse and Organics. Yet the marketplace is far too competitive for good brands to be enough on their own. Rivals such as L'Oréal have many strong brands too. Competitive rivalry is constant.

Spurred on by competition and by the opportunities presented by the European single market, Unilever managers decided in the early 1990s to organise their personal products business on Europe-wide lines. So instead of having factories, marketing departments and R & D laboratories in each of the major countries in Europe, Unilever concentrated its resources. For example, Elida Fabergé, the company's factory at Seacroft (near Leeds), specialised in producing aerosols and liquids such as Organics shampoo. It now exports such products throughout Europe.

Organics products from Elida Fabergé

Operating in this pan-European way places great strains upon a business. Effective communication is quite difficult in an organisation based in a single building, be it a school, a college or a manufacturing company. Imagine what it must be like coordinating sales, marketing, production and distribution between factories, depots and management teams throughout Europe – each speaking different languages! Yet Unilever believes this can and must be achieved successfully.

Unilever's starting point was to identify a clear objective. It was simple: to be number one in the world by the year 2000. This could only be achieved by strengthening the company's performance in Europe, where it lagged behind L'Oréal, especially in France. Although Unilever is an Anglo-Dutch company, such is its multinational status that much of the influence towards its pan-European approach came from an American. Bob Phillips, president of Personal Products Group USA was convinced that to become the world number one would require: 'Competitive innovation . . . to develop more new products and to get them faster to the marketplace . . . something unique . . . top class innovations . . . inevitably many will be copied . . . the only response to that has to be . . . having a constant flow of new ideas . . .'

This view was echoed by another senior executive, Antony Burgmans: 'The key word is "new". It is almost impossible to generate growth with concepts that have been around for five years.'

The conviction that success depended upon a continuous stream of new, innovative products led the senior management to draw a major conclusion. In order to generate the capital to finance a huge research and development budget (plus the marketing resources for many product launches) the company would need to get its costs down drastically.

After careful consideration, Unilever decided to pursue economies of scale by a Europe-wide factory reorganisation. By concentrating output of a product such as Organics in one British factory, 24-hour continuous production would minimise labour and overhead costs. Unilever set a target factory productivity level of one million units per worker per year by 1997.

Whether as part of an ambitious push into Europe or in a small manufacturing firm, the need for an integrated approach is paramount. Otherwise, ambitious executives in one part of a business proceed with a strategy that seems excellent, but pushes the business in the opposite direction to that desired by colleagues in other departments.

Although the need is obvious, achieving it can be difficult. The solution may seem to lie in holding plenty of meetings to ensure good communications between managers from different departments. Bright ideas can be discussed and the implications for the whole firm be identified. Unfortunately when groups of managers meet there is a tendency for caution to prevail over initiative. So although everyone is being kept informed of the ideas of others, the business as a whole may stagnate.

To combat this problem, modern businesses adopt a two-pronged approach:

- Management training and retraining in entrepreneurial skills, emphasising the huge competitive advantage of being first; the case study on Solero (see pages 15–17) illustrates this point.
- Ensuring that the business objectives and strategy are so clear that all departments know exactly which direction to move towards. For example, when Tesco moved upmarket in the late 1980s/early 1990s, all staff from store managers to advertising managers knew that the test of every decision was whether it fitted in with the new image.

CASE STUDY

Integration across the world – Magnum ice cream

Since its launch in 1989, Magnum has developed to become a billion dollar brand. It is as successful in Sweden, Thailand and the United Arab Emirates as it is in Britain. All this from the unlikely starting point of a children's brand called Nogger.

It was Wall's sister company in Germany, Langnese-Iglo, that decided to try a larger, better quality version of their chocolate-covered ice cream for children and to call it Magnum Nogger. Research showed that adults were the most enthusiastic about the product, though they rejected the children's image suggested by the name Nogger. 'Magnum' was born.

Once the target consumer was identified as adults, further development led to a thick coating of high quality chocolate, dairy ice cream and a distinctive foil wrapping. Magnum was an immediate success when launched in Germany, Belgium, Denmark, Holland, Sweden and Switzerland in 1989. In its first year it sold four times the forecast sales volume.

Magnum share of UK wrapped impulse market

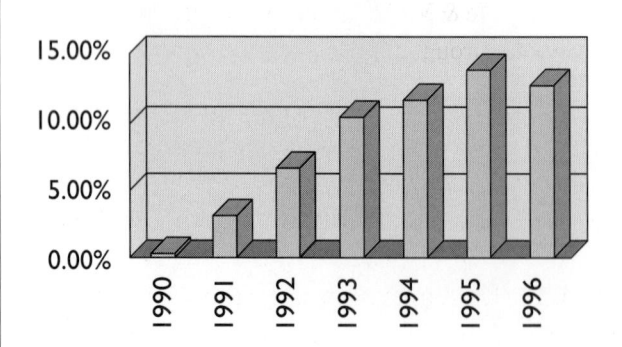

Source: Birds Eye Wall's

'Ich und mein Magnum'

Successful though the launch was, there was much to be learned still about the product and its consumers. Market research revealed that Magnum purchasers felt unusually intensely about the brand. According to Jean Callanan, international brand manager for Magnum: 'This brand has really got under the consumer's skin. People talk very passionately about it, across many countries.' Hence the advertising campaign 'Me & My Magnum', which has been successful throughout the world.

Klaus Rabbel, chairman of the Magnum International Brand Group, stresses that the success lies not in advertising alone, but in the entire marketing mix, including its 'wonderful product quality; global name, size and generosity; packaging and price'. In other words the input from designers, production teams and quality controllers is as important as that from the marketing executives.

This point can and should be taken further. For an ice cream to be successful, sophisticated distribution and production systems are vital. A week of good weather places enormous strains upon the supply chain, as demand can easily treble. So the 19 factories worldwide that produce Magnums have to be capable of rapid acceleration in their rate of production. No less importantly, the distribution system must be capable of rushing extra products to retailers throughout the world.

Ten years ago, a heatwave would empty the ice cream cabinets of Britain, leaving them empty for days. Now Wall's promises all its retailers to deliver their orders within a day, no matter how great the demand. This has only become possible through heavy investment in equipment and information technology. Here, as with every other aspect of the Magnum story, the heavy investment costs were always available from the parent company, Unilever. Without the financial strength, nothing else would have been possible.

So Magnum is a success story based upon good financial, marketing, production and design management. The future of the brand rests with an International Brand Group that has to coordinate and integrate the work of staff in 19 factories and 38 countries worldwide. It must also foster the work of the International Development Unit for Magnum, in Germany, which has been responsible for successful new variants such as Almond and Mint. Other product developments from the German team have included Walnut, Cappuccino and Coffee. These have not been introduced to Britain but are strong sellers in other countries.

Magnum is a rising star for Unilever and looks set to remain one for many years to come. In 1996, for example, all four Magnum flavours were in the UKs top ten best-selling impulse ice creams. Managing its rapid growth, coordinating the work of many thousands of staff worldwide and – above all – maintaining or enhancing the brand image is the task of executives such as Jean Callanan and Klaus Rabbel. To have taken a product for German children to millions of adult customers worldwide has been an extraordinary achievement of the brand's first six years. The next six years look likely to be just as exciting. Magnum in Tokyo? Magnum in China? You can count on it.

Is Europe a single market?

Impressive though the Magnum example is, not every brand can be developed in the same way. For although consumer tastes for impulse products or treats seem similar worldwide (Coca Cola, McDonald's, Magnum and Cornetto, for instance), there are many other product categories where tastes, habits and attitudes differ between countries. In Britain, for example, moisturising cream such as Oil of Ulay tends to be bought by older women. In Italy, the main market is among women under 30. So whereas Magnum can be marketed using the same product and image worldwide, Oil of Ulay could not succeed in Italy using the same approach as in Britain.

So what strategy could a British firm adopt if it wanted to expand into Europe, but knew that national consumer tastes were different? Just such an issue faces Cadbury's, with its near 30 per cent share of the UK chocolate market, but less than 1 per cent of the market in Germany, Belgium and Italy. One approach might be to copy Nestlé's 1988 takeover of Rowntree. At one stroke Nestlé's share of the UK market rose from 3 per cent to 27 per cent. It also acquired Rowntree's distribution strength and market knowledge, making it easier to launch successful new products. Yet such opportunities are rare and the cost can be prohibitive. Rowntree, for example, cost Nestlé £2.55 billion.

An alternative approach is to invest in acquiring local market knowledge and thereby see how best to market your existing products, and to see which new opportunities which may arise. For small firms, the only affordable way to proceed is through a local agent – a locally-based individual or business which handles local marketing and distribution in return for a percentage of the sales generated. Today, large firms tend not to use this approach, partly because of the difficulty of ensuring coordination with the marketing strategy in other countries.

Setting up offices, possibly a factory and certainly a distribution network in a country where current sales are small represents an expensive investment in the future. The Sony chairman, Akio Morita, has said that when he opened the first overseas Sony factory in South Wales in 1974 he expected it to take 15 years to make a profit. That may be exceptional, but any firm must expect quite a slow payback from expansion into a new market. There is so much to achieve before success is likely:

- Staff with the right combination of enterprise, integrity and experience need to be recruited and trained; the penalty for failure here may be as dramatic as the disastrous losses by the dealer Nick Leeson at Baring's Bank, Singapore.
- Gaining distribution for your products is vital, but expensive; often, firms achieve good distribution by selling to shops on the basis of sale or return; as they are taking no risk, many shops may stock the product; yet if customer sales prove slow, the products may be returned – often too close to the sell-by date to do anything other than scrap them in the case of consumables.
- Market knowledge needs to be acquired, and this is often largely a matter of learning from (often expensive) marketing mistakes, such as new product launches that flop; even experienced companies such as L'Oréal, Nestlé and Unilever have more new product failures than successes; for a firm new to a country, the chances of success are lower still.

Despite this daunting list of reasons to stay at home or to buy up a local business, the local approach can reap the greatest rewards. Both TI Group and Sony use the same phrase for their approach: 'global localisation'. Their intention is to bring together the benefits of research and development and production on a world scale with the enormous added value of local knowledge. In Britain today, Japanese firms such as Sony, Nissan, JVC and Honda have enjoyed huge long-term success from their investments in this country. Similarly, Unilever's decades of careful development of its subsidiaries throughout the world provided the infrastructure for a success such as Magnum.

A good test of which British firms are likely to be the successes of 10 or 20 years' time is their approach to overseas markets. Are they developing carefully in a series of markets (probably largely within the European Union)? Are they relying on agents? Or are they doing nothing?

Fortunately, few are likely to fall into the latter category. Most British firms are following the 60 per cent of our exports that go to European Union countries by developing stronger local sales and marketing operations. Whether a bottle of Organics shampoo, an aircraft's landing-gear or a Solero ice cream, British products are set to be an increasing feature of European life. Just as we will be seeing more and more European products in Britain. Integration is not only a vital part of company management, it is also likely to become an increasing feature of business life within the European Union and, later, the world. For young people who understand industry and are attracted by its challenges, there remains no limit to its scope.

ACTIVITY

Fizzing into Europe – a business role play

You have been appointed the European brand manager for 'Shhout!', a fizzy soft drink that has taken Britain by storm. With its exotic fruit flavour and creamy, frothy 'head', its widget-in-the-can has stolen a march on the major cola producers. Already, Shhout! has taken 10 per cent of the £2 billion UK fizzy soft drinks market, despite charging a 5 per cent price premium over the market leader.

You will have a £10 million budget for attacking the £8 billion market for fizzy soft drinks in the rest of Europe.

Your tasks:
1 Discuss with your colleagues the main pieces of information you need to know before you can decide how to proceed. It may be helpful to work under these headings: market research; competition; marketing mix; fixed and variable costs.

2 Now think up three alternative strategies you might adopt to make a success of Shhout! in Europe. Your strategies should fit in with the company's objective which is to build for profitable growth over the coming 5–10 years.

Make brief notes of your ideas. Your tutor may ask you to present the ideas of your group to the whole class.

Bibliography

Brookes, Richard, *The New Marketing*, 1988, Gower Publishing.

Drucker, Peter, *The Effective Executive*, 1994, Butterworth Heinemann.

Goldsmith, Walter and Clutterbuck, David, *The Winning Streak*, 1992, Penguin.

Handy, Charles, *Inside Organisation*, 1990, BBC Books.

Kotter, John, *The Leadership Factor*, 1988, Collier Mac.

Kotler, Philip, *Principles of Marketing*, 1993, Prentice-Hall.

Lorenz, Christopher, *The Design Dimension*, 1990, Blackwell.

McGregor, Douglas, *The Human Side of Enterprise*, 1987, Penguin Books.

Matthews, Peter (Ed.), *The Guinness Book of Records*, Guinness Publishing.

Mintzberg, Henry, *The Nature of Managerial Work*, 1973, Harper and Row.

Oates, David, *The Complete Entrepreneur*, 1987, Mercury.

Peters, Tom and Austin, Nancy, *A Passion for Excellence*, 1985, Random Century.

Peters, Tom and Waterman, Robert, *In Search of Excellence*, 1995, HarperCollins.

Pilditch, James, *Winning Ways*, 1989, Mercury.

Porter, Michael, *The Competitive Advantage of Nations*, 1990, Macmillan.

Rajan, Amin, *1992: A Zero Sum Game*, 1990, Industrial Society.

Ritchie, Berry and Goldsmith, Walter, *The New Elite*, 1987, Weidenfeld & Nicholson.

Scase, Richard and Goffee, Robert, *Theeal World of the Small Business Owner*, 1980, Croom Hill.

Scase, Richard and Goffee, Robert, *Women in Charge*, 1985.

Taylor, Frederick W, *The Principles of Scientific Management*, 1980, Norton Books.

Taylor, Robert, *The Future of the Trade Unions*, 1994, Deutsch.

Townsend, Robert, *Up the Organisation*, 1970, Michael Joseph.

Womack, Jim, Jones, Dan and Roos, Dan, *The Machine that Changed the World*, 1990, Rawson Associates.

Index

accounts 82-3
acquisitions 48
Adair; John 99, 100
advertising 25, 26, 31
Advisory Conciliation and
 Arbitration Service (ACAS) 73
aerospace industry 46
Allied Domecq 105-6
Apple Computers 38, 119
appraisals 68-9, 77
APV Baker (formerly Baker Perkins) 42
Assisted Areas 58
Austin, Nancy 43
autocratic management style 103
automation 7, 59
automobile industry 38, 46

Banham, John 98
bank loans 83, 85
Banks, Chris 105-6
batch production 50, 51
behavioural interviews 67
Bernstein, David 42
Bickerstaffe, George 99
Body Shop 25, 128-9
Bolton Report 111
Boston Matrix 21
Braebourne Ltd 120-3
brands 16, 19-20, 23-4
Branson, Richard 108-9
break-even analysis 89-91
British Airways 56
British Standard 5750 55-6, 75
Brooke Bond 21-2
Brookes, Richard 37
Brown, W. 95
budgets 92
bureaucracy 50, 107
Burgmans, Antony 131
business plans 115, 118-19
buying behaviour 13

CAD (computer-aided-design) 34, 37, 42, 43, 44-5
Cadbury Schweppes 7, 134
Callanan, Jean 132
CAM (computer-aided manufacture) 44-5
Canon 4
capital *see* finance
Carlson, Chester 37-8
cash flow 80-2, 121-2

Caulkin, Simon 7
CBI (Confederation of British Industry) 73-4
CBT (computer-based training) 69
centralised management structure 107
chain of command 105
channel of distribution 24
Chicken Tonight 21-3
chief executives 66, 99, 100
Clarks 107
Clutterbuck, David 107
collective bargaining 5, 73
commitment 7
companies *see* organisations; small businesses
competitive advantage 6-7
competitive pricing 24
complaints by customers 101, 102
computer-aided manufacture (CAM) 44-5
computer-aided-design (CAD) 34, 37, 42, 43, 44-5
computer-based training (CBT) 69
Confederation of British Industry (CBI) 73-4
consultative committees 72
Cornetto 44-5
cost plus pricing 24
costs
 of advertising 31
 of design 46
 fixed 49, 89
 of labour 3, 6, 50
 of product development 7, 45-6
 of production 51, 57
 variable 89
credit control 92
customer service 7, 100-2, 116
customers
 buying behaviour 13
 complaints 101, 102
 needs and wants 13-14, 35-6
 Pareto Effect 19
 target groups 17, 27

debenture loans 86
debt factoring 84
decentralised management structure 107
decision making 72, 107
delegation 107
demand 13, 23, 51
democratic management style 104

Denby Pottery 1, 125-8
Derwent Valley Foods 125
design 32-5, 37, 39
 computer-aided-design (CAD) 34, 37, 42, 43, 44-5
 costs 46
 and taxation 45
 of packaging 128
design-based innovation 33-5
differentiation 129
directors' salaries 99
diseconomies of scale 50
distribution outlets 24-5, 134
diversification 21, 27, 49
Dixons 100-2
Drucker, Peter 13, 95

ecobalance research 64
economic environment 1, 2
economies of scale 49, 49-50
EDI (electronic data interchange) 61, 76
Edwardes, Sir Michael 99
employees *see* personnel
employment statistics 4, 48, 111
empowerment 76, 109
Enterprise Allowance Scheme 120
Enterprise Investment Scheme 86, 125
entrepreneurs 114, 120
environmental issues 63-4
equity capital 125
European Investment Bank (EIB) 120
European single market 131, 134-5
Eurostar 56-7
Exchange Rate Mechanism (ERM) 2
exports 2

factoring 84
Fayol, Henri 95-6
finance
 for growth 125
 for small businesses 119-20, 125
 sources 83-6
 start-up 83, 119-20
financial services 6
firms *see* organisations; small businesses
fixed costs 49, 89
fixed-term contracts 77

flow production 50, 51
Ford, Henry 12
Ford Motor Company 54, 59
franchises 25, 129
Fuji 42

Gardiner, Paul 39, 45, 46
GEC ALSTHOM 28, 56
General Electric 35, 38
Giordano, Richard 100
GKN 28
Glaxo 46
Goffee, Robert 112, 113, 114
Goldsmith, Walter 99, 107
government
 economic influence 2
 grants 57, 58
 loans 86
 small firm initiatives 112
Green Party 63
green-field sites 58
Guinness Plc 7-9

Haden MacLellan 63
Hall, Sir John 130
Haloid 38
Handy, Charles 6, 103
Harrison, Sir Ernest 107
Harvey-Jones, Sir John 105
Hawthorne experiments 70
Herzberg, F. 70
Hewlett Packard 37, 42
hierarchy of needs 13
hire purchase 85
Hirsh, Wendy 97
Holdsworth, Sir Trevor 103
Horton, Bob 107
human resource management (HRM) 77
hygiene factors 70

IBM 2, 37, 38, 43, 55
ICI 46, 63, 105
incentive schemes 72
industrial inertia 58
industrial marketing 25, 28-30
industrial structure 9-11
industrial tribunals 73
inflation 2
information technology (IT) 61-3
innovation 13-14, 38-9, 45-6
 design-based 33-5
interest rates 2
international markets 134

interviews
   market research 15
   recruitment 66, 67
ISO 9002 56, 75, 76
IT (information technology) 61-3
iteration 39

Jacques, E. 95
Jaguar 58
Japanese firms in Britain 3-4
JC Bamford Excavators 45
job production 50, 51
job security 77
Jobs, Steve 119-20
John Crane 29-30
John Lewis Partnership 72
Johnson Matthey 63
Jones, Dan 54
just in time production 54-5

kaizen groups 55, 56
Kalmar 71-72
Kalms, Sir Stanley 100-1
kanban 54
Kodak 42
Komatsu 55
Kotler, Paul 32
Kotler, Philip 13
Kotter, John 98

labour
   costs 3, 6, 50
   flexibility 5, 71-2
   and production location 57, 58
labour intensive industries 112-13
labour intensive production 50
latent needs 35, 36
latent wants 13-14
lead times 43
leadership 7, 98-9, 100, 102, 105-6
lean production 52, 53, 54-5
leasing 85
Levi 501s 26-8
life cycle of products 20-1
limited liability 10-11, 86
LINC scheme 120
line managers 100
living standards 112
Loan Guarantee Scheme 83, 120
loans 83-6
location of production 57-9
long-term finance 84, 86
Lorenz, Christopher 35, 42
loss leaders 26

McGregor, D. 70
McWilliams, Douglas 6
Magnum ice cream 132-3
maintenance factors 70
management
   and decision making 107
   skills 7-9
   structures 105, 107
   styles 103-4, 108-9
   training 103, 132
management buy-outs (MBOs) 115, 125-8
managers
   effective managers 95
   and leadership 98-9, 100
   and promotion 66, 109
   qualities of 97
   role of 95-6
Mann, Robert 114
manufacturing industries 4-5
manufacturing resource planning (MRP II) 61-2
mark-ups 24
market niches 113, 114
market penetration 23-4
market research 14-15, 15, 36

market share 20, 27
marketing 12-13, 116, 122-3, 126-7
   industrial 25, 28-30
marketing mix 19, 132-3
markets 12-13, 17-18, 57-8
   international 134
Marks & Spencer 62-3
Maslow, A.H. 13, 70
mass production 50, 54
matrix structures 105
Mayo, E. 70
MBOs (management buy-outs) 115, 125-8
medium-term finance 84-5, 86
Mercedes Benz 58
mergers 48
Messier-Dowty 50-3
Mintzberg, Henry 96
Mitsubishi Electric UK 75-6
Morita, Akio 5, 39, 134
mortgage loans 86
motivation 69-71, 72-3, 77, 109
Motorola 2

needs 13-14, 35-6
Nestlé 134
Newcastle FC 130
NHS Trusts 87-8
niche markets/marketing 17, 113, 114
Nickson, Brian 69
Nissan 2, 4
Nittan 57
North Sea oil 3

Oates, David 114
oil production 3
ordinary shares 86
organic growth 48
organisations
   and European single market 134-5
   and international success 130-1
   structure 42, 105, 107
overdrafts 84

packaging 128
Pareto Effect 19
Parker, Alan 25
partnerships 10-11
pay see salaries
payback period 45
payment by results 72
people development 8
personal skills 7
personnel 65-6, 68-71, 77
Peters, Tom 43, 65, 107
PFI (Private Finance Initiative) 87, 88
Philips 55
Phillips, Bob 131
Pilditch, James 37, 42
Porter, Michael 6
preference shares 86
price discrimination 24
Price Waterhouse 87-8
pricing 7, 23-4, 34
primary business sector 10
Private Finance Initiative (PFI) 87, 88
private limited companies 10, 11
privatisation 2, 5, 10, 92-3
problem solving 8
production
   automation 7, 59
   cells 52
   costs 51, 57
   and the environment 63-4
   location 57-9
   and marketing 12-13

methods 50, 51
scale 49-50
strategies 53-6
and technology 61-2
value added 48
products 19-21
   and consumer needs 13-14, 35-6
   development costs 7, 45-6
   differentiation 129
   diversification 21, 27
   and environmental issues 63-4
   and international markets 134
   launching new products 15-17, 21-2
   lead times 43
   life cycle 20-1
   and new technology 37-8
   redesign 39
   transportation 24, 57, 58
profit sharing 72, 116
profits 1, 65-6, 82-3, 91
   reinvested 83, 86, 125
promotions 25-6
ProShare 11
psychological testing 77
public limited companies 10, 11
public relations 26
pyramid structures 42, 105

quality improvement teams (QIT) 76

Rabbel, Klaus 132
Racal Electronics Group 107
Railtrack 92-3
raw materials 37, 57
recruitment 66-8
redesigning products 39
redundancy 77, 112, 114
Regional Selective Assistance 58
reinvested profits 84, 87, 125
Renishaw PLC 37
research and development (R&D) 4, 38, 46-7
retail outlets 25
Richer Sounds 116-17
Riley, Stephen 126, 128
risk capital 125
Ritchie, Berry 99
Roddick, Anita 25, 128, 129
Rolls Royce 46-7, 49, 55
Roos, Dan 54
Rothwell, Roy 39, 45, 46
Rover 7, 55
Rowntree 134

safety margins 90
salaries 72, 99
sales promotions 26
Samsung 58
Scase, Richard 112, 113, 114
secondary business sector 10
SEG (socio-economic groups) 17, 18
service industries 4-5, 6, 58, 112
share-based incentive schemes 92-3
shares 11, 86, 125
shop stewards 73
short-term finance 84, 85
Simon Engineering 63
Sinclair C5 36
situational interviewing 66
skills 7-9
skimming 24
small businesses 111-13
   business plans 118-19
   definition 111
   and economies of scale 49
   and finance 119-20, 125

niche marketing 17
   starting 114-15
socio-economic groups (SEG) 17, 18
sole traders 10-11
Solero 15-17
Sony 14, 35-6, 54
   design-based innovation 33-5
   global localisation strategy 134
   locating in Britain 3, 4
   portable editor 39-41
   re-innovation policy 39
span of control 95
staff managers 100
Standard Life 66-8
standards of living 112
start-up finance 83, 119-20
stock control 54, 91
Stock Exchange 11, 86
strategic thinking 8
subcontracting 112
supply 23
Syrett, Michael 97

taxation 1, 2, 45, 125
Taylor, F.W. 69-70
Taylor, Robert 74
teamwork 35, 41-2, 54, 71-2, 76
technology 37-8, 61-2, 113
TECs (Training and Enterprise Councils) 120
television advertising 25, 31
teleworkers 61
tertiary business sector 10
Tesco 63, 132
Texas Instruments 42
Theory X 70
Theory Y 70
3i (Investors in Industry) 122, 125, 126
3M 19, 36, 39, 42
TI Group 28-30, 134
total quality management (TQM) 53, 55
Townsend, Robert 65, 72
Toyota 2, 54
trade credit 84
trade unions 3, 5, 73-4
training 69, 77, 103, 132
Training and Enterprise Councils (TECs) 120
transportation 24, 57, 58
Trust House Forte 107

unemployment 112
Unilever 130-2
Unipart 55
unique selling proposition (USP) 19
United Distillers 8

value added 48
variable costs 89
venture capital 83, 86, 125
Virgin 108-9

wants 13-14
Waterman, Robert 65, 107
wholesalers 24
Womack, Jim 54
women in business 114
worker participation 72-3
worker representatives 73
worker satisfaction 51
working capital 91-2
Wozniak, Steve 119-20

Xerox 38, 43, 55

YKK 3

Zaleznik, Professor Abraham 100